EMPIRE BUILDING

ROSIE LLEWELLYN-JONES

Empire Building

The Construction of British India: 1690–1860

HURST & COMPANY, LONDON

First published in the United Kingdom in 2023 by
C. Hurst & Co. (Publishers) Ltd.,
New Wing, Somerset House, Strand, London, WC2R 1LA
© Rosie Llewellyn-Jones, 2023
All rights reserved.

Distributed in the United States, Canada and Latin
America by Oxford University Press, 198 Madison Avenue,
New York, NY 10016, United States of America.

The right of Rosie Llewellyn-Jones to be identified as the author of
this publication is asserted by her in accordance with the
Copyright, Designs and Patents Act, 1988.

A Cataloguing-in-Publication data record for this book
is available from the British Library.

ISBN: 9781787388048

www.hurstpublishers.com

Printed in Great Britain by Bell and Bain Ltd, Glasgow

Dedicated to India's young historians,
Sami, Sudipto and Nimra, as well as
my dear friend Neeta.

CONTENTS

LIST OF ILLUSTRATIONS

1. 'The Capture of Port Hoogly' from *The Padshahnama,* c.1634. Royal Collection Trust/© Her Majesty Queen Elizabeth II 2022.

2. 'Rear view of the Cossimbuzar Factory House' (the East India Company's first Bengal factory) in 1795. Watercolour, artist unknown. © The British Library Board Add. Or. 3193.

3. 'The Trading Post of the Dutch East India Company' Chinsura by Hendrik van Schuylenburgh, 1665. Public domain via Rijksmuseum.

4. Old Fort William, Calcutta, date unknown. Engraved for *The Universal Magazine of Knowledge and Pleasure*, London, 1747–1803.

5. 'A view of Fort William, Calcutta, seen from the east with the Church of Saint Anne and the Governor and his guard' by George Lambert, 1731. Private collection.

6. The East India Company obelisk memorial at Plassey, with the gilt bust of *nawab* Siraj-ud-daula added in 2007.

7. Theodore Forrestie's map of Calcutta, 1742, showing (old) Fort William and the Great Tank. © The British Library Board K. Top. 115.40.

8. Piedmontese standard silk reeling machine. Note the small door (bottom centre) where firewood was inserted to heat the basins above. Courtesy of Karolina Hutkova.

9. 'Stamping Coinage in the Mint, Calcutta' by Arthur William Devis. Part of a series entitled 'Arts and Manufactures of Bengal', c. 1792. Ashmolean Museum, Oxford © Charles Greig.

INTRODUCTION

Chapter Outlines

London-born Job Charnock lies in the churchyard of St John's Church, Kolkata under the only city structure that can confidently be dated to the late seventeenth century. It is a curious two-storeyed octagonal building topped with a dome, so recognisable that life-size models of the tomb, fashioned from bamboo and canvas, have featured in the city's annual Durga Puja celebrations, when the old Bengal goddess is worshipped. Charnock was known as the founder of Calcutta (the city's former name) for over 300 years, and in 1990, on the tercentenary of its supposed foundation, much was made of the vision and determination he possessed in the face of indifference from his employer, the English East India Company. Romantic stories grew up around Charnock: his daring rescue of a beautiful Hindu widow from her husband's funeral pyre; his subsequent marriage to her, his adoption of supposed 'Indian practices' in the form of sacrificing a cock on the anniversary of her death; and above all the seminal moment at noon on Sunday, 24 August 1690, when Charnock and his thirty men clambered up a steep river bank to establish Calcutta, the second city of the British Empire. (London was considered the first.) It was a story that served the Empire well, a paradigm of how India's unexploited resources could be profitably turned to advantage by the British. The surprising thing is how long it took the people of Calcutta to challenge this accepted narrative: 313 years, to be precise, as we will see in Chapter 1.

Calcutta was not the earliest British settlement in India but it was to become the most important: the capital and centre of government until 1911, the first city in Asia to set up its own Chamber of Commerce and only the third city in the world to

1

have its central streets lit by electricity. The Bengal Presidency, an administrative division introduced by the East India Company, would later include not only the whole of northern India up to the Khyber Pass on the north-west frontier with Afghanistan, but would spread eastwards to Burma and Singapore as well. The original diocese of Calcutta embraced all Company territory including footholds in the Persian Gulf. It provides the best, but not the only, example of the construction of British India, which is the theme of this book and why our story is focused mainly on Bengal.

The title of the book reflects the physical changes that the Company achieved in India, with the words 'building' and 'construction' deliberately chosen to emphasise the work of its engineers. The role of these men, tasked with installing the mechanism of Company trade, defence and administration, has never been properly acknowledged. *The Military Engineer in India* by Lt Colonel E.W.C. Sandes, a former principal of the Thomason Civil Engineering College at Roorkee, was published in 1933, and there have been few resources since for the general reader who lacks access to specialist, and often highly technical, articles. In fact, all Company engineers in the period under discussion were termed 'military engineers' and held an army rank. They fulfilled an astonishingly wide range of tasks, from land surveying to taking meteorological observations, building palaces and establishing botanical gardens. Most of the early 'colonial' buildings admired today were the work of engineers, not architects. So the theme of engineering runs strongly through this book and is explained in simple terms, without technical jargon.

Few attempts have been made to examine the impact of the European Enlightenment on the subcontinent, yet it played a vital part in the discovery of India's own history that had been largely lost or forgotten by its own people. The importance of the Asiatic Society of Bengal, founded by Sir William Jones in 1784, cannot be overestimated. Chapter 3 shows how it inspired Europeans— mainly Britons—to explore the country, to familiarise themselves not only with its history, but with its geography as well as its numerous resources that included commercial plants like sugar cane, indigo, opium and tea, all of which became important trading items. A new genre of painting was developed as Indian artists were commissioned to illustrate local flowers, birds and animals for European connoisseurs. Learned articles in the Society's journal led to an appreciation of the country's literature and more importantly its languages. Normally monolingual Britons realised it was to their advantage to learn Persian rather than relying on interpreters (*dobashes*) or shouting loudly in English.

For various reasons discussed in Chapter 4, mapmaking had not flourished in Mughal India. This was something the Company had to address, both for military and administrative reasons, once it took on the task of revenue collecting. James Rennell, an accomplished marine surveyor who was commissioned into the Bengal Engineers, produced *A Bengal Atlas* in 1779, co-ordinating reports from different sources. The following century saw the Great Trigonometrical Survey, an ambitious scheme to map India from south to north, which took 70 years to complete. The introduction of steamboats on the Ganges and the Indus was followed by the development of railways, which accelerated commercial traffic and quickly became popular with Indian travellers. The Company had not foreseen this popularity, having originally established a railway line between Calcutta and the coalfields of Raniganj in order to provide the Ganges steamboats with fuel. Alongside these nascent tracks, the electric telegraph was developed, which had a similar impact on communications between the British in India as the internet would have internationally in the 1990s.

History allows us the pleasure of being wise in retrospect. Not every Company initiative succeeded. Its silk filatures in Bengal failed primarily due to lack of supervision over the cocoon breeders. Steamboats on the Indus failed because technical and other challenges could not be overcome. An exclusive enclave of British houses at Maidapur, strategically sited near Murshidabad, fell into disuse when the Bengal capital was moved to Calcutta. But some Company developments proved extraordinarily successful, much more so than their originators could have imagined. Chapter 5 traces the development of the cantonment, a military establishment hitherto unknown in India. For the first time officers and men were located outside forts and in large, well-designed army quarters, with bungalows, barracks, parade grounds, powder magazines, cemeteries and facilities for the soldiers (and later their families).

Today the cantonment is an integral part of the subcontinental scene, important as a military base, and often ecologically too, as a verdant haven with neat, tree-shaded roads. The rapid establishment of hill stations following the Company's capture of the Punjab was equally successful. Cantonments were built here too, although on a smaller scale from those in the plains. Houses were initially erected in Shimla, Mussoorie and other stations by army officers, but private entrepreneurs quickly moved in, building buy-to-let properties for Britons who wanted to escape the heat of summer on the plains.

By the end of our study a pattern had emerged in cantonments and towns under Company control. Facilities now often included banks, post offices, telegraph offices, railway stations and metalled roads. These are described in Chapter 6. As the Company extended its remit, intangible changes were introduced too, aimed at standardising what seemed like a bewildering array of local usage and customs. The Gregorian calendar had been in use for a century in the Presidency towns: now weights, measures, coinage and mileage were to be harmonised. Even time itself was 'Westernised' with the change from *pahars* to hours. The passage of time also led to societal changes. What had been seen as normal in the rumbustious eighteenth century was frowned upon in the nineteenth as the Evangelical movement replaced liberal Enlightenment thought. Some of these changes were humanitarian, like the crackdown on Arab slave-trading and the rescue of children trafficked from Africa. Others saw attitudes harden towards Britons who appeared to have pro-Indian sympathies, shown particularly by their dress and marriage partners. Colonisation can be a subtle process, not limited to military conquest, legal and administrative moves or indeed the spread of European buildings.

The East India Company

Although we know today that settlements already existed on the site that was to become Calcutta, the traditional date of its foundation, 1690, is a convenient starting point for our study. The end date may be harder to justify, but it is generally accepted that the events of the Great Uprising of 1857–8 (formerly known as the Mutiny) marked a watershed in the relationship between India and Britain. The East

India Company was abolished, and the British government assumed responsibility for areas previously under Company control. Other parts of the subcontinent which had remained independent were named as Native States, and Political Agents were deputed to oversee them, reporting back to the British Viceroy in Calcutta.

By 1860, most of the systems that were to govern British India for the next 87 years until Independence had been put in place. The Imperial (Indian) Civil Service (ICS) was established; a huge expansion of the railways had begun; army cantonments were enlarged and made more defensible; the Indian Medical Service (IMS), which had begun in an ad hoc manner with ships' surgeons, was formalised; the Indian Forestry Service (IFS) was under discussion; a Public Works Department (PWD) was already operating. In short, the foundations of modern India were being laid. The days when a man working for the Company, or a European mercenary working for an Indian leader, could make a real difference were over. For those who prized individuality above the routine business of running a country, the opportunities to show initiative, ingenuity and enterprise—not to mention cunning, trickery and deceit—were fast disappearing.

The eighteenth century was a crucial time when the foundations for foreign rule in India were laid down; when bold decisions (that were not always the right ones) were made; when luck often played as important a role in battle as military skill; and when the Mughal Empire that had once seemed invincible began to fail, allowing others to step in. It was a time of flux, when the old hierarchies were crumbling, to be replaced with new ones. Powerful groups led by charismatic rulers swept across the country and around the edges of the imploding Mughal Empire as smaller states were established in Awadh, Hyderabad and Bengal. This turbulent period used to be known as the 'great anarchy', a time when the breakdown of the established order enabled the East India Company to advance unchecked into the vacuum left by weak central rule. While it is true that the Company was quick to take advantage of local leadership changes that could benefit it with new concessions, it worked pragmatically, steadily extending its primary base in Bengal but conscious that political and military upheavals were inimical to profitable trading. The infrastructure that we associate today with colonisation and which is examined here was initially developed to support trade. How it turned, subtly, into something else with profound consequences is part of our theme.

Much has been written on India under the Company and its subsequent governance up to Independence in 1947. Some scholars have confessed to choosing the subject simply because its written records are so comprehensive. There was almost nothing that the Company did not minute in exquisite detail. Its records are divided today between India, Pakistan, Bangladesh and Britain. But within these post-Independence studies there is a noticeable divide between the social, cultural, political and economic histories and the architectural critiques. The latter concentrate on style and function but neglect the impact that the buildings had on the landscape—and on the people who used them—and the implied foreign values that they introduced, while the former seldom mention buildings of any kind except in passing.

This book will attempt to integrate several different disciplines to produce an analysis of how Company-directed initiatives affected both the built environment in India and the lives of its inhabitants. It explores the idea of 'political architecture', a term that embraces anything that introduced foreign structures and foreign concepts into India. It will argue that every structure erected by the British, although using Indian contractors and labour, made a political statement, even if unconsciously. It will also utilise visual material, paintings and drawings from India, which have been curiously neglected by many historians in the narrative of British India. The change from earlier private, native-controlled functions like education, justice and punishment, entertainment, trading and healing the sick to public, British institutions of colleges, law courts, prisons and hospitals will be considered, together with the creation of cantonments and hill stations. We will look at the problems and pragmatic solutions found by military engineers before architect-designed buildings became the norm, and we will consider the hitherto undervalued role of these engineers.

To assess the foreign impact on India's built and unbuilt environment is to consider briefly what India was like before the Portuguese, the Dutch, the Danes, the British and the French arrived. Early European travellers included the Frenchmen Jean-

Baptiste Tavernier and François Bernier, whose written accounts of what they observed give us a rich but partial picture. There were already some minor European interventions along the east and west coasts, but what both men reported seeing was a flourishing empire. Tavernier was a diamond merchant and thus more interested in the southern Golconda diamond mines than the urban structures of neighbouring Hyderabad. Bernier, a physician, who visited Delhi and Agra noted the shopping arcades that lined a few of the main streets. The arcades had rooms above them, creating a uniform pattern of two-storeyed terraces with flat roofs, which were used as sleeping areas in the summer months. Bernier points out at some length how the severe climate influenced India's buildings and why they were so constructed to catch every passing breeze during the hottest season. (This was something that was going to take the first British inhabitants time to figure out.) However, for the most part both men were fascinated by the alien, exotic customs they found, rather than the architecture. In particular Tavernier took a gruesome interest in *sati,* where widows burnt themselves on the funeral pyres of their husbands. He also noted the numerous 'pagodas', as Hindu temples were called, a word with a disputed etymology but which has been in common use since the thirteenth century.

Other discerning visitors would have noted the severe fortresses perched on rocky outcrops, the numerous *ghats,* or jetties along the great rivers, the caravanserai halts for merchants, the stepwells that allowed villagers access to water and the unending plains, broken only by the occasional cluster of thatched huts around a buffalo-haunted pond. Most Indian cities were walled, as in Europe, and within the walls lay extensive palaces with many forecourts. There were also pleasant gardens; Hindu temples, some of great antiquity; the spacious mosques; the equally revered sites of Muslim *pirs,* or saints; and the *ganj,* a fixed market with shops. The European traders arriving in the seventeenth century were in no position to build their own walled cities, and we shall look at how they defended, not always successfully, their small coastal settlements.

Mughal India was profoundly different in every respect from post-medieval England that sent its first Company traders to Surat and later Bombay, Madras and Bengal. It had not, for example, seen a damaging civil war that split families in half and whose repercussions were to echo for several generations. It had no territorial ambitions on other countries, which is why there was virtually no Mughal navy. It had no parliament, although the presence of noblemen at the *durbar* (court assembly) provided a forum for discussion and the exchange of views. The emperor faced no statutory checks or threats, apart from disgruntled members of his own family. India's wealth came from the labour of its peasants in the form of land revenue remitted to the royal treasury through a number of intermediaries appointed by the emperor. It came also from trade, particularly of spices and fine fabrics produced by skilled weavers. But it was mainly enterprising Arab traders who ferried Indian products east to the Malay peninsula and west to Jeddah where they were shipped onwards to Europe. Business communities like the Jains—an ancient, possibly pre-Hindu sect—and the Muslim Bohras, who made a living by trade, preferred to operate within the Indian subcontinent rather than outside. So when European traders began to arrive they were seen as successors, or rivals to the Arab entrepreneurs, and not as a threat to Mughal hegemony.

During the seventeenth century, when the East India Company was gaining a tentative foothold along the coasts (albeit treading where other Europeans had trod before), the Mughal Empire flourished. Akbar, Jahangir and Shah Jahan were among the great emperors, far superior in wealth and authority to the English Queen Elizabeth I, the last Tudor, and her successors, the Stuarts. The Mughal emperors ruled much of their vast country through a series of deputies, *nawabs* and *subahdars*, who were themselves immensely powerful men. So powerful, in fact, that at times they felt able to oppose the emperor by withholding the annual tributes of cash, jewels and costly fabrics, or by not attending court when summoned to the imperial capital. When this happened, punitive raids would be launched and compromises reached, which would last until the next time a deputy tried to assert his own authority. As the rule of the last great Mughal emperor, Aurangzeb, drew to a close, European traders prepared themselves for change and opportunities to exploit the fluid situation which they believed would follow. Aurangzeb had ruled most of India for nearly half a century, and at his death ambitious men were ready to step in to establish new centres of power around the periphery of the empire.

This meant that Europeans now had to negotiate with local rulers as well as with Aurangzeb's successors, at times playing master and deputy off against each other. But it was a dangerous game. Company men knew that if they were captured in battle they too could become slaves, and they would not always be ransomed. Courage and ingenuity weren't always enough. An estimated sixty Europeans, including Company men, were massacred at their Patna dinner table in 1763 during an attempt by the *nawab* of Bengal, Mir Qasim, to reassert his authority. Had these men been killed on the battlefield, they would have been duly mourned, and in fact a larger number of Britons were killed the following year at the battle of Buxar. But it was the reports of the Patna victims defending themselves with knives and forks, their only weapons, that had horrified their fellow countrymen. This was simply not fair play.

The English East India Company was in the East Indies to make a profit. So much effort went into this, so many premature deaths, so great an investment in ships and men, so much ventured, so many disappointments, so much rivalry with other European Companies, that the men who survived all this became cunning and bold. Yet these were not men insensible of their surroundings. They were negotiating in a foreign country where they met men who were equally cunning, equally interested in profit and often more casually cruel. These first Company men in India lived in a place where the average life expectancy for Europeans was below 30 years of age.[1] It was not a place for old men, but for young men in a hurry. Those who had the good fortune to survive returned home to England with as much profit as they had been able to realise.

The Company was moreover an entirely male organisation. Women were peripheral to it. Some officers and soldiers brought their wives to India, and some unmarried women were initially sent from England, at the Company's expense, to find husbands. Miscegenation only went in one direction, with European men marrying—or more often living with—Indian women. The high death rate meant the frequent loss of colleagues, partners and children. It meant that if an engineer died prematurely, projects he had started often remained unfinished. If he had not left written instructions, or briefed a colleague, the work was either abandoned or more often, as occurred at Fort William, botched.

In the domestic sphere there were far more servants than many Company men were used to in Britain, although each servant had their own very specific tasks which couldn't be re-allocated to anyone else. If a servant was thought to have misbehaved, he was personally beaten by his European master; there are many accounts of servants being given 'a thorough thrashing' for alleged misdemeanours. Corporeal punishment was the norm and was inflicted on European soldiers and *sepoys* by men who had themselves been beaten as boys, particularly those who had gone through the public school system in Britain. Slaves of various kinds were common and included children who were sent downriver to the cities from famine-struck areas, where the alternative was starvation. There were also African slaves, men, women and children who were shipped to India's west coast by Arab traders and distributed overland, usually to Muslim kingdoms.

British soldiers and civilians met their deaths during the Company's advances inland from the coastal cities of Bombay, Madras and Calcutta, although the numbers were insignificant compared to the Indian dead from the same encounters. But fear and expediency drove them on, as well as the adrenalin of youth. It was not only their fellow men they had to fear either. Death from wild animals, snakes and insects was not uncommon in this tropical country and they struck indiscriminately. Hugh Munro, the only son of the Company's commander-in-chief, Sir Hector Munro, was mauled to death by a tiger while on a hunting expedition on an island in the Bay of Bengal.[2] Highly poisonous snakes, including the krait and the cobra, lurked on jungle footpaths and in long grass which sprang up after the monsoon season, making road building through such areas particularly treacherous. Anopheles mosquitoes that thrived in damp, waterlogged areas spread malaria through their bites. And although malaria was not invariably fatal, it was extremely debilitating and could reoccur at intervals.

Given all these potential hazards, for some years the senior post of Agent at Calcutta, and by extension certain outposts in Bengal, fell to the oldest Company officer who had managed to survive India's perils. When he died, or was fortunate enough to retire and go home, the next in seniority replaced him. This provided a counterbalance to the hotheaded young men, but it also led to the caution and hesitancy that comes with old age. Job Charnock, the longest-serving officer in Bengal, was sixty-three at the time of his death, an old man who had outlived his Indian wife and many of his contemporaries. Like his fellow officers, he took his orders from the Company's Court of Directors in London. It took months for letters to reach India, and inevitably urgent decisions had to be taken locally. Directors would send instructions to men who had been dead for months, and requests from serving officers who wanted to retire due to ill health were frequently received in London posthumously. Nevertheless, the Company men in India did their best to carry out the Directors' wishes, and if they were unable to, because of changed circumstances, they forwarded their explanations.

Away from the small towns where the British settled were the vast tracts of countryside. The role of the *ryot* (peasant) in rural India ranged from a kind of serfdom, or bonded labour, to men and women who tilled rented land for the *zamindars*, or landholders. There was a significant cultural divide between the sophisticated cities and the farmed areas that provided the land revenue which sustained the rulers and their courts. Peasants working their small plots of rented land only became aware of significant political changes (which they were unable to influence) when events impinged on their everyday lives. A flourishing weekly market suddenly shut down without explanation, reports of an army on the march that was trampling growing crops and stealing livestock, a demand for increased land revenue—these were all indicators that things were changing somewhere far away at a place which could only be imagined.

By the beginning of the 1700s, the Company had been trading for nearly 100 years. There was nothing original in its choice of locations, and it was a latecomer to the subcontinent. In every case it was following in the footsteps of other Europeans, notably the Portuguese who had built their first Indian factory in 1500 and their first fort 2 years later. In a grand gesture, Francisco de Almeida was appointed Viceroy of India in 1505, and with the co-operation of local rulers he built further forts in south India. The Dutch had established themselves by 1605, initially on the Coromandel Coast, before venturing to Surat and Chinsura in Bengal. Both Portugal and Holland, although fierce rivals, paved the way for the English East India Company, which was by no means as innovative in its forays as laudatory histories would have us believe.

Chance and fortune played a large part in the Company's emergence as the most successful of the European traders. The Portuguese had been expelled from Bengal by the Mughal Emperor Shah Jahan, leaving that prosperous province open to exploitation by the Dutch, the French and the English. And the French, who had come even later to India than the English, never received the support they needed from their own country. After the Comte de Lally, a capable general, was forced to surrender the French enclave of Pondicherry in southern India to the English Company, he was made a prisoner of war and shipped back to France, where after being tried for treason he was beheaded. It is difficult to imagine a defeated English Company officer being treated in a similar fashion. At the battle of Pollilur in 1780, for example, when the English were worsted the unfortunate officer in charge, William Baillie, became an object of commiseration, particularly as he died in captivity. The victory of Baillie's opponent—Tipu Sultan, the ruler of Mysore—was ascribed to his having superior weapons.[3]

Gradually, through treaties, land purchases, superior naval power and the capture of rival trading posts, the English Company became the dominant power in Bengal, consolidating its position when its army under Robert Clive defeated the local ruler—Siraj-ud-daula, *nawab* of Bengal—on the banks of the river Hooghly at Palashi (Plassey) in 1757. But apart from Bengal, the English presence in the remainder of the subcontinent was still miniscule: a strip along the east coast, called the Northern Circars; a small but respectable circuit around Madras; and pinpricks at Surat, Bombay and Fort Victoria, some 60 miles south of Bombay.

Over the next 100 years, the map was transformed, as indeed was the English Company from traders to rulers over almost half of India. A vast, medieval country whose riches came primarily from land revenue and the enterprise of its inhabitants was being pushed and pulled into the modern era by foreigners. Clearly, this could not have been carried out without the active co-operation of the majority of the people who lived here. One of India's many strengths is her genius for assimilation. The small number of European men and a few women in India, estimated conservatively at around 7,000 towards the end of the eighteenth century, would not have been seen as remarkable. They were protected by around 20,000 European soldiers, amounting to a total of less than 30,000 exotic, white-faced foreigners. Conversely, the population of India is estimated to have approached 200 million during the same period.[4]

It seems extraordinary to us today that in 1783 the brilliant Whig orator Edmund Burke spoke passionately about how he perceived the Company's impact in India. He said in Parliament:

> England has erected no churches, no hospitals, no palaces, no schools; England has built no bridges, made no high-roads, cut no navigations, dug out no reservoirs. Every other conqueror of every other description has left some monument, either of state or beneficence, behind him. Were we to be driven out of India this day, nothing would remain to tell that it had been possessed, during the inglorious period of our dominion, by anything better than the orang-outang or the tyger.[5]

Burke could not have been more wrong, and rhetoric was no substitute for facts. For better or worse, modern India has been shaped by Britain, which has left numerous reminders of its rule. It is to India's credit and often advantage that she has maintained and developed the institutions and infrastructure put in place by a small group of foreign merchants who arrived on her shores four centuries ago.

Political Architecture

This raises the question of 'political architecture', a term I first used in 1985 to describe the costly projects foisted on the kings of Awadh by greedy Company officials.[6] Definitions of what 'political architecture' means today have become bogged down in discussions about the architect's role, rather than that of governmental or dictatorial policy. It is easy enough to quote examples of how most people would define political architecture: Albert Speer's grandiose plans for Nazi Berlin and Josef Stalin's triumphalist designs for Moscow are frequently cited, although both remained unrealised. More interesting is the colonial city of Asmara in what was previously known as Italian Eritrea, a country bordering the Red Sea. An Italian shipping company had gained a foothold here in 1870 when a local chief sold it some land to develop a coaling station for ships passing through the newly built Suez Canal. In the 1930s, the town was extensively rebuilt in the 'Fascist style', a mixture of authoritarian buildings and the modernist Art Deco movement then popular in Europe. Architecturally it is so striking that it is now a UNESCO World Heritage site. Politically it was a clear physical manifestation of who was in power.

Single buildings can be considered political too, as the grandiose palaces of various authoritarian rulers and their subsequent fates have shown. The Winter Palace in St Petersburg, which clearly proclaimed power made manifest in brick and stone, was a victim of an early twentieth-century mob, as were palaces in Romania, Libya, Iraq and Zimbabwe. As these regimes fell, it became almost a rite of passage for triumphant protestors to ransack these palaces, followed closely by television cameras which showed the world that an international 'dictators' style' does indeed exist, with lots of marble and gilt but no vernacular references. Nearer home, the British embassy outside Kabul, whose construction was agreed by treaty following the Third Afghan War, opened in 1927 and was described as a 'large and opulent compound'. The building was both political and provocative, given Britain's relationship with Afghanistan, and unsurprisingly did not survive to celebrate its centenary.[7]

Political architecture in India is closely linked to religious structures. The first mosque erected by rulers of the Delhi Sultanate in the Qutb complex south of the capital was hastily put together using columns from Hindu and Jain temples, which were deliberately destroyed to provide building material and to inform the population that it had new masters now. The Qutb Minar is also known as a Tower of Victory, just in case the message was not clear. At Gaur, the ancient capital of Bengal, the Firoz Minar fulfils the same function, and close examination of its doorway clearly shows that stone pillars, pillaged from destroyed Buddhist temples and decorated with carved images of the Buddha, have been incorporated in the haste to get the tower built. A more recent example is the Babri Masjid in Uttar Pradesh, which was

14

torn down by a mob in 1992 and replaced by a large Hindu temple dedicated to Lord Ram.

Clearly the Company's own buildings and infrastructure can be seen as political architecture: a visible, physical intervention by foreigners who had legitimately taken over the administration of Bengal, Bihar and Orissa by 1765. But it feels uncomfortable to attach the 'political' label to the buildings and infrastructures that are the subject of this book. Not only were they admired by local people, they were useful too: post offices, schools and universities, orphanages, hospitals, asylums, good roads, canals, steamships and railways. As we will see, wealthy Indians donated land and money for churches, colleges and a missionary society school. Poorer people found work at cantonments and in the construction of projects instigated by the Company. Perhaps most surprising of all, many independent or semi-autonomous Indian rulers enthusiastically embraced the new architectural style introduced by the Europeans and 'borrowed' Company engineers to erect something similar in their own native states, one even naming his new fort 'Little Calcutta'.[8]

Even at the worst point in the Company's history, the Uprising that took place across northern India in 1857 and 1858, there was little destruction of foreign buildings. While it is true that prisons were broken open to release prisoners, Company treasuries and record offices ransacked and officers' bungalows fired, there were no attempts to demolish buildings for their own sake, or for what they represented. Calcutta remained untouched, although jittery.[9] So as far as India is concerned, we need to reverse our gaze and admit that 'political architecture', though it clearly exists, is not always detrimental and that context is important too.

The Indian Response

There will inevitably be gaps in a book as wide-ranging as this, heading into little-explored territory. One which is hard to fill is what Indians themselves felt about the physical colonisation of their country. Did they resent the erection of foreign-looking buildings, the construction of new highways and bridges and the necessary deforestation that entailed? From the limited information available, it would seem not; in fact, there was praise and admiration for what the East India Company had created. True, objections did come from Indian rulers, notably from the *nawab* of Bengal, Siraj-ud-daula, on military grounds when the early European factories morphed into forts. But after his defeat at Plassey there appears to have been no criticism nor resentment of visible Company expansion. Of course householders grumbled if their dwellings were demolished to make way for new developments, but this was not solely a European habit, and there are plenty of examples of Indian rulers not only removing their fellow citizens' houses in order to build new palaces, but of re-utilising their bricks and timber too.[10]

Focusing on four books—two translated from Persian, one from Urdu and one written in English—we can at least draw a picture of Calcutta between 1772 and 1838 as seen through Indian eyes, from its rapid expansion to consolidation in the nineteenth century. (All four authors noted here were Muslims: at present we have no equivalent accounts by Hindu writers.) *The Travels of Dean Mahomet* was published in English in 1794 in Cork, Ireland. The author was born in Patna and joined the Third Brigade of the Bengal army before emigrating to Ireland. His adventurous life is well documented, and his descriptions of Calcutta, where he was stationed for 6 months in 1772 and which he revisited twice, are flattering.[11] It is a very flourishing city, he tells us, containing 'a number of regular and spacious streets, public buildings, gardens, walks, and fish ponds', with an estimated population of just over half a million souls.

Mahomet names various areas of Calcutta, including Chandpal Ghat, a favourite residential area for Europeans, and he notes the 'concourse of English, French, Dutch, Armenians, Abyssinians and Jews' assembled there who in turn attracted 'merchants, manufacturers and tradesmen, from the remotest parts of India'. While old Fort William was now being used mainly as offices, the new fort, a mile to the south, contained 'beautifully constructed buildings, that, in such elevated situations, have a very fine effect on the delighted beholder'. It was 'an astonishing piece of human workmanship'. Other principal public buildings were the courthouses, prisons and churches, including those of the English, Armenian and Portuguese religious communities. 'Pleasant villas' marked the summer retreats of the European gentlemen, with 'delightful improvements, aromatic flower gardens, winding walks planted with embowering trees on each side, and fish ponds reflecting, like an extended mirror, their blooming verdure'. Mahomet also mentions Tolly's Nullah, an old canal restored by the Company engineer William Tolly, which connected to the Ganges and facilitated the shipping of goods to different parts of Bengal.

Mahomet was writing in English for an English-speaking audience from his adopted home in Ireland, and *Travels* is noteworthy in that it is the first published book by an Indian author living in the West. The title page of his two-volume work makes it clear that Mahomet's early travels took place 'while in the service of the Honorable East India Company' under the command of Captain Godfrey Baker of the Third Brigade. Baker was a native of Cork, and Mahomet accompanied him there when the former retired and returned home. Mahomet's book was published by subscription, with over 300 prominent Irish families contributing to its cost. *Travels* largely avoids the political implications of Company rule, although the author was sympathetic towards the defeated Raja of Benares, Chait Singh. There is no reason not to take his description of Calcutta at face value and accept that his response to it was genuine and positive.

The second author to be considered, Ghulam Husain Salim, wrote *Riyazu-s-Salatin, 'Garden of the Kings'; a History of Bengal* in 1788 at the request of his employer, George Udny, the Commercial Resident of the Company's factory at Malda, in northern Bengal. The Persian manuscript became a standard reference work for later historians but was not translated into English until 1902–3, when it was published by the Asiatic Society of Bengal.

Salim begins his description of Calcutta factually. It is a large commercial port of the English Company and the residence of the English chiefs, officers and employees. 'The buildings are solidly made of lime and brick,' of two and three storeys and constructed 'after those of England: they are well-ventilated, commodious and lofty. The roads of that city are broad and paved with pounded brick. And besides the English Chiefs, Bengalis, the Armenians, etc. there are also rich merchants'. Salim explains that the soil is 'damp' and salty, and that drinking water comes from tanks, not wells.[12] Describing the new Fort William, Salim says, 'The English are wonderful inventors. To relate its praise is difficult [and] one ought to see it, to appreciate it … inside the fort there are large and lofty buildings. Wonderful workmanship has been displayed in the construction of the fort,' and other 'curious and rare workmanships are visible in this city. In point of beauty of its edifices and the novelty of its arts, no city is equal to it, barring Dehli, which is unique'. Calcutta's chief drawback was its unhealthy climate, with 'putrid air' and poor soil: complaints which the English were to echo.

Salim then breaks into verse:

> Wonderful is the City of Calcutta in Bengal:
> For it is a model of China and England.
> Its buildings please the heart and the soul,
> And tower to the height of the air.
> A master-hand has wrought such workmanship
> That everything is anaint [available] and everything beautiful.

The streets are clean and paved, he continues, full of elegant men and women. The bazaar contains rare goods from every corner of the globe. And he goes on to praise:

> People, whilst promenading in gardens
> Like wandering stars, meet each other in their walks.
> Such a city in the country of the Bengalis
> No one had seen, no one had heard of.
> The hat-wearing English who dwell in it
> They are all truthfull and well-behaved.

Although Salim was writing at the suggestion of the Englishman, Udny, and was himself employed by the Company as a *dak*-master (in charge of postal communications), he cannot have expected many English people to read or understand his flowery Persian (nor to agree that all their fellow countrymen were truthful or well behaved).

The third text, and probably the best known, is *Seir Mutaqherin* by Seid Gholam Hossein Khan, written in Persian in 1780 and translated into English 9 years later as *The Review of Modern Times Being a History of India*. This is a political history by a Muslim nobleman from Murshidabad, and while the author is good on recent military events and insightful into the character of leading Company officers, particularly Robert Clive, he dismisses Calcutta in a single sentence as 'an immense city, not unlike the ocean'.

Yusuf Khan Kambalposh, the fourth author, came from Hyderabad to Lucknow to serve in King Nasir-ud-din Haider's army. Anxious to travel abroad, he got permission to visit England and arrived there in August 1837. He stayed for 5 months, mainly in London (where he saw Queen Victoria's coronation procession), and subsequently wrote an entertaining account which was first published in Urdu in Delhi a decade later.[13] Although Kambalposh had spent 6 months in Calcutta before his journey, he does not describe the city until his return there in July 1838, when he wanted to see how much it had changed during his absence: 'I went with my [English] friends to see the buildings that I had seen before. I keenly observed their beauty and architecture.' He visited the Town Hall and the Indian Museum in Chowringhee, among other places, remarking that 'the quality of these buildings is beyond description'. Fresh from England he was impressed to find local Bengali boys fluent in the English language and praised the system of education introduced by the Company: 'Thus, with efforts made by the British, Calcutta has become a seat of learning.' Fort William impressed him too, with its 'hundreds of cannons', and he concluded that Calcutta 'is a great city and settlement. People with resources should go there to enjoy life as everything is available there. You find people of all nationalities.'

Like Mahomet, nearly 60 years earlier, Kambalposh commended the area around Chandpal Ghat which was still fashionable. There was verdure and greenery throughout the year and he noted that the British sahibs and their ladies drove out in carriages to enjoy the fresh air. 'Day by day, this place is beginning to resemble London. No educated man coming to this city would remain indigent.' The roads were smooth and as clean as a mirror: 'where is the question of dirt and dead animals on them?' he asked with a sarcastic swipe at native towns. Kambalposh was particularly impressed by the cambered roads, which he compared to the sloping sides of a fish, and which allowed water to drain away on either side. The streets were cleaned daily. 'There is no Hindustani city today that can be compared to Calcutta. These are honest and truthful remarks. I spent two months there ... but since I was running out of money and there was no-one to help, reluctantly, I decided to leave.'

Mahomet, Salim and Kambalposh all stress the broad, paved streets of Calcutta, its lofty buildings, its gardens and walks and particularly its commerce with goods and merchant communities from all over the world. From this we can extrapolate that the city's wide (and clean) roads, and in particular the great avenue that ran from Writers' Building to Salt Lake, were unusual features not replicated elsewhere. The notion of places where European men and women could promenade on foot or in carriages in their fine clothes in the cool of the evening also struck the authors, indicating that this was not an Indian custom. Nor, it seems, were lofty buildings or good workmanship associated with forts. Negative evidence is sometimes the only thing we have to work with, and while there were clearly exceptions—particularly in Delhi, with its handsome Chandni Chowk and Red Fort—these architectural innovations were not the norm. None of the writers indicate any resentment of the foreign buildings they saw in Calcutta, nor indeed of its builders. On the contrary, they were full of praise, commending the workmanship and enjoying the multinational community. None of them came from Calcutta, and although they might have been dazzled by the city, they were all well-travelled and sophisticated men.

So in the absence of further evidence we have to conclude that the local response to Company buildings and infrastructure was positive, certainly as far as Calcutta was concerned. And, further afield, response to the introduction of railways (although they only covered short distances at first), was overwhelmingly favourable, and far greater than the Company had anticipated.

Literature

In the three-quarters of a century since the British left India, there has been a considerable shift of emphasis in literature examining the British Raj and its predecessor, the East India Company. In 1948, a year after Indian Independence and the creation of East and West Pakistan, Holden Furber wrote what remains one of the best studies of empire building in his book *John Company at Work: A Study of European Expansion in India in the Late Eighteenth Century.* This was probably not a book that could have been written at the time by an Indian or British author; the events of Partition and its implications were still too recent, too raw and too undigested. It needed an outsider, an American professor, to look impartially at the first country to slip out of Britain's embracing net of empire.

The first scholarly post-Independence study to examine and classify colonial architecture came 20 years later, in 1968 with Sten Nilsson's book *European Architecture in India 1750–1850*. Nilsson is a Danish academic, and his book was about neoclassical buildings erected in India, mainly by Europeans. Following its publication, a number of books appeared detailing India's colonial architecture, which included *Stones of Empire: The Building of the Raj* by Jan Morris and Simon Winchester (1983) and The Penguin Guide to the *Monuments of India: Islamic, Rajput, European*, edited by Philip Davies (1989). In the same year as Davies' book appeared, the American academic Thomas Metcalf published *An Imperial Vision: Indian Architecture and Britain's Raj*, the most thoughtful look at the links between architecture and imperialism. It focused on 'high architecture', that is, vice-regal palaces, the Indo-Saracenic versus the Gothic debate and the building of New Delhi. It concentrated on how the various design movements in Britain, including the Arts and Crafts revival, influenced styles abroad. Metcalf's book was one of the last to consider British building in India as a whole.

Following it, research and photography diversified into several strands: chatty and informative books about single towns, like *Simla: Summer Capital of British India* (1992) by Raja Bhasin, and grand coffee-table editions, including *The Royal Palaces of India* by George Michell and Antonio Martinelli (1994). In the same year, the well-regarded Indian publisher Marg produced *Architecture in Victorian and Edwardian India*, a collection of essays edited by Christopher London. Marg subsequently chose to examine cities in a wider context than the purely architectural, as, for example, the author's collaboration with Neeta Das on *Murshidabad, Forgotten Capital of Bengal* (2013). Single-city books continue to be published, now with a broader frame, like the recent *Colonial Lahore: A History of the City and Beyond* by Ian Talbot and Tahir Kamran (2016). Once-popular books like *Murray's Handbook for Travellers* are now collectors' items, and most guidebook information today is online.

What has happened, outside the increasingly narrow range of academic books (books written by academics for other academics), is a new wave of writers who take a critical look at colonial India and in particular at the role of the East India Company as a phenomenon in its own right. This began in 2006 with Nick Robins' book, *The Corporation That Changed the World: How the East India Company Shaped the Modern Multinational*. Interestingly the author is not an historian, but has a City of London background. More recent is Shashi Tharoor's indictment *Inglorious Empire: What the British Did to India*, Jon Wilson's *India Conquered: Britain's Raj and the Chaos of Empire* and William Dalrymple's *The Anarchy: The Relentless Rise of the East India Company* (2019). Clearly, there is a contemporary critical theme here that has moved away from history as narrative to something rather less objective. Historians like Tirthankar Roy, John Keay and Zareer Masani who view the Company's achievements more positively are currently in a minority.

But in examining India's past, and indeed other histories, we must be aware of the dangers of retro-liberalism, that is, imposing the sensibilities of today on the behaviour of the past. We have only to see how things have changed within a generation in Britain to be conscious that we do not think like our parents did and much less like our grandparents. It is impossible to put ourselves in the shoes of men like Charnock and his contemporaries, nor should we condemn today what they considered perfectly normal, even commendable, behaviour in a foreign country. This book therefore seeks to bring a practical context to recent narrative accounts of the East India Company; to examine its physical structures and infrastructures, and its motives for construction; and most importantly to visualise what British India looked like before 1860.

1

MERCHANTS OR SOLDIERS?

Look at a recent tourist guide map to Kolkata and you will not find Fort William on it. This doesn't mean the fort has been demolished. In fact, it occupies a considerable area of land on the Maidan, the large, open ground on the bank of the Hooghly River. The guarded gates of the fort are clearly visible during a drive to the river or when walking across the Maidan. What the casual spectator won't see, however, is the fort itself, firstly because it is hidden in a substantial, man-made valley, and secondly because it is not open to the general public, for obvious reasons. It is the headquarters of the Indian army's Eastern Command, and the army also owns and controls the Maidan. But it cannot control Google Earth, so we can see the fort 'star-scatter'd on the grass' from an aerial view.

And it is indeed like a star, or rather two stars, one within the other, making fourteen 'points' in all. Within the star fort, as this particular type of defensive structure is called, is a small military town, with two churches (one Protestant and one Catholic), the armoury, the old powder magazine (now a small museum), several substantial barracks, parade grounds, a nine-hole golf course and the mansion where the governor lived before Government House was built outside the fort. As many as 10,000 troops of today's Indian army can be accommodated here, while one of the churches has become a library, with the marble plaques of deceased Britons neatly incorporated among the shelves. If it seems strange that Eastern Command should be housed in a fort named after a British king, then equally strange is the fact that a British-built structure over 250 years old is still considered fit for military purpose today. Another curiosity is that this fort has never been besieged and has never had to defend itself, unlike its predecessor that stood a mile to the north, also on the riverbank. It is this first Fort William, although long since demolished, which still casts its shadow over the beginnings of British incursions into Bengal.

In 2003, the Calcutta High Court considered a report by five distinguished academics who stated that the origins of the city lay not with the enterprising East India Company, as had previously been thought. The site was already an important trading centre before the Company men arrived, and a place of pilgrimage too. When Job Charnock first anchored here in 1686, the group of villages and a harbour were under the custody of an ancient Brahmin family, who had been granted it as a *jagir* by the Mughal Emperor Jahangir 80 years earlier. A *jagir* was initially granted for a person's lifetime, often as a favour, and served as a source of income, a reward and occasionally a way of paying off a debt. Harvests from the land, together with the right to levy duties on its peasant inhabitants, produced an income which could be considerable if the land was properly managed. In theory a *jagir* reverted to the crown on the *jagirdar*'s death, although ownership could become an hereditary right. It could also be taken back by the emperor or his deputies and allocated elsewhere, in this case to the East India Company.

As we start to unpick the story, we find logical explanations for the rise of pre-British Calcutta and why Charnock was so determined to plant his Bengal factory here. The Hooghly River, a branch of the great Ganges River which flows onto the plains from the Himalayas, had scoured out a deep-water harbour next to the village of Sutanuti. Charnock was familiar with river navigation up and down the Hooghly because he had been the Company's agent at two small English settlements above Calcutta: Cossimbazar and Hughli, a former Portuguese stronghold which took its name from the river. Charnock had also travelled by ship to and from Madras more than once and had been ordered to Chittagong on an ill-fated mission by the Company. Calcutta's natural harbour was the furthest point upriver to which large cargo ships could travel at the end of the seventeenth century. Beyond Calcutta, only smaller country boats could sail north, because the river was shallower. It also meant that the Company's warships could get up as far as

Calcutta to defend it if necessary. Portuguese trading vessels had been using the river from 1530, transferring their cargoes to country boats at a makeshift port opposite Calcutta, so the area and the river capabilities were well recognised.

The small settlement of Sutanuti Haat—a village market for cotton and cotton thread, as its name implies—lay on the east bank of the Hooghly. It may well have been a temporary market, as one still finds today in the subcontinent. Unprocessed cotton is seasonal, being harvested in the spring, so the market would have been busy in the early months of the year. By 24 August 1690, the traditional date of Charnock's third arrival in Sutanuti, along with thirty soldiers, he found the place 'in a deplorable condition, nothing being left for our present accommodation, and the rain falling day and night'.[1] As it does, during the monsoon. Many of the market traders would have returned to their own villages to sit out the monsoon before cotton planting began again in the autumn. Charnock had hoped that some of the thatched mud huts built in a small defensive enclosure during his previous visit 2 years earlier might still be standing, but he found only three ruined earth hovels. The men lived on their boats until new huts were built and Charnock began negotiations for 'ground whereon to build a factory'.

The East India Company had not bought the land here and was in fact unable to do so because it was not for sale. It belonged, as we have seen, to the emperor and was leased out. Because the emperor was personally unable to oversee all grants of land, he deputed the task to various trusted officials. In this case, it was to the *subahdar* or *nawab* of Bengal, who was empowered to allocate land on behalf of his master. The post of *subahdar* was one of immense power and influence, and it generated its own number of deputies, whose palms had to be greased before the *subahdar* himself could be approached. Often the post was given to a relative of the emperor, but Ibrahim Khan ibn Ali Mardan Khan, who was appointed *subahdar* in 1688, came from a family of Persian origin. He was responsible not only for Bengal (which then encompassed the whole of present-day Bangladesh), but for the *subahs*, or provinces, of Bihar and Orissa as well. The capital of the *subah* was at Dacca some 130 miles north of the port of Chittagong. After negotiations, Ibrahim Khan agreed that Charnock and his men could trade at Sutanuti on payment of an annual fee of 3,000 rupees. In effect, the Company was renting the land but was permitted to build on it. Just as important as the *subahdar*'s permission was agreement from the East India Company's Court of Directors in London that Charnock could go ahead and construct a modest factory as long as it was done in a frugal manner, with no unnecessary expense. Frugality was to be the theme throughout the sixty-year life of the first Fort William, with ultimately fateful consequences.

What did the Company get for its 3,000 rupees a year? A stretch of the east bank stood somewhat higher above the river, not quite a cliff, but certainly a raised area that would be the most suitable place on the flat Bengal plain for a settlement. Beyond it was a long, thin strip of land and an unpaved road that ran from Sutanuti in the north to Kalighat in the south, a distance of some six miles.

Not everyone travelled by river. Goods were moved on land by buffalo cart or carried on the heads of porters. There were pilgrims too, worshipping at the ancient and important Kali temple which had indeed stood next to a *ghat*, or landing stage, before the river changed course. Various suggestions are made about the origin of Calcutta's name, but 'Kalighat' is really the most convincing. Today we can follow the pilgrim route almost precisely by road, walking south down Chittaranjan Avenue to Chowringhee. Or we can take the Metro, opened in 1984, which runs beneath this major highway from Sutanuti to Kalighat neatly linking the two significant sites which had been in existence before Charnock's arrival. To the east of the pilgrim road, the land degenerated into a malaria-prone swampy area, heavily wooded and described as an animal-infested jungle where tigers roamed. It gave Calcutta a reputation for unhealthiness and soon filled up its European cemeteries.

This had to be balanced against the site's advantages and Charnock's insistence that the major permanent English factory had to be developed here and nowhere else along the Hooghly. The eastern swamp and jungle, horrid though it was, provided a defence against attack. The river was a natural barrier to raiding parties from the west, and strategically employed ships could guard the northern and southern approaches to the settlement. Rudyard Kipling was correct when he imagined, two centuries later, the city's voice declaring, 'I am Asia. Power on silt, Death in my hands, but Gold!' If one survived the 'two monsoons' which were reckoned to measure the average lifespan for a European here, then there were fortunes to be made.

So a clearer picture of the area begins to emerge. The present-day Holy Church of Nazareth lies just south of the Howrah Bridge, on Armenian Street. It was built within the old burial ground for the Armenian community, replacing the earlier church of St John's which had burned down. The earliest tomb is that of Rezabeebeh, the wife of the late Charitable Sookias 'who departed from this world to life eternal on 11 July, 1630', some 60 years before Charnock's arrival.[2] And while the Englishman was erecting a few thatched mud huts on his second visit to Sutanuti, he must have been startled to see the wooden tower of St John's Church rising a mile to the south, a Christian symbol in a foreign land. The new church was opened in June 1688 and had been built with funds raised by the Armenian community, which argues that the community was not only long established here but substantial too. Armenian Ghat is nearby, on the bank of the Hooghly.

The final indication that Calcutta, as it became, was rather grander than the conventional picture painted by earlier historians comes from an unreferenced statement by the historian and politician Henry Cotton that 'the only conspicuous masonry building [Charnock] acquired ... was the cutcherry of the Mojumdar family who were the local jagirdars and here were lodged the Company's official staff and the records'.[3] Within its grounds, continues Cotton, was an old tank (a man-made pool), which later became part of the Great Tank in Dalhousie Square at the heart of Calcutta.

'The Mojumdar family', as Cotton calls them, were part of the extended Sabarna Roy Choudhury clan, and the Mojumdar name comes from one of its members, Ray Lakshmikanta Gangopadhyaya Majumdar Choudhury, a noted scholar. Tasked by the emperor with the administration of this area of Bengal, Lakshmikanta built the two-storey *kacheri* (courthouse), ordered the clearing of jungle round the area and built a road to the south. Forty years after his death in 1649, the name Majumdar was still associated with the courthouse. In playing down what the medieval settlement looked like, Charnock's part in its development is played up. It was not, as we see now, a few poor huts scattered along the riverbank, but a trading port which had been in use by foreign ships from the early sixteenth century. It exported cotton, among other things, and facilitated enough business to support the Armenian community and doubtless others who left no trace. It attracted pilgrims to the Kalighat temple, it had named *jagirdars* who held land in trust from the emperor and there was civil administration in place which justified a proper, brick-built courthouse.

One of the most significant indications of early European infiltration into India, yet one of the least studied, is the rise of the fortified factory. It was an insidious, stealthy and usually underhanded process, as Company officials bribed various princes, *subahdars* and *nawabs* who were frequently at odds with each other. There was no co-ordinated response to the white-skinned foreigners, either at provincial or national level, in fact they were frequently welcomed as useful allies and entrepreneurs who would encourage trade. They were a source of wealth in themselves too and initially behaved like other merchants, giving gifts in return for favours, offering bribes and paying customs duties on their goods.[4] Local rulers, acting either on their own initiative, or as representatives of the emperor, were wary of foreigners but receptive to the benefits they could potentially bring. Greed and caution often played equally in their minds.

To see how a trading post or factory morphed into a military establishment, we need to study pictures and maps of early European forts in Bengal, where the greatest number were established. The first Europeans to settle in substantial numbers were the Portuguese, who arrived at the port of Hughli on the eastern bank of the river, some 30 miles above what was to become Calcutta. By 1537, a sizeable foreign town was developing which became known as Golin, the Portuguese version of Ugolym, or Hughli.[5] A small fort was built together with a governor's palace, and the Portuguese were clearly as interested in trading for souls as they were for goods. The Jesuit missionaries of St Augustin built a Catholic cathedral and a church, and a convent, school and hospital were also established. Unlike other European settlers in India, the Portuguese, through their priests, were ardent proselytisers who converted local Hindus and Muslims to the Catholic faith, often by various unpleasant means.

The *Padshahnama*, an exquisitely illustrated manuscript produced during the reign of the emperor Shah Jahan and now in the Royal Collection at Windsor Castle, has one of the first descriptions of how Europeans were able to establish themselves in Bengal. A group of Frankish (another term for *feringhees* or foreigners) had settled themselves on the banks of the river, and:

> on the pretext that they needed a place for trading, they received permission from the Bengalis to construct a few edifices. Over time, due to the indifference of the governors of Bengal, many Franks gathered there and built dwellings of the utmost splendor and strength, fortified with cannons, guns, and other instruments of war. It was not long before it became a large settlement ... The Franks' ships trafficked at this port, and commerce was established, causing the market at the port of Satgaon to slump. Of the peasants of those places, they converted some to Christianity by force and others through greed and sent them off to Europe in their ships ...

The emperor 'decided that when he gained control over this region he would eradicate the corruption of these abominators from the realm'.[6] And this is what he did over 2 days in September 1632. The accompanying illustration to this account shows Portuguese men wearing lacy collars and ruffs, wide-brimmed feathered hats and padded doublets, armed with muskets and rowing desperately away from Hughli. They are accompanied by a couple of fair-skinned women and a number of turbaned men. One of the escape boats is sinking, and a couple of Portuguese are swimming for their lives, their hats floating forlornly on the surface of the water.

Behind them is the substantial town of Hughli, with the large cathedral of St Paul's in a prominent position amid a forest of domes and spires. Men are carrying valuables out of the Portuguese governor's house, which has been mined by the Mughal engineers and from which rises a cloud of black smoke. On the west bank the army has set up cannons, while the Mughal soldiers are sailing across the river armed with crossbows and matchlock rifles. A number of Portuguese were killed during the encounter, and captured prisoners were force-marched to the Mughal court, then at Agra. The battle of Hughli marked the end of Portuguese settlements in northern India, although pockets of Portuguese remained, including a convent. Apart from their forced conversions of local people—'peasants', as the text describes them—there were tensions here which resurfaced a century later when the English Company was establishing itself at Calcutta. At Hughli, there was the pretext of a trading post and the granting of local permission 'from the Bengalis' and not from the emperor; the indifference of the *subahdars* of Bengal to what was happening; the magnificence of the fine, European-style buildings leading naturally to royal envy and the transfer of commerce away from previously prosperous, Indian-controlled areas. (In fact, the port of Satgaon was silting up and the course of the river was changing.) It illustrates too the ongoing conflict between provinces on the periphery of the Mughal Empire and how the centre based at Delhi or Agra could not always control powerful local *subahdars*. When a fellow Jesuit, the cartographer Joseph Tieffenthaler, visited Hughli more than a century after the expulsion, he noted that the governor's palace and the fort had been abandoned, and that the Augustine convent and the churches were 'entirely ruined—nothing at all remains of the Jesuit habitation,' he wrote sadly. [7]

With the Portuguese gone, trading faltered, but only briefly. As the Portuguese were leaving, the Dutch were moving in next door, to the adjoining village of Chinsura. Both countries were competitors for trade, not just in India but in the wider world of seventeenth-century expansion out of Europe. The Portuguese had initially sailed west, across the Atlantic to South America where they were to colonise Brazil. The Dutch had gone east, to the Spice Islands of Indonesia and Java, to establish a capital at Jakarta in 1619. Bengal was therefore not the chief area of interest for either country, but a place where the trading of luxury goods like muslin, saltpetre, opium and spices could augment larger profits made elsewhere in the world.

In the absence of any physical remains of forts or fortified factories in Bengal from this early European period, we have to examine other sources, mainly visual. The first is a bird's-eye view of the Dutch factory at Chinsura, painted by Hendrik van Schuylenburgh in 1665. [8] It shows an elegant, walled structure that the governors of Bengal could justifiably argue was an adornment to their province. The walls enclosing the factory stand 10 feet tall, topped with tiles. High as the walls are, two riders on elephants in the foreground can easily peer over them. What they will see inside the walls is a *charbagh*, a garden with plants and trees laid out in four squares bisected by paths. The main entrance to the factory has an elaborate gateway, thronged with Indian merchants. It leads into an interior courtyard flanked by warehouses and offices. Closing the courtyard at the far end is the two-storeyed house of the Dutch governor. Prominently displayed in a smaller courtyard is the flag of the Vereenigde Oost-Indische Compagnie, the Dutch East India Company, usually referred to as the VOC. Built into the tile-topped walls are small apartments for the Indian staff who are needed to service the factory, and there are stables with horses neatly lined up in their stalls. Two wells within the walls are visible. The Hooghly runs nearby, busy with Dutch sailing ships and an Indian barge which is being rowed vigorously towards the factory. It too is flying the VOC flag. To the extreme right of the painting is a corner of the original Dutch cemetery, before its removal a century later to its present site.

It is an enchanting painting in its detail. We can actually see the Dutch factors in their plumed hats emerging from the warehouse, conversing with each other in the courtyard as they stroll outside the factory with an armed guard. A Dutch woman in a fashionable tall black hat is strolling through the *charbagh*. Coolies in loincloths are carrying bales of goods on their heads, watering the gardens, making ropes and tending to the horses, while Indian merchants are negotiating with the foreign factors. It is a vision of harmonious existence. The foreigners are bringing trade and prosperity to this part of Bengal. Local people have employment and *gomastas* (middlemen) have a flourishing market for their wares. The VOC from its eastern headquarters in Batavia had created what was known, rather grandly, as the Directorate of Bengal in 1655, and the Dutch factory was its chief asset here.

Outside the factory walls, an important man—the *subahdar* Shaista Khan—is holding court in a large, tented enclosure. A procession of white-clad Indian men walk past him, their leader holding the VOC flag. Horses and camels are paraded in front of him. The *subahdar* was anxious to woo the Dutch, not only because they stimulated trade along the river but also because he needed military assistance in recapturing the port of Chittagong in east Bengal, which had fallen to an unlikely alliance of Arakanese and Portuguese invaders. At this point, in 1665, there are no obvious signs of fortifications around the Chinsura factory, but further upriver the British—in their pre-Calcutta days, operating from the small and undefended factory at Cossimbazar—still 'regarded with envious eyes the modest defences which the Dutch, through bribery and a display of some military power, were allowed to erect around their factory at Chinsura'.[9] In return for assisting Shaista Khan in his own small wars, the Dutch were permitted to fortify their factory, which was named Fort Gustavus in 1743. The National Archives of the Netherlands in Amsterdam hold a map of the fort, drawn in the same year.[10]

Gone now is the simple wall around the old factory. In its place is firstly a moat, next a substantial outer wall, inside that a ditch and finally the walls of the original factory. There are bastions at each corner for cannons. The main gateway where Indian traders would meet and gossip is now a forbidding place, with high walls, ravelins and a barred door. The path to the river, once a tree-lined avenue, is now equally fortified with water-filled ditches, and a drawbridge leads into the fort. A redoubt, or outpost, stands in place of an earlier tree-surrounded bungalow. The VOC flagstaff has been moved from inside the factory and now stands aggressively on the riverbank.

There were a number of similarly named, European-owned structures around the Indian coasts: Fort St George at Madras and Fort St David south of Madras, both established by the English Company. The Danes had Fort Dansborg at Tranquebar, and the French Company had Fort Louis at Pondicherry as well as Fort d'Orleans at Chandernagore, which had been established in 1673 with permission from the same *subahdar*, Shaista Khan. So Charnock starts to look less like a pioneer and more like someone who sees competing Europeans taking the best places along the Hooghly. The area he selected for the factory, later to become Fort William, was to the south of Sutanuti, near the *kacheri* of the Majumdar family. Kipling writes about Calcutta being 'chance-directed, chance-erected', but there was nothing casual about this first substantial British intervention. The old courthouse gave authority to the neighbourhood. It was already being used by the Company for living accommodation and the storage of account books and papers which had been moved there from the thatched huts. Both convenience and familiarity must have played a part in the choosing of the fort site, as well as an unvoiced feeling that this was the centre of the place called Calcutta, no matter how small it may have been. When Charnock died on 10 January 1693, he was interred in 'the burying ground' due south of the area mapped out for the factory. The position of this first Anglican cemetery reinforces the idea that this was cultivated land but on the outskirts of a small settlement. It was only later that this cemetery was incorporated into the present St John's churchyard.

The factory site was marked out in 1693 by the Company official Sir John Goldsborough, who was not only admiral of the East India fleet but also chief of the Company. He chose the raised area on the riverbank and mapped out a large, rectangular site, slightly wider at its southern end.[11] There is a hint that a European building already stood on the site, inhabited by 'papist priests', the robust Anglican description of Catholic missionaries. Goldsborough wrote: 'I turned their priests from hence and their Mass house was to be pulled down in Course to make way for the factorie ...'[12]

The appointment of an admiral to supervise the initial layout of the factory had not been a whimsical gesture. 'A passing commander,' wrote the Court of Directors, 'will instruct you therein and give you his opinion what is necessary to be done to make your buildings more commodious, strong and tenable, ffortification being one part of the usuall Study of accomplisht Marriners'.[13] This might have had something to do with the rather haphazard nature of the factory's construction. Company officials sent out to Calcutta as factors were generally resourceful men, but they did not necessarily count engineering among their qualifications. Strange as it may seem, it was often seamen—and particularly gunners—who were involved in designing the earliest fortified European buildings around the Indian coast. This was because the first English guns employed on land came from the Company's ships, either brought from English foundries or captured at sea from enemy ships. The gunners advised on the mounting of ordnance on land, and particularly at the factories where corner bastions were built to accommodate the cannons. The angle of elevation—that is, the extent to which the cannon could be raised or lowered on its carriage—determined the height of platforms within the factories' walls.

Old Fort William had begun modestly enough. We only have written records here, which show that Goldsborough, before his sudden death 3 months after his arrival in Bengal, had ordered the construction of a 'mud wall' around the new factory. This would have been a simple ramped-up wall of compacted earth, topped with tiles to stop it washing away during the monsoon. There was no natural stone at hand. The nearest quarries were 240 miles upriver at Rajmahal or at Chunar, even further away at 400 miles. Kiln-baked bricks, described as *pukka*, were cheap and easily produced, and they formed the building material of Bengal, as they still do today. Also known as 'burnt bricks', to distinguish them from sun-dried (*kaccha*) bricks, they could be bought for a rupee per thousand, and 'wood costs nothing', as Goldsborough told the Company's Directors.

Within the central courtyard of the factory was the president's house,[14] warehouses for goods awaiting shipment, offices for the clerks or writers who recorded prices and transactions, and a carpenters' yard. The president was the executive director of the enterprise, living onsite in a Company-provided house, responsible to his masters not only for turning a profit on the annual exchange of goods but also for supervising his staff, who included Portuguese, Indians and Anglo Indians, as well as young Britons hoping to become junior merchants and make their fortunes. The European 'factory' was not a place where anything was made: it was the place where 'factors' or traders worked. Thus a 'factory' can be better understood as a trading post. A factory was also home to the Europeans who worked there, in effect a miniature town with an established hierarchy.

When Company officials were not engaged in actual trading— counting the bales of cloth, negotiating with *gomastas*, directing the loading and unloading of ships and the upkeep of the factories during the monsoon season—they were pursuing two important goals: gaining permission to trade and gaining permission to fortify their factories. Early correspondence between the Court of Directors and their servants in Bengal, Madras and Bombay emphasise that permission to trade, with the blessing of the emperor and his local rulers, was paramount. Bribes and legitimate payments for the right to trade were factored into the profits expected from the English settlements. At the same time, there was a cat-and-mouse game played between the Company's men and watchful local officials. If the new factories started to look more like small forts than simple trading posts, then they were liable to be attacked on the grounds that the paramountcy of the local chief was threatened. On the other hand, if the trading posts were *not* fortified, even by something as simple as a mud wall, then they were at risk of attack and plunder, either by legitimate local rulers or by marauders roving across northern India. Meanwhile, Company officials complained about their 'fenceless factories' and took covert measures to fortify them, adding a bastion here and a curtain wall there.

Concerns about security went hand in hand with expansion outside the factory. The latter was supposed to pay for the former. The more land that the Company could rent, the higher its revenue would be, revenue that would be invested back not only into increasing trade and shareholder profits, but into better defence and more guns too. It seemed a perfect circle, and the Court of Directors grew bold in its instructions to the men in Bengal. They were instructed to hire 'from the zamindar [landholder] of that country 3 or 4 miles circumjacent to your factory at the rent of 800 or 1,000 rupees annually or rather than fail, double that Sum by which hereafter in peaceable times a great revenue may accrue to the Company'.[15] It was therefore annoying to find that the local *zamindar*, one of the Majumdar family, was not prepared to rent land direct to the Company. He argued that he didn't mind renting his land around the factory to his fellow countrymen (who could in turn rent it to the Company), because he could always retrieve it from them when he wished. But he held that if the land was rented to the Right Honourable Company, then it would be 'wholly lost to him, that we [the Company] are a powerful people and that he cannot be possessed of his country again when he sees occasion'. There were mutterings inside the factory about problems with local inferior *zamindars*, and it was decided to approach the newly appointed *subahdar* of Bengal, Prince Azim-us-Shan, successor to Ibrahim Khan.

Azim-us-Shan was the grandson of the Emperor Aurangzeb and had been appointed prince by his grandfather. Word came to the Company men at Calcutta that the prince had requested a number of gifts to ease the forthcoming negotiations, and these included various kinds of alcohol, pistols, broadcloth and a watch. Three small brass cannon were added together with 'some new Flint ware', a durable and elegant kind of china. The Majumdar *zamindars* offered a straight bribe of 6,000 rupees, but the Company's pockets were deeper. For a sizeable payment of 16,000 rupees, the Company secured the *subahdar*'s agreement that land around the fort could be leased to the Company. The annual rent for the three villages of Dihi Calcutta,[16] Sutanuti and Govindpore was to be 2,500 rupees.

The *zamindars* protested loudly, 'making a great noise being unwilling to part with their Country [and] threatening to Complain to the King [the Emperor Aurangzeb] of the injustice of the Prince in giving away their country which they had so long in possession'.[17] It was true that the Majumdar family had held the land for almost a century, but ultimately it still belonged to the emperor. In the end, they agreed to accept 1,500 rupees to relinquish their title, and a deed of purchase was drawn up and signed. This was how the Company established its hold over what was to become Calcutta: not by conquest, but with a legal document reluctantly signed by the previous landholders.

This was a highly significant step, and the Court of Directors pointed out that, although it had cost a lot 'and made a large hole in our Cash', it meant Company officials 'may go on now in making any necessary Additional Strength to our ffortification without fear of giving Umbrage to the Moors, because they can't pretend to make an inquisition in a Place where they having nothing to do withall'.[18] At the same time, it was necessary to begin recouping the rent, and this was done by levying duties on the people in the rented villages. The Company now had jurisdiction over the rents, the leases, the uncultivated land, the ponds, the groves; rights over fishing and woodland; and the right to collect taxes from the resident artisans. A grain market was set up and a small fee was charged for buyers and sellers, which was called the 'grain fines'. Petty taxes and other duties were imposed but did not amount to very much; in fact, it amounted to only some 160 rupees in November 1694, which would not go far towards meeting the Company's financial obligations. Caution was urged, however: 'Yet we cannot lay any Impositions on the People, though never so reasonable, til such time as we can pretend a Right to the place which this farming of the Towns adjacent will soon cause, and procure us the liberty of collecting such duties of the inhabitants as is consistent with our own Methods and Rules of Government—til we procure a grant for our firm Settlement.'[19]

The Company's losses had been steadily mounting in the decade before work had even begun on the construction of the Calcutta factory. It was estimated that the small English factories in Bengal and Bihar (at Hughli, Cossimbazar, Malda and Patna) had suffered losses estimated at £700,000 or so and that this had been caused by outright plunder, demolition of warehouses, burning of goods, extortion and greedy demands for 'presents' from the foreign traders.[20] It was figures like this that were to determine Company policy on fortifying its factories and would lead to the transformation of Fort William from a simple set of warehouses surrounded by a mud wall into something that gave the appearance (falsely, as it turned out) of a defensible fortress.

In 1696, 3 years after Job Charnock's death, Charles Eyre, his son-in-law and successor as senior factor or agent, obtained a further concession from the then *subahdar* Ibrahim Khan that allowed him to put up proper brick walls around the Calcutta factory and replace the thatched mud warehouses with permanent brick buildings. Sir Thomas Roe, the English ambassador to the Mughal court at the beginning of the seventeenth century, had written succinctly to the East India Company that 'a war and traffic [trade] are incompatible'. He continued, 'if you will profit, seek it at sea, and in quiet trade; for without controversy, it is an error to affect garrisons and land wars in India'.[21] This policy of strength at sea and 'quiet' trading on land was being abandoned for pragmatic reasons by the end of the century.

The rise of the East India Company is often seen as the result of an irresistible, unstoppable force resulting from the vacuum left by the collapsing Mughal Empire. This is not entirely true. The Company's rise was not a discrete event, isolated from its Indian surroundings or even from its English origins. It observed (initially, at least), even if it did not always obey, the hierarchy of Mughal administration. Permissions continued to be sought for trading and the right to fortify factories, with a mixture of outright payments and bribes. Under Emperor Aurangzeb and his unceasing small wars, the Mughal Empire expanded to its greatest territorial size, its largest revenue and sowed the seeds of its rapid downfall after the emperor's death in 1707.

Aurangzeb himself wrote, 'Death drops the curtain even on Emperors,' and with his passing, a new and unsettling scenario emerged. In little over a decade after his death, three provincial *subahdars*, formerly deputies of the emperor, declared themselves independent and established dynastic rule in the areas to which they had been assigned. In Bengal, Murshid Quli Khan—who had served under Aurangzeb in southern India—set himself up as *nawab* and transferred the administrative functions of the province from Dacca to Murshidabad, then a small township on the Bhagirathi River, some 140 miles north of Calcutta. But this didn't mean that the old order was overthrown—far from it. This was not a revolution in the post-medieval European sense. No one was more anxious that the status quo should be maintained than the new *nawab*, and in fact land revenue increased thanks to his administrative reforms. Murshidabad grew in size and importance, and Murshid Quli Khan held court in his new palace of Chehil Satun. He was able to remit to the emperor as tribute not only money, but elephants, horses, 'wolf-leather shields', fine fabrics, ivory, musk and, interestingly, 'European manufactures and presents received from Christians,' which he dutifully passed on.[22] It was a later successor—the sixth nawab of Bengal, Siraj-ud-daula—whose assault on the Company's factory in Calcutta was to alter the course of India's history.

Aurangzeb had been on the throne for nearly half a century during the establishment of European trading posts at Bombay, Madras and Bengal. His relationship with foreign traders was pragmatic: if they threatened or attacked him he retaliated, but he otherwise made no move to expel or kill them as his father Emperor Shah Jehan had done at Hughli.[23] On Aurangzeb's death, a number of short-lived successors came to the throne. Some were overthrown by assassination or lost through an early death like the ill-fated Emperor Rafi-ud Darajat, whose reign lasted less than 3½ months.

The Court of Directors had long anticipated the emperor's death and the 'civil wars' that were likely to follow, and it advised that the way to avoid 'our estates [being] in danger' was to strengthen the fortifications. 'But,' the Court added:

> if a regular fortification will make the Moors suspicious ... you may do something that may answer the end pretty well in building your factory very strong with brick and lime and on occasion the windows may serve for Port holes, making the main timbers of the floor very substantial fit to bear a great Gun and the corners of the factory may have each an angle built as if designed for Closets ... Strengthen your Selves whether by this way or building strong Points in proper place on pretence of warehouses ...[24]

This directive, issued in 1699, marks a significant turning point in the role of the fortified factory in Bengal. It was signalled by the fact that the main building, which had up to this time been referred to as a 'factory', would now be known as Fort William, after the English king, William of Orange. At the same time, the Company's men at Calcutta got a welcome boost: 'In consideration of the great investments made years in Bengall,' wrote the Court of Directors, 'our being now possessed of a strong fortification and large Tract of Land and prospect from thence of raising a considerable Revenue in due time and of your having been made independent of our other ffactories, hath inclined us to declare Bengall a Presidency.'[25] This was a title that had been held by both Madras and Bombay since the 1680s. There were now three coastal towns in India governed by appointed presidents.

The policy of the Court of Directors was twofold; firstly, to build factories that would be defensible against powerful Indian rulers, from the emperor at the top to his deputy the *nawab* of Bengal and putative rivals; secondly, to increase profits for the Company by renting more and more land around the factories, which by subletting and imposing various taxes, duties and fines would bring in more revenue. The days when a factory was only lightly walled to deter burglars and roving bands of *dacoits* had gone. Now the factory had become 'politicised' as a powerful foreign enclave fortified to repel 'the Moors' in whatever form they presented themselves. At the same time, Company engineers were criticised for what the

Directors in London saw as unnecessary expenditure on defensive measures, with the result that Fort William was never properly supported financially from home. The suggestion that the fort's walls should be made 'very strong with brick and lime' was partially implemented, as was discovered when the site was excavated in 1880 for the foundations of the new Eastern Railway headquarters. It was found that exterior walls had been made of large bricks 'with a thin coat of lime plaster of a rich crimson tint and articulated in imitation of stone work'. Large oyster shells were found embedded in the walls and fillings. So outwardly the fort appeared to be a solid stone structure, its bricks painted red to imitate granite blocks.[26] Inside, it was far less impressive, or defensible. The suggestion that the bastions at the corners of the fort should be disguised as lavatories was not apparently taken up.

Although nothing remains today of the old fort, a ghostly outline of it still exists in the streets of Kolkata behind the General Post Office. Set into the post office steps are thin brass lines marking the outline of the south-east bastion. Street patterns, once established, tend to endure the passage of time; it is the buildings along them that change. So we can walk past what was the fort's eastern wall, where the great gateway stood facing St Anne's Church and the town. Turning left along the north wall towards the river, we find that what was the shore line in 1700 is now several streets inland and that the Hooghly can only be glimpsed through alleys leading off the vanished west wall of the fort. At the south-west bastion site, we turn right and return to the post office. The whole walk takes less than half an hour, a useful indicator that old Fort William was one of the smaller European factories, unlike those at Chinsura and Chandernagore. It was also one of the least elaborate, being simply a fortified enclosure around a raised platform. On the platform stood the president's three-storeyed house, completed in 1702, the same year that the Union flag was first flown.

Northwards was a low and dismal row of brick-built cell-like offices where the clerks or writers worked. These were, however, an improvement on their earlier 'thatched lodgings', which were repeatedly blown down during the monsoon season. Another hazard for thatched huts was fire, and a number of such places belonging to the Company's sailors and soldiers were destroyed in a fire that 'consumed the whole Bazar' while the fort was being constructed. Only the president's house had any pretension to decoration, with stucco mouldings above the windows. Apart from that the fort was a utilitarian structure, with a single crane on the riverside wharf to lift goods in and out of the ships. There were no pleasant gardens, as we saw in the Dutch fort at Chinsura, nor was there a place for worship like the Catholic church securely built within the French Fort d'Orleans at Chandernagore. The Court of Directors was very clear that the Company fort was strictly for business, and that its defence came second to the trade it was expected to generate.

As the Company's trade and land acquisitions expanded, more British staff and soldiers were needed who in turn required accommodation, food and drink, entertainment and a place to worship. It was estimated in 1704 that 'a hundred Europe soldiers' were necessary for the fort's defence and the surrounding area. Initially, both soldiers and sailors had had to find their own accommodation outside the factory, probably in the same kind of thatched lodgings as the clerks. But problems arose, as they still do today when military men and seamen are billeted in civilian areas. There were reports that the men were 'strowling about and hastening their own deaths in intemperance or the Natives Jealousyes', a clear indication that trained men were being lost to drink and ambushes by the local people, probably not without reason either. It is easy to imagine the havoc that drunken Britons deprived of female company could wreak on the Bengali settlements around the factory, not to mention the pollution and desecration of the little Hindu shrines that had sprung up as traders and handicraft workers moved into the area. Complaints from the very people that the Company was trying to encourage to settle around the factory are not recorded, but it is clear there were problems, so a barracks was built for the soldiers inside the factory. However, with the expansion in numbers, extra lodgings had again to be found outside. By 1709, new barracks were added on to the Company hospital, which stood about half a mile south of Fort William, conveniently next to the Burying Ground. 'And see a good Decorum [is] kept among them,' added the Directors.

Because there was little or no civilian accommodation inside the fort, Company officials had to make do with what they could get outside. Rooms were scarce and could be commandeered at times for storage of imported and exported goods. At one point, several Company servants who had found lodgings above a *godown*, or warehouse, had to move out for 2 years so that 'flint ware and Armenian goods' could be stored there. Senior Company officials, unwilling to live in thatched bungalows, began to get their own brick houses built around the fort, forming a large residential semicircle that encompassed the Great Tank which had been part of the Majumdar property.

Because the land was rented by the Company, the house-builders were in effect its sub-tenants, and the question arose of how they were to be regulated. Nominally, only the Company could lease land here, so a general order was issued that 'if any English build or improve any land near our factories or Habitations, they shall hold them at a very moderate ground rent'. If the English house-builders took out a mortgage, the president of the fort had to be informed. But it was one thing to give orders and quite another to enforce them. Not everyone was a Company servant. There was a sizeable Portuguese population, large enough to have built a new church after their original 'Mass house' had been seized and demolished by Admiral Goldsborough. Whose jurisdiction did the Portuguese come under?

There was clearly something of a building boom once Fort William was so named and the settlement became a Presidency. In an attempt to regulate rapid development, the Company decided to issue leases to house-builders, initially for thirty-one years. It was reported that 'several of the English inhabitants [were] willing to take Leases for ground rent having laid out considerable sums of money in handsome buildings', so it would seem that housebuilding came first and legal details second. There are mentions of individuals applying for building permission: Mr Benjamin Bowcher was given a 'parcel of ground lying between the row of trees which stands from Mrs Meverell's house to the water side' in return for building two brick *godowns* for the Company where goods awaiting export could be stored. Street patterns began to emerge, based in part on the north–south roads already in existence. During the following decade, early town-planning measures were carried out, which showed how quickly Calcutta was growing and with it the confidence of its British inhabitants.

For the first time Fort William was being considered in relation to its surroundings and not as a stand-alone site. The fort was described as 'very much choaked up and close sett with trees and small country thatched houses and standing pools of stinking water'.[27] The thickset stands of trees were thought unhealthy, and an order was given that they should be thinned out and kept in rows (rather like *sepoys* on the parade ground), and that all bamboos were to be cut down. Potholes that retained the stinking water and attracted malarial mosquitoes were to be filled in, the ground to be levelled and trenches dug on both sides of the road to convey the standing water into a large drain.

The most ambitious project was to extend the handsome avenue which began immediately outside the east gate of Fort William and ran due east along Bow Bazaar to Beliaghata. Houses that stood in the way were removed. The townspeople were reported to be pleased with the new four-mile-long walk to the lake (part of the salt-lake complex), and the deforestation was considered to have made the town healthier. New building was to be regulated and the streets surrounding the fort were to remain clear so that the fort guns, if necessary, could be brought to bear on an advancing enemy and would not be impeded by random buildings. In addition, 'the Houses may be at such a distance from the fort as not to prejudice any part of it in case by accident or design they should be set on fire'. The burial ground south of the fort, where Job Charnock's bones lay, was to have proper mud walls around it, built to a height of seven feet, to prevent the 'great offence … given by the Hoggs often breaking over and other Inconveniencys'. By 1709, the first Anglican church, St Anne's, had been constructed by public subscription and stood facing the fort's east gate, on the northern side of the Avenue.

While it is comparatively easy to chart the passage of early English building around Fort William through the East India Company's obsessive record-keeping, maps and paintings, it is almost impossible to discover what was happening in the much larger area of Indian-inhabited Calcutta. There are several reasons for this: many of the craftsmen and women who moved into the rapidly expanding villages of Sutanuti to the north, Govindpore to the south and Dihi Calcutta between the two were illiterate. This was also true of many of the merchants who, while they knew how to keep account books, did not keep letters, much less diaries. We will never find a Bengali Pepys for the eighteenth century. The State Archives of Kolkata begin in 1758, when the town was pulling itself together after its capture 2 years earlier by the *nawab* of Bengal, Siraj-ud-daula, and its subsequent liberation.

There is an archival collection which is housed in the Hazarduari Palace in Murshidabad, the last home of the *nawabs*, but it is uncatalogued and so far there are no reports from scholars working there. It is possible that some of the great families like the Jagat Seths, who were bankers, or the Tagores, who were landholders, may have family archives, but if so, they have not been made public. So we are left with a distorted picture of early Calcutta, seen almost exclusively through British eyes that are focused for the most part on British buildings and events. Only occasionally do we get a glimpse of the town outside this small, fort-centred area, which usually tells us more about the British than about the Indians who are being described.

It was a mixed community, with its old-established Portuguese and Armenian trading families settled in the Bara Bazar area north of Fort William in Grey Town. Further north, stretching along the riverbank as far as Chitpur, was Black Town with its predominantly Indian population, and around the fort was White Town, where regular streets and handsome English houses were being built. Using the terms black, grey and white to distinguish different areas of settlement has no derogatory overtones, as might be construed in the West, and it is how Bengalis themselves describe the city today. Little information can be gathered at this period on civil administration by the Company other than vague talk about the 'protection' offered to traders, weavers and other workers. The Court of Directors recommended to the Company that they practise 'an impartial administration of justice to all your inhabitants ... and the natives will soon see the difference between the mild English government and the arbitrary tyranny of the Moors'.[28] The word 'government' was used in the loosest sense of keeping order because the whole of Bengal was officially under the immediate jurisdiction of the *nawab* of Bengal at Dacca, who was responsible to his overlord, the emperor. The administration of justice in Calcutta was therefore the responsibility of the *nawab*'s officers, following established Mughal law.

As we have seen, a *kacheri*, or courthouse, was already here, set up by the Sabarna Roy family at the beginning of the seventeenth century. Added to this was the police station, the *kotwal*, and the jail, both 'in the bazar'. But British miscreants would not find themselves locked up here, and neither would Indian rogues be taken to the Company jail which lay directly south of the Avenue. There was a clear division between how convicted criminals of different races were treated. British civilians were dealt with by the president of Fort William and imprisoned, if found guilty, in the Company jail. British soldiers or sailors who misbehaved, usually by getting drunk or petty thieving, were locked up in the Black Hole, a room in the arched veranda on the east wall of the fort. Convicted Indian prisoners, described as 'burglars and felons', were chained together and put to work on strengthening the fortifications to which the Court of Directors had grudgingly agreed. They were joined by labourers, hired by the day, who worked in gangs of thirty men and women who were supervised by *sepoys*.

Unlike the other two Presidency forts at Bombay and Madras, Fort William did not have permanent engineers onsite. Men had come and gone, some dying shortly after their appointments, like Admiral Goldsborough. So improvements and additions at Fort William continued to be supervised by unnamed gunners, with interventions from the various presidents who were anxious to make their mark before they too were called home or died in office, as was the case with President John Beard, whose house was seized with almost indecent haste after his death to provide additional lodgings for new staff. This meant there was no overall plan and little continuity in strengthening the fort against any anticipated 'Attacks of the Moors'.

Confusing advice continued to come from the Court of Directors, who were not engineers themselves and who were unfamiliar with building materials and labour costs in Bengal. It was frequently suggested by the Directors that further fortifications were certainly desirable but were to be concealed 'with some specious pretence of the necessity of warehouses or other Buildings' in order not to alarm the 'Moors'. 'Some of you,' continued a letter of 1713, 'must have heard how jealous the Moors are of any thing that looks like a strong house of Fortification ...' Outright deception was recommended: the less Fort William was referred to as a fort, the better. There should be nothing to suggest to the casual observer or spy that it actually *was* a fort, but it should appear 'plain and snug' as if it were just a well-built factory in a compound.[29] This was increasingly difficult, as there were now bastions at each corner of the fort, and the whole site was surrounded by a crumbling ditch whose sides were falling in. Brick was thought too expensive to use for repairing the ditch, but the Directors helpfully suggested planting some small bushes or other vegetables whose roots would hold the earth together. 'Do what you think best to make the place tenable ... for we don't propose it as a Fortress to withstand a Royal Army,' they wrote. The only thing clear about this long and confusing missive was that it had been put together by people with opposing views who could not visualise what things were actually like on the ground, or how defensible the fort should be. The Directors were sharply informed that the Bengal soil consisted of two or three feet of clay above a foundation of sand, which was unsuitable for a ditch unless it was faced with brick properly cemented with good mortar, as opposed to root vegetables.[30] Nevertheless, by the winter of 1716–17, the Fort was considered complete: a utilitarian structure with cannon, that stood in Dihi Calcutta, expecting the worst from the Moors.

At the same time, something of equal—if not greater—significance was taking place. A Company delegation from Calcutta had arrived at the emperor's court at Delhi in July 1715, bearing gifts to the value of several lakhs and led by three English officers, an Armenian translator and William Hamilton, a surgeon. The group also carried with them the original *farman* (decree) issued to Job Charnock when he had been given permission to rent the three villages. The group was finally admitted to the presence of Emperor Farukh ul Siyar, after much careful groundwork by the Armenians of Delhi. Their petition contained a number of complaints from the other two Presidencies of Bombay and Madras, but more importantly it also held a number of requests: firstly, to obtain possession of thirty-eight villages around Calcutta; secondly, to be given use of the Mint at Murshidabad to strike Company coins;

thirdly, that anyone, native or European, who owed money or goods to the Company should be extradited to the Presidency at Calcutta 'on the first demand'; and, fourthly, that a passport or *dastak* signed by the President of Calcutta should be able to exempt specified goods from customs duties levied locally.

Fortuitously (for the delegation, at least), Hamilton was able to cure or relieve the emperor of symptoms of a chronic illness, and in return the surgeon begged that the Company's requests should be granted. More money changed hands, and eventually the group was able to return to Calcutta in 1717 bearing a new *farman* that granted the Company's wishes. If this event reads rather like a fairy story— ailing emperor, clever surgeon, happy ending—then this is because it is. Company officials at Calcutta and further upriver—not to mention the Court of Directors in far off London—had failed to realise the impact that the present *nawab nazim* of Bengal, Murshid Quli Khan, was making in reshaping Bengal. The Company and its Directors had made the mistake of seeing Muslim rulers and chiefs as an undifferentiated mass, referred to generally as 'the Moors'. In their eyes, there were good Moors and bad Moors, depending on how they treated the British, but the realpolitik of the fragmentation of the empire and the subsequent rise of autonomous, non-Mughal states was not properly appreciated.

Admittedly, in retrospect it was a period of confusion with rapid changes of personnel among the various Indian factions. There were assassinations: Emperor Farukh ul Siyar was murdered in 1719, 2 years after issuing the *farman* to the Calcutta delegation, and he himself had arranged the murder of his predecessor, the emperor Jahandar Shah. It was difficult sometimes for the Company to know who to bribe, and a large part of the gifts and lakhs of rupees given to Farukh ul Siyar was more or less wasted, as subsequent events were to show. Had the English officials at Calcutta been content to remain simple merchants, content to make a profit which involved the stimulation of trade in Bengal, then they might have been allowed to continue even though they were regarded with suspicion as *feringhees*. But circumstances, either perceived or real, were increasingly shifting the Company's emphasis from trader to landowner to soldier, the latter now established to protect the former two.

Despite the Company continuing to pay lip-service to the emperor, with the breakaway kingdoms emerging around the increasingly impotent Mughal Empire, legal agreements lost their power and rented land became, by default, the property of those living on it. Although the emperor had granted a number of important concessions to the Company, Murshid Quli Khan was more alert than his predecessors to the dangers of the steady infiltration into Bengal by foreigners. He could see control of the River Hooghly slipping out of Bengali hands. The 38 villages that the Company wished to rent lay on both sides of the river, from Baranagar, 5 miles north of Fort William, to Kidderpore to the south-west, situated at a bend in the Hooghly. Preferring not to be seen directly disobeying the emperor, Murshid Quli Khan quietly instructed the local *zamindars* not to rent any land to the English under the threat of severe penalties if they did so. The Company was able to evade this prohibition to some extent by using Indian brokers, who would buy the land rights on their own behalf and then lease them to the Company. But it was regrettable that the thirty-eight villages could not be rented outright, because the revenue they produced would have enabled more soldiers to be employed 'to defend them against the Moors'.

The plan to use the Murshidabad Mint 3 days a week to strike Company coins also failed. In spite of a substantial bribe being offered to the *nawab*, this was refused on the grounds that the Mint Master was dangerously ill and thus unable to supervise work. In fact, the real reason was that the powerful Jagat Seth family, who were bankers to the *nawab*, had opposed the request because they wanted to maintain their monopoly on coinage in Bengal. So the Company had to continue using coins struck in their own mints at Bombay and Madras.[31]

Although the emperor's *farman* was only partially implemented, it gave the Company a psychological boost, as can be seen in increased activity around Calcutta where it did have authority. More warehouses were built to deal with the increase in exportable goods, which included exotic 'elephants teeth' (ivory) from Pegu and saltpetre from Patna. Goods which the Company hoped to sell in Bengal included looking-glasses, firearms, silk druggets (a kind of coarse wool/silk textile) and perpetuanos (another variety of woollen cloth). Company traders continued to believe that the one thing Bengalis really wanted were woollen fabrics, though, to be fair, many of these were probably re-exported to Delhi, Lahore and other places where the winter months are colder.

Indian merchants who lived near the Hooghly were encouraged to build wharves in front of their houses at their own expense, and further upriver at Cossimbazaar, where the Company had a small footing, the wharf in front of the factory was rebuilt. A set of 'convenient stairs for the Gentoos [Hindus] to wash themselves' was added, again paid for largely by the merchants who contributed 2,750 rupees, a sum which the Company topped up by 250 rupees. Wherever possible, it was Bengalis who contributed to the building of Calcutta, both financially—with their own money—and through taxes, ground rents, leases and duties levied on bazaar goods.

In order to collect all these various dues (and there was nothing that wasn't taxed, from Armenian arrack to domestic oxen whose owners paid 8 annas, 6 pice per annum), the Company adopted similar methods to those already in use by the *nawab* of Bengal. *Zamindars* were employed, generally well-connected men who were landowners themselves, although it would be more accurate to see them as businessmen with a portfolio of varied properties which were 'farmed' to extract the maximum yield. Districts of Calcutta were offered annually at auction as 'farms', to be secured by the highest bidder. It was then up to the buyer, the *zamindar*, to collect a specified sum from the inhabitants of his 'farm', a proportion of which went to the Company.

There were perquisites for the *zamindar*, of course, which is how some of them became very wealthy men. The *zamindar* of Shobha Bazaar in north Calcutta, for example, got 10 per cent of the revenue imposed on goods bought and sold on market days. Rice, sugar, ghee, tobacco, salt and other essentials were all taxed, and the more assiduously it was collected the higher the profit. Major *zamindars* did not themselves go around collecting dues; this task was 're-farmed' out to others who in turn would expect a smaller share of the revenue. In order to meet the obligations of the auction, *zamindars* took out loans from bankers, then paid them back as money came in. It was an ancient and intricate system but it worked, and the Company was content to continue with it. To those who were being taxed, it made little difference who actually collected the money. There were of course endless opportunities for corruption, and there were frequent complaints of frauds by the underservants at the *kacheries* where the daily collections were deposited.

Population growth is a good indicator of how well a town is doing. The Bengali historian Jadunath Sarkar estimated Calcutta's population at around 15,000 in 1704, and rising to more than a *lakh* (that is, 100,000) by 1750.[32] This latter figure has generally been accepted, but Sarkar did not have access to the minutely detailed figures compiled by John Zephaniah Holwell, the Company official appointed as town magistrate and White Zamindar in 1752.[33] It was Holwell's self-imposed duty to weed out corruption among Bengali employees of the Company, which he did with a vengeance. He produced facts and figures and began by listing the number of houses in Calcutta, broken down into eight districts which included Dihi (central) Calcutta, Sutanuti, Govindpore and four bazaars. Dihi Calcutta, the district around the fort, had the largest number, with a total of 9,451 houses. Holwell could be precise because the house-owners were *pottah* holders: that is, each owner held a numbered document showing how much ground rent and taxes they had to pay.

In addition, there were a considerable number of houses within the Company bounds, but they belonged to proprietors who were independent of the Company. Their houses numbered 5,267 in all, and Holwell chose to include them because their owners bought goods which were taxable by the Company. Adding together the two sets of figures produced a total number of houses within Company territory of 14,718. Holwell named the house-dwellers as 'principal tenants' and estimated 'agreeably to the exactest judgment I can make, as well as the best information I have acquired' that each principal tenant had five under-tenants living in separate houses or thatched huts. So he calculated that the real number of dwellings 'properly in Calcutta' was 51,132. But each house or hut also had multiple occupants. Holwell reckoned that each dwelling place contained eight people, 'at a very modest estimate', so he calculated the number of souls in Calcutta as 409,056, which seems an astonishingly high figure.[34] If correct, and there is no reason to think Holwell was not an honest person, this would mean that Calcutta was even then the largest city in the Indian subcontinent. By comparison, the population of Delhi, within the walled city, was only 153,000 a century later.

The Company had admitted that the inhabitants of Calcutta were 'chiefly poor', so it was the wealthier merchants who were pressured to provide extra facilities. Their incentive was that the more people who could be attracted to Calcutta, the more the Company revenues would increase and with them extra trade for the merchants. Calcutta was expanding, although it was the Bengalis who paid for most of it. They had paid for the town gaol and they paid for the regular maintenance of road, bridges and drains, which in 1730 amounted to 8,000 rupees, of which the merchants were ordered to pay 5,000. It was pointed out that repairs to these essential structures was a public benefit to all the inhabitants.[35] But this time there was a revolt, and the Court of Directors ultimately advised that taxation should be based on the relative value of the taxpayers' properties and not on their perceived wealth.

A further quarrel arose over the building of a town hall, a significant symbol embodying the Company's imposition of civil administration along British lines. Disputes among the inhabitants had previously been taken to the Mayor's Court, set up in 1726 by Royal Charter. When the Court of Directors queried whether Bengalis should be asked to contribute towards the new town hall, where it was proposed the Mayor's Court would be held in future, Company officials replied sarcastically that, judging by the register of cases, the Bengalis were 'so fond of Bringing all manner of Causes thither, as not to end any by arbitrations, nor to have them decided by the zamindar as formerly ...' They claimed grandly: 'We are the Lords Proprietors of the Land' and added that it was not fair that the Company should pay for a place where the Bengalis could pursue their endless litigations.[36] All the city's inhabitants had been taxed without exception to build the gaol and the town hall, but since there was a much larger number of Bengalis than British in Calcutta, the greater part of the building funds came from Indian taxpayers.

The wealthy Jagat Seth family had obliged the Company by planting the Chitpur Road with trees at their own expense, a subtle reproach perhaps for all the trees which had been felled around the fort. But research showed that these descendants of Mukundarama Seth, who had settled in Govindpore in the sixteenth century, got a rebate on the rent they paid for their gardens, provided that they 'keep in repair the high way between the Fort and landmark to norward on the back side of town'. (Pyramids of mud and brick covered with stucco were 'landmarks' that had been erected to mark the boundaries of the Company's remit.) Although the Seths owned much of the land at Govindpore, south of Fort William, it was swampy and uninhabitable. A creek, later known as Tolly's Nullah, divided Govindpore from Kidderpore, one of the thirty-eight villages that the Company wished to rent. A bold plan was made to drain the swamp by building a high road—that is, a raised road across the swamp—felling more trees so the winds could have 'free passage' to the town, installing drains and filling potholes with rubble and crushed bricks. By 1723, the land was 'tenantable', and people began to build on it and enclose lands there.

A *ganj*, or bazaar was established near the Hooghly, which had to be reinforced the following year when piles were driven into the bank and a proper wharf made with three pairs of stairs for unloading goods for the bazaar. Just as the Company employed *zamindars* for collecting revenue, so it contracted out building works, and here again there were opportunities for fraud. The Hindu businessman Govindaram Mitra was a particular bugbear for Holwell, who described him as an 'arch plunderer'. He was already the Black Zamindar for a considerable number of 'farms' in Calcutta, some of which he held in his relatives' names and others where he lied about the amount of revenue collected. Mitra was also in charge of repairs to roads, bridges and *kacheries*, and Holwell claimed he had grossly overcharged the Company for work for years. Much of Mitra's wealth, however accumulated, went into building the enormous Navaratna Kali Temple on the Chitpur Road, which was painted in its prime by Thomas Daniell and in its decay by Charles D'Oyly.[37]

It was Bengali initiative and money that led to the digging of the Maratha Ditch in 1742. Again, the Seth family were involved, Vishnuda, Ramakrishna, Rasvihari and Amichand Seth borrowed the enormous sum of 25,000 rupees from the Company treasury with a promise to repay it within 3 months. The ditch was planned as a 7-mile semicircle aimed at protecting Calcutta's north, east and southern boundaries. The River Hooghly made a natural western barrier. Only about 3 miles of the ditch seem to have been excavated, and work stopped once the Maratha threat had passed.

The threat had not been an idle one, though. Led by powerful chiefs, the Marathas—described as a Hindu warrior group— fanned out across central and northern India from their homeland on the western coast. Roaming Marathas had captured the former Portuguese fort at Hughli, upriver from Calcutta, but still too near for comfort. Apart from the ditch, the small English base at Cossimbazar was fortified and plans drawn up for protecting the Presidency town. Smaller ditches were dug, gates leading into the city were walled up, gunpowder and rifles were purchased. Cannons were laboriously dragged to seven crucial points along the roads, including one at Jorosanko, where twin bridges crossed a creek flowing from the river.[38] A parapet wall was erected around Fort William, forming an outer cordon, and barricades were erected around the Great Tank.

But in the end it was not the Marathas who were to be the undoing of old Fort William. They had reached the limit of their expansion across India. The Moor's revenge came from Murshidabad, from the new *nawab* of Bengal, Siraj-ud-daula who inherited the *masnad* in April 1756 at the age of twenty-three. He has been memorably described as 'a compound of temerity, cruelty, ambition and avarice',[39] but this is the English view. To many Bengalis he is seen as a hero, the last truly independent *nawab*. Siraj-ud-daula recognised the increasing power of the Company, so clearly demonstrated by the rapid growth of Calcutta, and he was determined to stop it. A month after his accession, he warned the president, Roger Drake, that he intended to level the English fortifications 'on account of their great strength', adding that unless they were demolished and the Maratha Ditch filled in, the Company would be expelled from Bengal.

Siraj-ud-daula followed up on this threat early in June with the capture of Cossimbazar, which had been trading peacefully for a century and had in fact been the Company's first factory in Bengal. Its defences against the Marathas, put in place 14 years earlier, were insufficient to save it. This should have been a wake-up call for

Calcutta. Instead, Company officials panicked, and by 20 June Fort William and the surrounding town had fallen to the new *nawab* and his troops. The tower of St Anne's Church, which overlooked the east gate, had provided a useful high vantage point for the *nawab*'s soldiers, who were able to fire from it directly into the fort. The warehouses had been built adjoining the fort's southern wall, which meant there was no clear field of fire, and they were also quickly overrun and set on fire.[40] In retaliation, Company ships under the control of Admiral Watson captured the town of Hughli and set fire to its houses and granaries. The *nawab* protested indignantly to Watson that 'these are not actions becoming merchants!' and added that he was prepared to compensate the Company for its losses in Bengal 'If the English, who are settled in those provinces, will behave like merchants, obey my orders and give me no offence ...'[41] But it was too late. The Company had discovered it could be both merchant and soldier. Within months, the militant *nawab* was dead, killed on the orders of his former commander-in-chief, Mir Jafar, after the disastrous defeat at Plassey by Robert Clive. Eight years later, in 1765, the Emperor Shah Alam granted the Company the *diwani* of Bengal, Bihar and Orissa, giving it the right to collect land revenue from the three provinces and effectively to take on the role of government.

2

ENGINEERS, ARCHITECTS AND BUILDERS

If the East India Company men in Calcutta had been initially uncertain whether they were merchants or soldiers, then the Company's engineers were equally unsure of their roles. This was exacerbated by the lack of training that was provided in Britain during the eighteenth century, coupled with the belief by the Court of Directors that employing engineers often led to unnecessary expenditure: these two factors had both aided the capture of Calcutta. At the same time, the remit of the engineer was so wide that it embraced both terrestrial and nautical surveying, astronomy, meteorology, architectural design, the manufacture of gunpowder and the minting of coinage, as well as more conventional skills like fortifications and the building of canals, roads and bridges. This was to lead to the curious situation where many of the early 'colonial' buildings still extant on the subcontinent and much admired today were seldom designed by architects onsite, and often not by architects at all. An example is St Mary's Church, Madras, the first Anglican church in India, which was constructed by the master gunner William Dixon between 1678–81, specifically to resist artillery fire.[1] Two of the best-known Company buildings, the Government House in Calcutta and the Residency at Hyderabad, were designed respectively by the military engineers Charles Wyatt and Lieutenant Samuel Russell. Because there were little or no Company criteria, we have to extrapolate what went on from the lives of men described as engineers before looking at the often thankless task of the European architect during this period.

During the summer of 1742, the Italian engineer Theodore Forrestie was summoned to Fort William to advise on the fortifications of Calcutta. (This was before its capture 14 years later.) Forrestie had been working in Patna for the Company and was regarded as a good engineer and 'an Ingenious and Knowing man in his Business'. He had certainly been well rewarded by a monthly salary of 80 rupees, with food, lodging and servants all provided. Forrestie had unfortunately fallen ill in Patna, where he had been 'detain'd Sometime by Sickness', but he set out on 11 July, arriving in Calcutta 19 days later. More misfortune happened on his journey: he was robbed by a Maratha gang in the Nuddea district of Bengal and lost 300 Madras rupees (then worth slightly more than the Bengal rupee). Forrestie hoped that the Calcutta Council would reimburse his loss, which had happened while he was answering its summons, and in fact the Council not only did so but also appointed him engineer at the enhanced salary of 120 rupees per month.[2]

His brief was to draw up plans for the immediate defence of Calcutta against the Maratha threat, and Forrestie worked quickly with the English Surveyor of Works, John Olliffe. The two men provided three different estimates: the 'large plan, the middle plan and the small plan', each of which involved demolishing a large number of houses and a considerable amount of money. After the Company had enticed people to live in Calcutta in order to increase its own revenues, the estimates for destroying their houses were not well received by the Calcutta Council. Together with Forrestie's plan of Calcutta they were shipped to London for the Court of Directors' scrutiny and approval, although by the time an answer was received the Maratha danger would either have passed or would have overwhelmed the town. By the same ship went a separate plan, drawn up by Major Charles Knipe at the request of the Calcutta President and Council. Knipe had paused at Calcutta on his way to Madras to take up a new post, and during the autumn of 1742 he spent 6 weeks and an immense amount of trouble to take the exact dimensions of the proposed fortification suggested by the 'Italian Engineer', as he called Forrestie.[3] Knipe claimed that his own plan could be carried out 'at less than half the expense of the Scheem intended by the Italian Gentleman', and not surprisingly the Bengal Board, who had commissioned him, preferred this cheaper version, while at the same time continuing to pay Forrestie his salary.

When the response from London was finally received, the Directors told the Bengal Board that they thought Calcutta was already sufficiently well-defended and only needed the addition of a few more defensive batteries to mount cannons. They approved the Board's idea of raising a local militia of *lascars*, buying some more guns and stationing some sloops (armed sailing boats) at strategic points on the Hooghly. As for Mr Forrestie, they wrote: [He] 'may be an Ingenious Skilful engineer, but We don't see any Occasion that We have for him, such Persons have generally Expensive Schemes in their heads, therefore he must be Discharged from our Service.'[4] So Forrestie disappears from the story, his only contribution a map of Calcutta now in the British Library in London,[5] and, as we have seen, the poorly defended town was easily captured in the next decade by Siraj-ud-daula.

What this episode demonstrates, apart from the British distrust of clever foreigners, was a more serious disjuncture between the Company's civil officers and its engineers, frequently exacerbated by sudden deaths. Six months after Knipe's own plans for the Calcutta fortifications had been accepted, the veteran officer was dead. Engineering in Britain had not yet fashioned itself into a profession, and it was initially tied to the British Army with the first regular corps of engineers formed in 1716. It was another quarter of a century before the Royal Military Academy was established at Woolwich, in south-east London. Writing in *The Military Engineer in India*, E.W.C. Sandes found little evidence of training for the Company's early engineers: 'they seemed to have been trained only in the hard school of experience, which is perhaps the best school'.[6] But Sandes did not have access to information about the backgrounds of the men appointed by the Court of Directors, which was clearly having difficulty finding suitably qualified people. Grandiose job titles were offered, including: 'Chief Engineer of all Our Settlements', 'Engineer General', 'Chief Engineer Bombay' and so on.

The curiously named Lieutenant Colonel Caroline Frederick Scott came with a formidable if questionable history. Serving in the British Army in Scotland during the Jacobite Rebellion of 1745–6, 'he gained a reputation for atrocities and reprisals against Highlanders'. In spite of—or perhaps because of—his past, he was appointed Engineer General to the East India Company in 1752 and was dead 2 years later in Madras. In introducing him to the Calcutta Council, the Directors described Scott as 'a Gentleman of distinguished abilitys and Character',[7] and he was appointed to manufacture gunpowder for the Company. As a young man he had been educated at the well-regarded University of Leiden after his widowed mother had moved to the Netherlands to give her sons a good education.

On 20 January 1748, Captain Alexander de Lavaux was appointed 'Chief Engineer of all Our Settlements' and Captain of the train of Artillery at Fort St David in Madras by the Court of Directors.[8] A week later, he was given a captain's commission to enable him to serve in the East India Company's army and take up his new position. Eighteen months later, he was discharged from the Company's service, with no reason being given. De Lavaux was born in Berlin about 1704 and had served in the Prussian Army as a lieutenant and engineer. He was appointed as a cartographer in the Dutch-held country of Suriname, where he is said to have been involved in punitive actions against runaway slaves. After being found guilty of desertion from the Dutch Army and judged insane due to his harsh imprisonment before court-martial, he was nevertheless taken up by the Court of Directors.

A Swedish engineer, Captain Jacques de Funck, was appointed Chief Engineer of the Bombay Presidency and Captain of Artillery in 1752. His job was to report on the defences of the town, and as the Seven Years War between Britain and France intensified, further fortifications were added under his guidance. However, the familiar complaint of expense was made by the Court of Directors, and when a replacement was sent out de Funck resigned after an attempt to court-martial him. He had been receiving two salaries while employed: a token £40 per annum as engineer and an additional £200 per annum as Captain of Artillery, a fairly clear indication of the Court's priorities.[9]

The point about these briefly related careers is that all three men had been educated in Europe, not Britain, which was slow to acknowledge that engineering was not something to be tacked on to a cadet's training, as the following story of Robert Barker reveals. When the Englishman arrived in Madras in 1749, he joined the

Presidency's artillery unit as a cadet. After several years' service, and after his undoubted talents had been noticed, Barker was ordered to Bengal, and he was with Clive at the capture of Chandernagore. He had learnt surveying, and he was asked to produce a measured sketch of the Fort d'Orleans and the small town surrounding it immediately after the French surrender on 23 March 1757. Following Clive's orders, the fort was dismantled and its bricks and timbers taken downriver to Fort William, which was in urgent need of materials and repairs after its recapture from Siraj-ud-daula a month earlier. Robbing one building to repair or erect another was common among men who wanted something built in a hurry, and in this case the Company's need for materials was desperate. Britain was at war with France and by proxy in India, which is why Chandernagore had been captured: Siraj-ud-daula was gathering his troops, including some of the defeated French soldiers, for another assault on Calcutta.

Barker, as a soldier and not an engineer, was asked by the president, Roger Drake, to survey Calcutta as a matter of urgency and to nominate an area suitable for fortification against a fresh assault. Fort William had been badly damaged; the parapets around its four bastions needed rebuilding, as did the riverside façade. The powder magazine had been destroyed, and the fort's supply of gunpowder was being temporarily stored on a hired ship, *Speedwell*, anchored in the Hooghly. This was expensive at 2,000 rupees per month, and clearly unsatisfactory as well as dangerous.[10] Everything was in short supply, and the engineers appointed by the Court of Directors had yet to arrive. Barker suggested that the damaged fort should be rebuilt in a new area to the east, away from the river, and he carefully laid out his reasons for the move. But, having been asked for his views, Barker was promptly ignored and ordered instead to supervise repairs to the existing fort. This is where things went wrong. Barker found himself dealing with two separate workforces: one hired direct by the Company, whose men often seemed curiously absent apart from 'a few poor peons' (foot messengers) selected from among the coolies, and the other supplied by the *bakhshi*, the Indian paymaster and his merchant backers. The Company was attempting to get Calcutta's wealthy merchants to pay for the repairs to Fort William on the reasonable assumption that once the city got back to normal, trade would resume and everyone, Indian and British, would benefit. Barker now had a managerial role, overseeing a large number of workmen supplied from two different sources.

In a long letter of complaint to Drake and the Board, Barker said he had tried to introduce a regular pattern of working among the labourers and had appointed overseers to keep lists and accounts of the workmen and women. This had not gone down well:

> I was sorry to see the Company imposed upon by a parcel of Cooley's who laugh'd at me as they sat in Groops Smoking their Hookers … the Cooleys and People employ'd on the Works have been found Sculking in all Holes and Corners either Sleeping, Smoking or counting of Cowries … not above one Third of the People Employ'd really work, so that the Company are at a terrible Expence …[11]

Barker said he had made 'use of a Rattan', a small cane, to beat the workmen with, which not surprisingly had led to their raising strong objections. There were problems with getting materials too: the wrong things were supplied, which delayed the repairs for 2 or 3 days when time was at a premium. The battle of Plassey was yet to take place, and with the uncertainty of what might happen, Barker's fears and frustrations are clear. His complaints failed to garner sympathy, and he was told it was not his business to order supplies but rather simply 'to walk round the Works and point out what was to be done'. He responded with some sarcasm that he had obviously mistaken the nature of his new job and had 'spent 6 or 7 years to very little purpose in not making my self acquainted with the Business of an Engineer; though I must Confess I never Imagined my self as Acting in that Station in Bengall' and having to work under the *bakhshi* 'whose Orders and Directions have been Obey'd, when mine have been refused'.[12]

Barker's letter was discussed by the Board, and in mitigation the warehouse keeper of supplies said: 'I am very sorry he did not consider a little the Times and the Situation we were then in when these Works were carrying on, when there was hardly an Inhabitant in the Place much less Shops and Markets … hardly any thing was to be got'.[13] The Company's Committee of Fortifications became involved and suggested that the 'ablest' European invalids and pensioners should be employed to oversee the labourers who were mocking Barker. The Committee also confirmed that there was a severe shortage of materials, because the 'Country People' had not immediately resumed the manufacture of bricks and *chunam* after the liberation of Calcutta from the *nawab* of Bengal's troops. As a result, the whole of Bengal as far as Dacca had been affected, and any material that was available was at such an 'Extravagant Price' that only essential supplies could be afforded. Barker had to struggle on with what he could get until Clive's victory at Plassey the following month relieved the pressure on Calcutta. But his comments about not imagining, as a cadet, that he would be asked to act as an engineer rang true.

Things did not improve, and by 1763 the Court of Directors had to tell Bengal:

> We would gladly comply with your request for sending you young persons to be brought up as assistants in the engineering branch, but as we find it extremely difficult to procure such, you will do well to employ any such who have a talent that way amongst the cadets or others.[14]

It was not until the end of the eighteenth century that the Company arranged with Woolwich Academy to get a number of its cadets trained in engineering, and it was another few years before the Company's own Military Seminary was established at Addiscombe, Croydon in 1809. Although the majority of pupils at Addiscombe studied to qualify for infantry or artillery units, an average of fifty military engineers a year, who could potentially be employed in India, was produced during the half-century of the seminary's existence. The Addiscombe syllabus included mathematics; the art of fortification; natural philosophy (science); and chemistry. Measured drawing was taught—essential for presenting plans and elevations—and photography was introduced as its advantages became apparent. Pupils were shown how to construct gun-carriages, and there was a sand-modelling hall where real or imaginary terrains were laid out for the purpose of teaching and practising strategies and tactics.

But before the Company had any dealings with Woolwich or Addiscombe, the problems arising from the acute lack of qualified

British engineers in India persisted. In December 1783, Colonel Henry Watson wrote a long letter to the governor general Warren Hastings in Council that began:

> Gentlemen—I think it a duty incumbent on me as Chief Engineer to represent to the Board the present disadvantages which the Gentlemen of the Corps [of Engineers] labour under for the total want of opportunities to improve themselves in mathematical learning except by an application to books only, but the very limited as well as imperfect Knowledge which can be obtained by such slender aids even with the most anxious desire of improvement are well known.[15]

Watson continued by saying that engineers needed an intimate knowledge of many branches of mathematics which was seldom achievable without tutors. Hastings was urged to set up a mathematical school inside the new Fort William so the existing (and presumably practising) Corps of Engineers could be taught theory and practice. He felt there was a serious lack of surveyors, and, while it was part of an engineer's duty to survey small districts, there was no one able 'to determine with precision the Longitude and Latitude of places and therefore unable to perform extensive surveys with the requisite exactness'. There was also a 'very great want of astronomical knowledge' among those engineers who could carry out surveys and even fewer who could do nautical surveys, 'which I believe are more wanted to the eastward of Bengal than any other part of the globe ... where such [estuarine] branches of commerce are daily carried on'.

Watson laid out his argument well, appealing both to Hastings' military as well as his financial interests. Without decent, large-scale surveys it was difficult to plan future actions that the Bengal Army might become involved in, and of course one needed an uninterrupted flow of trade vessels to and from China and the West. Fortunately, Watson was able to recommend just the man to Hastings, someone who was 'eminently qualified to instruct the Corps in every branch of the Mathematics, and who besides possessing a perfect knowledge of the theory has joined thereto the most extensive practice both as an astronomer, a surveyor and a teacher'. This was 'Mr Reuben Burrow who has been induced to quit his native country in search of the supposed hidden treasure of ancient learning which he hopes to meet with in the Hindoo and Mohammedan repository of Asia'.

In recommending Reuben Burrow, Watson was taking a gamble. Burrow was certainly a genius. He was a working-class man, practically self-taught, who had left his father's small farm near Leeds to walk to London and find a job. On arrival, he managed to set up his own school, and his ability at mathematics and its practical use in navigation came to the notice of the Astronomer Royal, Nevil Maskelyne. Burrow was offered a minor post at Greenwich Observatory, which he soon quit. He then worked as a 'mathematical teacher' in a training school for artillery officers—the forerunner of the Woolwich Academy—and he carried out surveys of the south coast of England against a possible French invasion. But this highly talented man had an equal gift for rubbing people up the wrong way. He was more than fond of alcohol, and this led to drunken fights. Burrow seemed to quarrel with everyone, including the Astronomer Royal, and it was probably with some relief that his former employers saw him leave for India under Colonel Watson's patronage. On the outward journey, he criticised the captain of the ship for his poor navigational skills.

Burrow arrived at Madras in April 1783 and travelled north to Calcutta. India seemed to settle him. He learnt Sanskrit and Persian to add to his Latin, and he began teaching mathematics to the Company's engineers. Curiously little is known about Burrow; he does not appear in histories of eighteenth-century Bengal, nor in William Hickey's extensive and gossipy diaries. Yet he is an important figure as someone who explored India's rich mathematical heritage and who worked with Indian men on academic projects. Among his acquaintances was the equally clever Tafazzal Hussain Khan, a scholar and scientist whom Burrow described as a 'very ingenious native', and with whom he proposed to translate Isaac Newton's *Principia* into Arabic.[16] He also wrote a number of highly technical articles, including 'A proof that the Hindoos had the binomial theorem', which was not published until 1799, 5 years after his death.

It is clear that Burrow's chief interest was in mathematics and how it could be practically applied to disciplines including navigation, surveying and astronomy. He failed in his attempt to get

Warren Hastings to set up an observatory in Calcutta, the Company arguing that one was already established in Madras and another could not be afforded. Meanwhile, it is difficult to evaluate how influential Burrow's teachings were on the young men of the Corps of Engineers in Bengal. They may have seen him as an eccentric, sometimes drunken, figure, the kind of quirky tutor whose faults and excesses are forgiven for the nuggets of real knowledge imparted. Burrow was in India for less than a decade, dying from malaria at Buxar in 1792. He left behind his English wife, a son and daughter who had joined him in India 2 years earlier as well as an illegitimate son with his Indian *bibi*, Betsy Roshni. He is an important, if little-known, interface between Hindu scholarship and the introduction of new ideas that were carried back to Britain from the East, and he deserves a full-length biography.

Burrow had been elected a member of the Society of Civil Engineers, established in London in 1771 as the first engineering society in the world. Its founder John Smeaton coined the term 'civil engineer' to distinguish its practitioners from the engineers trained at the Woolwich Academy. He attracted a number of men associated with the Lunar Society, the Birmingham-based group of inventors and artists which included Matthew Boulton and James Watt, who were later to provide equipment for the Company's Mints. John Rennie and William Jessop joined as civil engineers and Colonel Henry Watson did too, which showed that the line between military and civil engineers was not then rigidly enforced. This might have been how Watson first encountered Burrow, perhaps at the King's Head Tavern in Holborn where the early meetings were held. It was from this Society, also known as the Smeatonian Society after its founder, that the Institution of Civil Engineers emerged in 1818.

By the mid-eighteenth century, military engineers were no longer being referred to as 'Mr' but by their army rank of lieutenant, captain, colonel or major. (This is why the Berlin-born engineer Alexander de Lavaux had to be commissioned as a captain in the East India Company's army before he could be appointed as its chief engineer. His Prussian Army rank of lieutenant was not recognised.) Engineers working in India before the 1850s were invariably military engineers, and it was not until near the end of the Company's administration that civil engineers were admitted into

India to work. This coincided with the establishment of Roorkee College, examined in a later chapter, which for the first time taught engineering to young Indian men as well as British officers and private soldiers. But for almost a century this had meant that, in addition to defensive structures, everything needed in British India was erected under the supervision of army engineers: courthouses, police *thanas*, jails, cantonments, administrative offices, Residencies, churches, hospitals, post offices, rest houses, roads, bridges, canals, docks and *ghats*. This also included drawing up plans, overseeing construction and supervising regular maintenance.

The physical impact on the Indian landscape by the British is one of the themes of this book, but the psychological impact on the Indian psyche needs to be considered too. The Company's engineers brought change, often for the better, as swamps were drained, 'cuts' made to prevent flooding and roads improved. But how did it appear to the city dweller or rural inhabitant, always to see foreign soldiers supervising Indian workmen and women? In some cases, as we have seen with Robert Barker, they just laughed and continued smoking. But for some it cannot have been a laughing matter as they toiled under their new masters. However, it was not slave labour, for the men and women were paid proportionately, and in times of hardship projects were set up so they could continue to earn small amounts. These were known as famine works and included road and canal building.[17]

The extensive role of the engineer does not mean that architects were not involved in designing buildings for the Company or other clients, although few (if any) were described solely as architects. As we understand it today, architects design buildings and engineers make them stand up, but the line between the two was shaky in eighteenth-century India and it was often the case that the same man fulfilled both functions as well as other unrelated roles. Lieutenant Paul Benfield arrived in Madras in 1764, appointed by the Court of Directors as 'Civil Architect and Assistant Engineer' and a man 'exceedingly well recommended to Us as having been regularly bred an Architect, Surveyor and draughtsman, and for his knowledge in Fortification and other branches of Mathematicks'.[18] Trained by his father, who was a carpenter, Benfield had a very lucrative career and was praised for his work at Fort St George. He subsequently built the Chepauk Palace in Madras for the ruling *nawab* of Arcot (an early example of a Company engineer working for an Indian prince), and he retired to England with a fortune, gained mostly from money-lending and trade, rather than from architecture or engineering.

Venetian-born Edward Tiretta was listed as the Company's civil architect in Bengal, although it would be more accurate to describe him as a property developer. His eclectic career had included a youthful assistantship to Giacomo Casanova, the great lover, before arriving in India around 1781 where he was appointed Superintendent of Roads in Calcutta, despite not having an army rank. He was the Land Registrar, recording the ownership deeds of householders as well as defining and marking out the limits of the town. Tiretta's name is remembered today in the eponymous bazaar he set up in north Calcutta, which quickly attracted a number of Chinese immigrants and is still a popular place for Chinese food. Late in life, he purchased a plot of land beyond the existing town boundary as a burial ground. His child bride was re-interred here, and this site too carried his name well into modern times.

Tiretta's successor in 1804 was Richard Blechynden, an even more unlikely architect, who had trained as a mathematical practitioner in navigation and marine surveying. Like others, he had arrived in India 'to make his fortune', and he was soon listed as an architect and civil engineer who built houses for private clients and designed bridges. But in the same year, and possibly as a result of Blechynden's over-smooth succession as Company architect in Bengal, the Council agreed to subsume the role of civil architect into that of garrison engineer, meaning that it was the Company's military engineers who controlled the procurement, design and construction of buildings and the Public Works Department. It was not until 1850 that the PWD was detached from the Military Board, and another 5 years before it took over the supervision of civil buildings, roads, irrigation works, railway and military works. At the same time, the Military Board—which had been all powerful for half a century—was abolished.

There were sufficient reasons why most British architects shunned a career in India during the early period of Company administration. Unlike their fellow artists who eagerly travelled east, painting landscapes as well as portraits of the rich and famous and bringing saleable portfolios home, there were no independent architects outside the Company's structure. And as we have seen, the few within it had other, more profitable, interests. Although the reason for this was the desire by the military engineers to maintain their privileged position as sole providers of the British-built environment, there was another, more aesthetic, reason, which was spelled out by a retired officer, Captain Thomas Williamson: 'India is not the soil to which a man of science, or of taste, should repair, under the hope of being liberally repaid for his trouble and expences; much less of being cherished for his genius and acquirements.'[19]

The disjuncture between architect and engineer is also clearly spelled out in an exchange between the governor general Lord Amherst and the Military Board. A Calcutta-based engraver and paper manufacturer called Ernesto de la Combe had written to the government chief secretary in August 1825 with a proposal to publish a portfolio of 'Architectural Drawings and Plans of Buildings adapted to the Climate of India': a sensible idea, one might think. Because de la Combe was an independent trader, he sought financial backing from the government, and his request echoes Williamson's complaint that India in general lacked an appreciation of the fine (that is, Western) arts:

> Limited as the European society of India is and narrow minded as the rest of its population are, I cannot expect to obtain any return for the great expenses I must necessarily incur and in defraying the expense of printing, much less reap any reward for my labor ultimately, unless I receive in this stage of the undertaking some encouragement from the Government.[20]

The portfolio was to consist of engravings made from designs by the civil architect Charles Knowles Robison 'and some of his friends'. Robison was a young Scots architect working in Calcutta who had provided, without charge, designs for a new school for 'native females' which was opened in 1826. We do not know what this building looked like, but Robison's later buildings in the Bengal capital included the neoclassical Metcalfe Hall, its design based on Grecian temples, and the striking Ochterlony monumental pillar, with its Egyptian base and a Turkish-style kiosk at the top.

So 'architectural drawings and plans' suitable for an Indian climate were likely to be based on buildings that already existed in tropical or semi-tropical areas, though not, it seems, on indigenous buildings in India. Amherst sent de la Combe's proposal to the secretary of the Military Board, who in turn passed it on to the chief engineer, Colonel Charles Mouat, who gave it a guarded response. He thought the portfolio would be useful to the barrack masters' assistants 'by establishing the improvements and a superior style of Architecture with respect to elegance and novelty'. But he issued a warning that theoretical designs, as Robison's were, had little worth and that it was better to rely on buildings already standing, presumably on the grounds that they hadn't fallen down. Mouat continued:

> The Artist conversant in the practice of Building often meets with difficulties after having made Drawings of every part and alternatively examined the whole. The selection of Plans and Elevations in the work ... will no doubt unite convenience and comfort in the interior distributions, with simplicity and conformity in the exterior thereby combining the useful and the beautiful as practiced by the Principal of our English architects.[21]

It was a qualified yes, though there was no discussion of buildings being adapted to the climate. The proposed portfolio, when published, would be useful for junior offices in the Corps of Engineers and even among some of the officers of the barrack department who might gain 'many hints and precepts which may prove useful and necessary in the prosecution of their Architectural duties'. It was recommended that thirty copies of the portfolio be published, but this is the last we hear of it. No copies exist among the Company records, either in London or Delhi. It looks as if de la Combe decided not to go ahead with this expensive venture, which had not met with a particularly enthusiastic welcome. And Robison's designs may simply have been too 'modern' for military engineers at the time.

The transmission of information from west to east was straightforward. Illustrated manuals, ground plans and elevations could be shipped out as well as engravings and received within a year of request. If some of these prestige buildings and others look familiar to the Western eye, it is because they were based largely on buildings, or parts of buildings, in Britain. Government House Calcutta was inspired by the architect James Paine's designs for Kedleston House in Derbyshire. These had been published by Paine as *Plans, Elevations and Sections of Noblemen's and Gentlemen's Houses* in 1783, and Captain Wyatt adapted them as a prototype, though not a straight copy. There were other useful illustrated publications too, including *The Builders Magazine, or Monthly Companion for Architects, Carpenters, Masons, Bricklayers, etc. Consisting of Designs in Architecture in every Stile and Taste*, compiled by 'A Society of Architects' and published from London in various editions between 1774 and 1817.

The problem was that buildings designed for a cold northern climate did not necessarily sit well on an Indian plain. The Residency at Lucknow is a good example of a building transposed with little thought for its surroundings. This was the home and office of the British Resident in Awadh, an important if controversial post, and it was built on a small hill overlooking the River Gomti. We do not know the name of the engineer who built it, nor the date of construction, but it was well established by the time the artist Sita Ram painted it in 1814. It sat among smaller, separate buildings, including a domed well which still exists today, so we can pinpoint the spot where Ram was seated as he painted. The Residency, as he depicts it, is a stolid, Palladian rectangle, three storeys tall, with a sweeping exterior staircase on one long side leading to an entrance at first-floor level. The lower storey is rusticated. A parapet surrounds the flat roof, the only concession to its location, which would have provided a seating or sleeping area in the heat of summer. Its many windows, lying flat in the façades, are shuttered with wooden venetians, but this is the only defence against the glare and the heat. There are trees, but unfortunately not near enough to provide any shade.

By 1840, the Residency was almost unrecognisable. Its original core had sprouted extensions, loggias and elaborate shades over every window, some fixed and others of striped cloth. The exterior staircase had gone, to be replaced with a large, pillared portico—so much more practical during the rainy season, when carriages could drive under it to discharge their passengers in the dry. What breezes there were during the hot season could be filtered into the rooms through the verandas, while awnings at every window diverted the sun's fierce gaze. Nothing demonstrates more clearly the distance that separated the expectations of the incoming British, with their grand notions of English country houses, from the practical, climate-proof built environment already existing in India.

Captain Williamson had much more to say about the British in India quite apart from their lack of appreciation of creative and talented people from home. Williamson himself was not only an officer of 20 years' standing in the Bengal army, but a composer, artist, author and, during his retirement, a music publisher.[22] He was forced to retire on half-pay in 1801 after criticising in print the Company's military policy, a fact that may have influenced his opinions, especially as he had a large family to support. He is not known to have worked as an engineer, although he clearly knew a lot about building, and his book *The East India Vade Mecum, or Complete Guide to Gentlemen Intended for the Civil, Military or Naval Service of the Hon. East India Company* (1810), contains, among much general information, helpful advice on how to choose or build one's own house. He tackled head on the architectural prejudice and ignorance of his fellow countrymen: 'When the English first visited India they adopted a mode of building by no means consistent with common sense and displaying a total ignorance of the most simple of nature's laws.' Houses 40 to 60 years ago were constructed:

> more like ovens than the habitations of enlightened beings. The doors were very small, the windows still less, in proportion, while the roofs were carried up many feet above both. Those roofs were in themselves calculated to retain heat to an extreme, being built of solid terras at least a foot thick lying horizontally upon immense timbers chiefly of teak or saul wood.[23]

There are further remarks on how British families, new to Calcutta in the 1780s, lived in the first floors of their houses, keeping their carriages and cellars on the ground floor. Because hot air rises, these lower rooms would have been cooler than the floors above, but it took time for the British to appreciate this simple scientific principle. When they did, the ground floor rooms were increased in height and adapted for living rooms, while the carriages were moved to a separate stable. 'We therefore, must coincide with the habits of the natives, to a certain extent, if we mean to retain health, or to acquire comfort,' he added.

Williamson was also a keen observer of how Indians built their own houses, and he commented in detail not only on the materials used but on the skill of the craftsmen: 'Some of the *rauz,* or bricklayers, in India, are very clever, so far as relates to mere practical operations; but they have not the smallest idea of planning from paper, or on paper.' Although 'it is true, that many of the bricklayers, employed under regular architects, may be seen to use our tools of every description', this only happened when they were supervised by a European; otherwise, they preferred to use native tools.[24]

Stucco decoration was ubiquitous in European-style houses in India, on both interior and exterior walls. Delicate stucco swags were looped below ceilings in reception rooms and Wedgwood-inspired foliage hung over doorways. Known locally as *chunam,* the stucco was a mixture of lime, brick-dust and sand mixed with a binding agent, and it could be coloured or left white to contrast with the walls. Williamson noted that these intricate patterns were created by workmen using small, specially shaped trowels rather than being simply moulded or stamped, which would have been quicker and more uniform. Instead, the native workman would carve the design with 'great ingenuity, consummate patience, and often, great delicacy; but, with respect to design, taste, composition, perspective, consistency and harmony ... he will prove himself to be completely ignoramus.' At the same time, Williamson admired the workmen for quickly learning new skills and found that 'The Hindu is both bricklayer, plasterer, tarras-maker, etc. and that the blacksmith and carpenter are often the same person.'

Colonel James Achilles Kirkpatrick, who designed the Residency in Hyderabad, had a slightly different description of the *rauz,* whom he called a 'native architect ... or expert accomplished mason, conversant in the different orders of European architecture'. The word *raz,* of Persian derivation, means 'builder, mason, or bricklayer', a loose term, but seemingly different from that of *mistri,* which is usually associated with carpenters and smiths. But Kirkpatrick also said that 'the maistry bricklayers I require must work themselves in brick and mortar as an example to the native Hyderabad Bricklayers who will work under them, and be masters of the art of laying on fine chunam'.[25] This is a hint that a different class of craftsman was emerging, one that was conversant with European architecture and who could supervise and teach the ordinary workmen new skills. Kirkpatrick was also careful to differentiate between the various skills, unlike Williamson who found that a single workman, in his case a Hindu, could do many jobs. Clearly there were regional differences, and the Hyderabadi workmen were more likely to be Muslim, rather than Hindu.

The scope for frustration and misunderstanding between Indian craftsmen and their European supervisors was clearly large. Williamson was a (reasonably) sympathetic observer, but conflicts would have been inevitable between a short-tempered British military engineer and a meticulous, but slow, Indian craftsman who couldn't translate an image from *The Builders' Magazine* into something three dimensional. So there had to be a number of intermediaries between the two.

When Calcutta lawyer and diarist William Hickey wanted a country house built at Chinsura, he bought a piece of land 'in a delightful situation' between the River Hooghly and a beautiful park. He had already employed an Indian architect to add a veranda to his town house in Calcutta, and he approached the same man now to furnish him with plans for his new residence. 'He accordingly gave me three different drawings; I adopted the one that most resembled my town residence, though upon a much smaller scale, it was three stories in height.' The building, begun on 1 January 1796, was finished by 15 June the same year, much to everyone's surprise. Hickey explained 'but as I had supplied Aumeen, which was the builder's name, with cash whenever he required it, he employed a great number of workmen, executing the job in a very masterly and capital style'.[26] Hickey was wrong in thinking that 'Aumeen' was the man's given name: it simply means 'supervisor', and in this case it described a competent man who could supply a foreigner with the paper plans he required, in addition to organising a large workforce. There was a hierarchy in construction, just as there is today: the client, in this case Hickey, and his project manager 'Aumeen'. For larger buildings, there was a contractor who supplied materials, recruited the workpeople and paid them. It was here that financial profits were to be made by unscrupulous men who overcharged for bricks, timber and *chunam* and cheated the workpeople out of their meagre pay.

While we know from Hickey's account that his Indian architect drew up plans for him, we cannot say for certain whether Indian architects working for Indian clients also presented them with drawn plans and elevations on paper or canvas. The complete lack of anything we would recognise today as such is puzzling. Possibly fragments may come to light in future, but the fact that we have no eighteenth-century indigenous drawn plans means we need to rethink how information was conveyed from architect to client, and from architect to builder, outside the European context. The answer may lie in the model, the architect's three-dimensional representation of a projected building. Architectural models could be made from many materials: plaster, clay, wood, paper, ivory, bamboo, shola and in fact anything that could be easily fashioned into a miniature house, palace, temple or mosque. Information is sparse, but there are clues.

In 1749, the Court of Directors had instructed the Bengal Board on further defensive measures for Fort William, stating bluntly that, in case the work was 'interrupted by any casualty that may happen to you', designs were to be drawn up to a large scale. If the drawings alone were not 'sufficiently instructive you are in that case to cause large and durable models to be made'.[27] None of these survive, and in fact no models of any proposed eighteenth-century buildings in India are known today. However, there is a handsome early nineteenth-century ivory model of the Hazarduari Palace at Murshidabad. It was made by Sagore Mistri, assistant to the military engineer Captain Duncan Macleod, who had been seconded from the Bengal Engineers to build the palace. Mistri's model was sent to England and presented to William IV as a gift from the Murshidabad *nawab*, Humayan Jah. It may have been made as a working model and contains extra wings which were not in fact built, but it demonstrates that the art of model-making was well understood and, in this particular case, exquisitely executed.

The Murshidabad palace is one of several major buildings erected by the Company's military engineers working for Indian princes. Murshidabad had been the last capital of independent Bengal, and one of the most poignant exhibits in the Victoria Memorial Hall, Calcutta is also one of the most overlooked. Placed at the far end of the gallery of Western paintings is a low, black, circular table, 6 feet in diameter, with a faceted rim and a Persian inscription. It currently has no accompanying label, so visitors don't appreciate its significance unless they can read the inscription: 'this auspicious throne was made at Mongyr in Behar by the humblest of slaves Khaja Nazar of Bokhara on the 27th Shaban 1052 hijra'.[28] This corresponds to 1643 and the time of Sultan Shuja, the *subahdar* of Bengal. Carved out of a single piece of hornblende, a basalt-like substance, there are small holes along one side where poles supporting a canopy could be inserted.

The throne, or *masnad*, was made during the reign of the emperor Shah Jehan, but it is its afterlife that gave it resonance during the troubled eighteenth century. This was the throne on which the governor, Robert Clive, had placed Mir Jafar, the new ruler of Bengal, after his aid had led the Company to victory at the battle of Plassey. More importantly, this was the throne on which Clive sat side by side with *nawab* Najm ud daula at Murshidabad in April 1766, the start of the Bengal new year and the date on which the Company took over the administration. For a century and a half, the throne remained on the terrace of the Mobaruk Manzil (House of Fortune) at Murshidabad, occasionally extruding drops of reddish liquid, caused by iron deposits in the stone, which were fancifully imagined to be tears of blood, wept for the lost province. Lord Curzon on a visit to Murshidabad ordered that the throne be brought to Calcutta where his vision of the Victoria Memorial Hall was taking shape as a tribute to the late empress of India.

Warren Hastings had been British Resident to the Court of Murshidabad immediately after the Company's victory at Plassey, and he was later to oversee the shift of administrative power to Calcutta, when the revenue office and the two courts of civil and criminal justice were transferred there in 1772. Hastings declared that 'the whole power and government of the province will centre in Calcutta which may now be considered as the capital of Bengal'.[29] A severe famine the following year and the decline in trade meant that Murshidabad would lose its premier position to the British in less than half a century. Which makes it all the odder that subsequent *nawabs* in the former capital should deliberately choose to embellish their now half-empty city with European palaces and a distinctly foreign style of architecture erected by British engineers.

The construction of the hugely expensive Government House in Calcutta, completed in 1803, had clearly inspired Azad-ud-daula, the Murshidabad *nawab*. But it would take three decades before work began on the Hazarduari Palace, standing at a right angle on the riverbank of the Bhagirathi. Colonel Duncan McLeod was an experienced man of long standing and already known among Indian princes for a small palace constructed in Lucknow, the Khurshid Manzil. The Hazarduari Palace, completed in 1837, was infinitely grander and severely neoclassical in design. Its great external staircase rising to the first floor echoes that of Calcutta's Government House. But why a European design at all? All we know is that there was a fashion, almost a craze, among the post-Mughal rulers of Murshidabad, Awadh and Hyderabad for buildings in the new, foreign style.

In 1773, Warren Hastings, the newly appointed governor general of Bengal, was asked by the ruler of Awadh, the *nawab wazir* Shuja-ud-daula, to find him a European architect 'to direct the construction of some Buildings and compleat the Works of his new Town of Fyzabad'.[30] Hastings suggested Colonel Antoine-Louis Polier, a man of French parentage born in Switzerland, who had worked for 2 years on the new Fort William at Calcutta. Polier does not seem to have received any engineering or architectural training before his arrival in Madras at the age of sixteen when he served as a cadet in the Company's army and reached the rank of major, the highest rank a foreigner could achieve. Clearly a gifted man, he became a field-engineer and surveyor as well as leading the *nawab wazir*'s troops in the siege of the fort at Agra.

A decade before Polier's arrival, a large, new fort had been built at Faizabad on the riverbank, which had the curious name of Chhota Calcutta (Little Calcutta). It certainly didn't look like any of the European-style buildings erected at the Company's headquarters. But the 1764 date for the completion of 'Chhota Calcutta' is significant: this was the year when the *nawab wazir* Shuja-ud-daula and two powerful allies had failed in a bid to defeat the Company's army at Buxar in Bihar. The immediate result was that Shuja-ud-daula was forced to surrender part of Awadh, including Benares and Allahabad, to the Company. So was it an ironic gesture that prompted him to name his new fort after the Company's Calcutta capital? Or was it an attempt at flattery? Clearly the *nawab wazir* liked European buildings erected by European engineers, a liking that was continued by his son and heir Asaf-ud-daula when he transferred the Awadh capital to Lucknow in 1775.

In Hyderabad, it was the British Resident James Achilles Kirkpatrick who initiated the construction of the handsome, Palladian-style Residency in 1803. But it was the *nizam* Ali Khan, Asaf Jah III who sanctioned the building in his capital, who allotted extensive land for it and who paid for it. Kirkpatrick had been unsuccessful in obtaining funds from the Company, which had been shocked at the cost of the new Government House in Calcutta built by the governor general Lord Wellesley. The Hyderabad Residency was constructed shortly after Government House and the two buildings share some similar features, including a grand exterior flight of stairs. The engineer Russell described in detail the rationale behind the Hyderabad building: the central portion with its large, handsome rooms was for the Resident and official functions, the east wing contained the kitchen and ancillary offices and the west wing was for staff. The building was strictly neoclassical in style, with a portico of the Corinthian order and oval rooms with Ionic pillars.

The reason this Residency was so much more successful in functional terms than its Lucknow counterpart, as well as much grander, is because Kirkpatrick took an active part in its construction, writing that he was 'desirous of it being erected both with taste and solidity' and selecting a 'Madras Native Architect and a few artisans' for whom he was willing to pay their travelling expenses and top up their monthly wages. The building was thoughtfully designed for its surroundings and climatic conditions, and as a result needed none of the add-on verandas and loggias of the Lucknow Residency.

Because India could not provide all the materials that the engineers needed for building and defence, large quantities of metal and heavy items were exported from Britain. In 1771 alone, the following quantities were shipped out to the three Presidencies:

Bengal—145 tons copper, 136 tons lead, 70 tons iron, 1,270 barrels of gunpowder

Madras—100 tons copper, 95 tons lead, 50 tons iron, 1,000 barrels of gunpowder

Bombay—255 tons copper, 186 tons lead, 60 tons iron, 25 tons steel[31]

The previous year, 25 tons of steel had gone to Bombay on the *Syren Snow*. Why was all this needed? Iron was used extensively for the new docks being built in the Presidencies, and in Calcutta Colonel Henry Watson had established wet and dry docks at Kidderpore, as well as a marine yard for repairing and equipping vessels. India had been producing iron for almost two millennia, as the iron pillar of Chandragupta II, now at Delhi, demonstrates. But this was 1771, not 371 CE, and there was a difference between 'Hindustanee iron' and the perceived superiority of iron exported from Britain. Lead was needed for bullets, and steel for the cranes that began to hover over the new docks.

Locally made gunpowder was considered inferior to that produced by the British, and with some justification, as we will see. It was part of the Company's Charter agreement that a certain amount of saltpetre (500 tons per annum) had to be provided to the British government. Saltpetre was the main ingredient of gunpowder, mixed with sulphur and charcoal in a ratio of 75 per cent saltpetre, 15 per cent sulphur and 10 per cent charcoal. Awadh and Bihar were the primary sources of saltpetre, with Patna acting as the chief distributor to other parts of India, including the Bombay Presidency and Bengal. The export of saltpetre to Britain, which could only produce a limited amount at home, was a highly profitable business, and Company men jostled with each other to purchase the concession to supply it. But shipping gunpowder to India in kegs, as the barrels were called, was a dangerous business. The average keg contained 100 lbs of gunpowder, and an explosion on board of even one barrel—let alone 1,000—would inevitably be fatal. It was also an expensive business, with a single barrel costing 80 rupees.

So the Court of Directors agreed to the establishment of gunpowder factories in India supervised by Company engineers. It was in Bengal that the largest factory was built at Ichapur in 1790 under the Military Board, replacing an earlier gunpowder factory at Akra, south-west of Calcutta. The new factory of Ichapur was on the east bank of the Hooghly, some 16 miles north of Calcutta, and thus convenient for supplying Fort William as well as cantonments upriver, including Monghyr.[32] The factory site was spread out over a mile, with separate sheds for different processes, and was the largest single industrial unit in India. In fact, as the Industrial Revolution began in the west, Ichapur was one of the largest units anywhere in the world, employing between 2,000 to 2,500 seasonal workers.

The Scotsman John Farquhar had been employed at the Akra factory, and he moved to Ichapur when it opened to become the Agent of Powder Works. Accounts of his early life differ, but he seems to have had no formal training as an engineer. By his twenties, he was working in Barrackpore, and it was his skill in chemistry, mathematics and mechanics that led to the Ichapur appointment, a position he held for nearly a quarter of a century. This was an almost unique length of time for a European to be employed in a single post, when death often halted or reversed ambitious schemes. It allowed Farquhar to develop the Ichapur factory along certain lines which frequently brought him into conflict with the Military Board. For example, he was reluctant to employ other Europeans as assistants and even more reluctant to provide proper accounts, which may be how he returned to Britain in 1814 with a fortune of £500,000. Nevertheless, he introduced some unusual features for the time, including small pensions for the relatives of victims who had died in explosions at the factory. There were also occasions where the Indian workers withdrew their labour in the expectation of higher wages, and Farqhuar was prepared to meet their demands in defiance of the Military Board's rules. Something of Scottish Enlightenment ideas and ideals seem to have inspired Farquhar, who relied on his Indian foreman, Ganga Der, to organise and pay the large workforce. News of the Ichapur factory spread, and men and women from as far afield as Chittagong, over 400 miles distant, were prepared to travel there for work.

In the first year of its establishment, Ichapur was producing 13,680 pounds of gunpowder per month. But 10 years later, in 1800, the output had risen to around 445,000 pounds per month, a substantial increase, which meant even more workers were employed.[33] The local manufacture of gunpowder by hand was labour intensive, involving much grinding, sifting and mixing, and previously had often been carried out by women and children working in thatched huts, producing poor-quality powder. The Ichapur factory was mechanised to a certain degree, in that bullocks were used to rotate the large metal cylinders containing the final mixture to ensure that it blended properly. Twenty-four bullocks were attached to each mill onsite, and they required stabling, feeding and veterinary care. It was this attention to processing that made Company-produced gunpowder superior to that of indigenous manufacturers. Trials were conducted after the Second Anglo-Sikh War using a mortar to fire a shell propelled first by Bengal powder, then Sikh powder. The former projected the shell 75.5 yards, whereas the latter could only reach 19 yards.[34] Ichapur supplied gunpowder not only to Fort William and other arsenals in Bengal, but also to the Bombay and Madras Presidencies during times of shortage. The Company's Ichapur factory had changed the manufacture of gunpowder from an amateur, almost cottage, industry into a professional operation, resulting in a superior product.

This was not the first time that the Company had moved from purchasing goods to producing them with an Indian workforce using Western technology. Silk was one of the Company's earliest exports, after spices, from the east. By 1708, there were already complaints in the small town of Calcutta about the shortage of warehouses in which to store bales awaiting shipment and to sort out the raw silk produced in northern Bengal, primarily around Cossimbazar. The Dutch East India Company was a keen competitor too, and there was a well-established network of native merchants that bought silk, both raw and as piece goods, to sell to the European Companies.

Like the indigenous manufacture of gunpowder, processing silk was a labour-intensive industry that employed women and children in its initial stages. Sericulture was carried out in the subcontinent wherever mulberry trees could be grown successfully. The sturdy Himalayan mulberry flourished in Bengal and fed a variety of silkworm, including the superior 'annual worm', the *desi* or local worm and the China or Madrassie worm.[35] Cocoons generated by the silkworm were traditionally gathered from the mulberry leaves and dried in the sun, which could lead to uneven results and discolouration. A 'good' single cocoon, when carefully unwound, could give up to 1,000 feet of silky filament, but the trick was then to reel and twist the strands together to produce an even thread that was strong enough to handle. This was called raw, or 'country-wound', silk and was processed either by the villagers themselves on a simple hand-held reel or by specialists who travelled around the villages. Both the drying and the reeling methods were to change significantly when Company engineers began to involve themselves in silk production.

Italian silk was highly prized and had been manufactured in the Piedmont region since the seventeenth century. It was here that machinery was developed that could reel off and twist two threads simultaneously, resulting in a stronger and more even thread, ready for the weaver. Jacques Wiss, born in Switzerland in 1734, was of Huguenot extraction, with that community's skills in silk weaving. He moved to Italy where he was apprenticed at an early age in the silk trade at Novi (now Novi Ligure). How he came to the notice of the Company is not clear, but by 1769 he was on his way to Bengal with seven fellow Italians, a number of Frenchmen and two Englishmen, contracted to implement the 'Piedmontese system' there. Wiss, who now went by the anglicised name of James, had been appointed as one of four superintendents in the Silk Investment, a project instigated by the Company's Committee of Commerce. The Company was in business to make a profit, but it was also ready to invest substantial sums of money and expertise in manufacturing items that could be exported.

The date of Wiss's arrival was no coincidence. Following the grant of the *diwani* in 1767, the Company deliberately sought to create employment for Indians now under its jurisdiction. More importantly, from the Company's point of view, it now needed to remit the surplus revenue home. Britain had no domestic raw silk of its own, so if the Company could increase the supply of raw silk from India, it would not only fill a gap in the market but would transfer some of the *diwani* profits to Britain.[36] It was an elegant solution, as long as the quality of Indian raw silk could be improved. Bringing the production of raw silk 'in-house' with new equipment, rather than dealing with individual merchants or groups of merchants, seemed the way forward. *Zamindars* were encouraged to plant mulberry trees, and concessions were given including reduced rents for those who did. Land newly cleared of jungle and uncultivated areas were declared rent-free for 2 years if they were planted with mulberries.

The Silk Investment was an ambitious project to establish four filatures or factories based on the Italian model, where raw silk could be processed on a commercial scale using imported machinery. The sites chosen were:

Commercolli (Kumarkhali)	200 furnaces
Rungpore (Rangpur)	104 furnaces
Bauleah (Rajshahi)	104 furnaces
Cossimbazar (Kasimbazar)	104 furnaces

The first three sites are now in Bangladesh, and all four factories were adjacent to rivers.[37] Inside the factories, wood-fired furnaces heated water where the cocoons were washed free of their natural gum before being reeled through the machines.

On his appointment, James Wiss ordered 'a considerable quantity of reels, wheels and other implements to be made at Novi for the use of the filatures'. These were shipped in twelve large cases, which on arrival were divided between the sites. Wiss carefully supervised their construction, giving precise guidelines about the distances required between different parts of the machine.[38] It was soon discovered that the wooden cog wheels used in Italy were not suitable because they split and warped in the extreme Indian climate, so brass wheels were substituted, with the axis made of hardened steel.

There were other, more serious problems too. Wiss had initially been allocated £2,200 to erect a temporary filature at Commercolli with sixteen furnaces, and he began construction in February 1771. However, he soon had to modify his design because of the 'better Information he had received of the Effects of the Wind and Rain in this country'. Professional expertise would have helped, but Wiss quickly became his own engineer. Once he got going, he was, in his own words, 'possessed with the Rage of Building' and had 'run on the foundation of 50 or 60 Pillars as an extension' to support the first floor.[39] This was done on his own initiative and using money from his own pocket, which he naturally found difficult to reclaim from the Company despite the fact that the Committee of Commerce had authorised him to expand the filature.

While building was going on, Wiss had become friendly with a fellow European, who by coincidence had also worked in the silk trade for a short period in Lyon, not so far distant from Novi. This was Captain Claude Martin, who had had his own disagreement with the Company but was now employed as one of the surveyors working on what would become the *Bengal Atlas*. The two French-speaking men, with a common interest in silk, wrote to the Company justifying the extra expense.

Wiss explained he had sought an unbiased opinion from Captain Martin, who had visited the Commercolli filature three times: at the start of construction, during construction and on its completion. He had also lent Wiss his surveying instruments to make a plan of the building. Martin was lavish in his praise, reporting that 'The Materials are all good the Bricks, Timbers, lime etc. The Place for the cocoons is very well raised and the filature exceedingly spacious.' He compared it to the Rangpur filature with its large central pillar, which blocked the supervisors' view of the reelers. At Commercolly, Martin continued, the design was:

> very convenient for being able at one View to see if every Body be at Work and also on Account of it receiving hereby an additional Quantity of Air ... Your Ovens are strong enough to resist a Siege in short the Canals, passages etc. which you have constructed the whole in so short a time with your own money and at the risque of not being reimbursed ... had you constructed a temporary Filature according to your Orders, how often must it have been repaired and God knows but it might have been set on fire in which case, How much would the Companys loss have been? Which you have guarded against by erecting a substantial one which, neither You nor I will ever see the End of.[40]

(The canals referred to were actually channels for the discharge of smoke, that is, chimneys.) Wiss planned to call the local *gomastas* (the Company's paid agents) to show them how to establish 'the new mode of winding throughout the Country'. He himself had found it easy 'in teaching the Natives to wind off Silk under your own eye' but now needed to delegate this task so he could concentrate on running the filature. The first batch of raw silk from the Commercolli filature reached Britain in 1772 and it was reported that 'Mr Wiss had succeeded to admiration in drawing a tolerable silk from the most ungrateful cocoons that the sickliest worms under the most unfavourable Season could produce'.[41]

The Rangpur filature, to which Claude Martin had alluded, had run into structural problems, and the British Resident there, Robert Phipps, who was charged with its building, complained that the natives were unaccustomed to using bricks and *chunam* 'in this part of the country'. He also found 'a most extraordinary Degree of Dilatoryness and Indolence in the inhabitants', and when he started building in 1771 he had to take a number of experienced (and expensive) workmen with him to Rangpur. Even so, the filature there, though adapted from that at Commercolli, required 'constant attendance and a competent knowledge of architecture'. As we have seen, transposing a European-style building to India was not straightforward, and neither Wiss nor Phipps were architects or engineers. The intrusive central pillar at Rangpur, criticised by Martin, was almost certainly propping up a poorly designed structure. Three years later, Phipps was still having problems. The soil was poor, he complained, it was too sandy and difficult to make bricks with it, there was a scarcity of *chunam* and the bricklayers were delayed for a year. Even when they did start, part of the building fell down, and the surveyor reported it as 'defective'. Nevertheless, the filature was operating, although it only had fifty-six furnaces in April 1774.

The four filatures were buildings of considerable size, two storeyed, with handsome European-style façades and corridors of furnaces. They were the first industrial buildings to be erected in Bengal, and their importance has not previously been recognised, possibly because none appear to remain today. These brick-built factories would have been all the more striking in an area where only forts, palaces, temples and mosques were constructed of substantial materials. Major James Rennell, ensign in the Bengal Engineers (and better known as a cartographer) reported: 'There are few towns of note in the Province of Bengall but the Villages are innumerable; in the course of 150 miles I could not discover one

Brick House, all the Country Houses being built of Bamboos and Mats.' He even found the brick-built buildings in Dacca to be 'very mean, altho' mostly of Brick, but of one Story only'.[42]

The filatures represented a large investment, both in financial terms and in manpower. The largest site, at Commercolli, eventually cost over £10,000—an enormous increase on the modest sum originally allocated to it—and it employed around 625 reelers (three to each furnace). It also required stokers for the furnaces and water carriers to top up the basins where the cocoons were immersed, as well as sweepers to keep the factory free of dust and guards to keep it secure. Approximately 1,000 men would have been employed here, and around 700 at each of the 3 smaller filatures. But in spite of the Company's investment, the production of raw silk was not the success it was hoped it would be. Various excuses were made: the quality of the worms decreased over the years, although new strains were introduced from China, notably by Colonel Kyd in 1788. The Himalayan mulberry did not produce such good silk as the white mulberry trees used in Italy; the worms themselves were not always well-managed by the *chassers* (the peasants rearing the worms); control could not be exercised over all the reelers; and the system of grading raw silk in categories from A to E was often ignored, leading to an uneven supply of exports.[43] Quantity was preferred over quality, and there was simply a lack of senior management, which perhaps, given the large distances between the filatures and the difficulties of travel, was not surprising. By 1833, when the Company had to relinquish its commercial activities, the four filatures were sold to private manufacturers and disappeared from view. Having set them up, James Wiss moved to London in 1776, where he was appointed Inspector of Bengal Raw Silk, a post he kept for many years, and where he was presented with a generous bonus of £1,000 by the Court of Directors 'as a mark of their approbation'. He died in Pimlico in 1816.

A more successful and longer-lasting Company enterprise was the introduction of steam-operated machinery to manufacture its coinage. Coins were hand-struck in Mughal and pre-Mughal Mints, a process that involved hammering a small disk of gold, silver or copper between two dies which were engraved with the obverse and reverse of the required coin. In theory, Indian Mints were licensed

1. 'The Capture of Port Hoogly' from *The Padshahnama*, c.1634. Royal Collection Trust/© Her Majesty Queen Elizabeth II 2022.

2. 'Rear view of the Cossimbuzar Factory House' (the East India Company's first Bengal factory) in 1795. Watercolour, artist unknown.

3. 'The Trading Post of the Dutch East India Company' Chinsura by Hendrik van Schuylenburgh, 1665.

Engraved for the Universal Magazine for J. Hinton in Newgate Street.

A Perspective View of FORT WILLIAM in the Kingdom of BENGAL; belonging to the East India Company of ENGLAND.

4. Old Fort William, Calcutta, date unknown. Engraved for *The Universal Magazine of Knowledge and Pleasure*, London, 1747–1803.

5. 'A view of Fort William, Calcutta, seen from the east with the Church of Saint Anne and the Governor and his guard' by George Lambert, 1731.

6. The East India Company obelisk memorial at Plassey, with the gilt bust of *nawab* Siraj-ud-daula added in 2007.

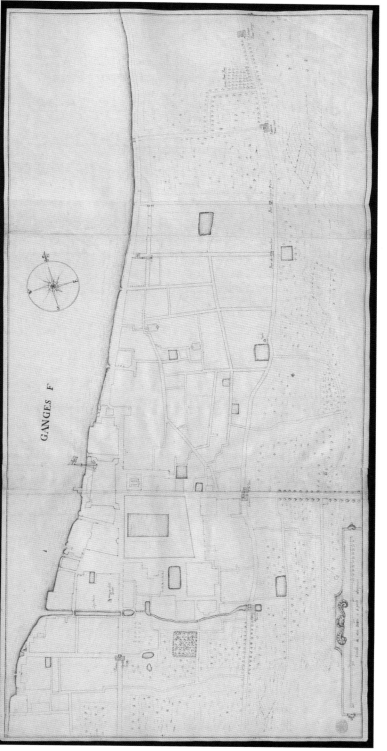

GANGES F

7. Theodore Forrestie's map of Calcutta, 1742, showing (old) Fort William and the Great Tank.

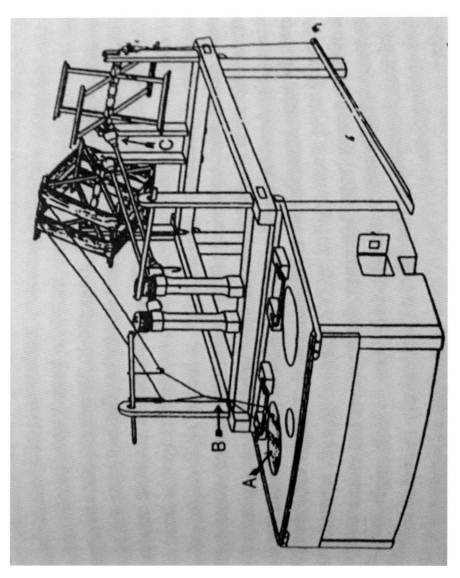

8. Piedmontese standard silk reeling machine. Note the small door (bottom centre) where firewood was inserted to heat the basins above.

9. 'Stamping Coinage in the Mint, Calcutta' by Arthur William Devis. Part of a series entitled 'Arts and Manufactures of Bengal', c. 1792.

10. 'Rooms of the Asiatic Society in 1828' from *Asiatic Museum Illustrated*.

11. Memorial to Colonel Robert Kyd, Botanic Garden, Calcutta.

12. Close up of the Colonel Robert Kyd memorial, Botanic Garden, Calcutta.

or approved by the emperor, and coins carried his name and regnal year, but in practice this could not be enforced. Provincial governors who established strong local bases struck their own coinage, so the Company was not setting a precedent in establishing its own Mints. The first was at Bombay in the late seventeenth century, set up by Gerald Aungier, Agent of the small town, and struck under the Mint name of Surat.

The first Calcutta Mint was established in old Fort William, in that uneasy period between the sack of Calcutta by *nawab* Siraj-ud-daula and his defeat at Plassey. The *nawab* granted the Company permission for the Mint on 9 February 1757, and workmen came from Murshidabad to set it up while two officials, William Frankland and Thomas Boddam, were appointed to ensure that the Calcutta coins were equal in weight and fineness to those produced by the *nawab*'s Mint. [44] By 4 July of that year, less than 2 weeks after the Plassey battle, the Mint Committee reported that 4,000 sicca rupees had been coined from imported Mexican dollar bullion. Shroffs and traders could get bullion coined at the Company's Mint for a small charge, and, after 1765 when the Company began to administer Bengal, its coins continued to carry the name Murshidabad because it was still then the capital.

A second Calcutta Mint was set up in 1790, and two Bengal engineers—Lieutenant Golding and Lieutenant Humphries—supervised the construction of the manual screw machine, working from instructions sent from England, and quite possibly with a model too.[45] Six years later, nineteen screw machines were purchased from Matthew Boulton at the Soho Mint at Birmingham, which though still hand-operated could reproduce the entire die on each coin. None of the Company's Mints could however produce enough coinage to prevent the acute shortage of specie experienced in the late eighteenth century, which was particularly noticeable in Bengal and Awadh.

An unsuccessful attempt to redress this had been made by the enterprising vicar's son, John Prinsep, who had joined the Company as a cadet but on reaching Bengal in the early 1770s went into trade. After his discovery of copper at Rotasgarh, in Bihar, Prinsep was given Company permission to mine and mint copper coins, an early example of the exploitation of India's natural resources, though not sufficient to satisfy the need for small coinage. The solution came when the Company began importing copper coins from the Soho Mint under the directorship of Matthew Boulton.

Great quantities of coins were shipped to India in wooden casks—17 million coins to Bombay in 1791 alone—and by 1809, the year of Boulton's death, an estimated 220 million coins had been made and shipped to the Company.[46] Boulton, with his partner James Watt, had been experimenting with steam-pressed coinage, and its advantage over the old hand-produced methods was immediate. For the first time, coins could be made that were perfectly round, of equal diameter and uniform appearance. A 'collar' in the coining press avoided mis-strikes (where the image on the coin is off-centre), and adaptations led to the edges being milled, or even engraved. It also meant that counterfeiting or clipping coinage became almost impossible. Dies from the Soho Mint were sent under escort to the Company's subsidiary Mints at Dacca and Patna.

Although the Company was aware of the advantages of a steam-powered Mint and had in fact asked for estimates for machinery from the Soho Mint in 1808, nothing further was done for a decade. Then the Bengal engineer Lieutenant William Nairn Forbes was sent from Calcutta to Birmingham to report on, and order, a steam-powered Mint capable of producing 200,000 rupees a day.[47] The equipment including the steam engines, melting furnaces and die machines arrived in October 1823 and was installed in the third Calcutta Mint, a grand and imposing building inspired by a Grecian temple and built on reclaimed land facing the Hooghly. Forbes had been commissioned not only to design the Mint itself but to supervise its 'complicated machinery' and become its Mint Master, where he remained until 1854. He was an extraordinarily gifted man with a range of skills that demonstrate how broad the definition of 'engineer' still was in the last half-century of Company rule. He had prepared the mines that were detonated at the siege of Bharatpur, he was Surveyor of Embankments in Bengal and Orissa and he designed St Paul's Cathedral in Calcutta[48] Like Farquhar at the Ichapur gunpowder factory, Forbes was in charge of the Calcutta Mint for a lengthy period of time, and, although answerable to the Military Board, he was given a free hand to develop and implement improvements.

Some of the Company's most successful enterprises in India marked the change from indigenous amateur efforts, which were frequently hindered by local disputes and factions, to a single, unified professional goal. The majority of the Company's officers and engineers were foreigners in India who came in with new ideas and imported new technology. Often ignorant of local customs, or choosing to ignore long-seated hierarchies and prejudices, they introduced new ways of working. These were not always popular, or indeed adopted, by the people in India. Locally made gunpowder using the old labour-intensive methods continued to be manufactured. The Nizam of Hyderabad, the richest ruler in India, continued to have coins in his Mint hammered by hand until the end of the nineteenth century. These traditional ways of working certainly distributed low-grade employment to more people, including women and children, but the Company generally set them aside in favour of enhanced production methods and bigger profits, aided by its engineers.

3

THE SPIRIT OF ENLIGHTENMENT

During the monsoon season of 1785, a curious audience gathered on Calcutta's Esplanade in anticipation of a spectacular event. Advertised in the *Calcutta Gazette*, it was the launch of the first hot-air balloon in India, and the crowd was not disappointed when a balloon six feet in diameter rose successfully from the street on 29 July and flew off. It was unmanned, and all we learn from the *Gazette* is that the flight was organised by a Mr Wintle. This may have been James Wintle, the Bengal civil servant and judge of the Court of Appeal at the time. It is not clear if it was indeed the same man, but to construct and launch a balloon in the 1780s required money, contacts and expertise; it was not something that a travelling entertainer could afford to do.

The first hot-air balloons had been launched in France 2 years earlier, and technical information was soon widely shared and circulated. By August 1785, a plan and drawing of the Wintle balloon was being exhibited at the house of a local auctioneer, Joseph Quieros. Later that year, Claude Martin (whom we met as a surveyor at Comercolli) was launching his own unmanned hot-air balloons in Lucknow to the amazement of the *nawab wazir* of Awadh.[1] There was a sudden craze for ballooning, particularly in Britain and Europe, which lasted for 15 years or so before fading, due in part to some inevitable tragic accidents. Late eighteenth-century balloons became deeply entwined with Enlightenment ideas during 'The Age of Wonder', as the historian Richard Holmes dubbed the period from 1760 to 1830. The paperback edition of his book of the same name has the Montgolfier Brothers' hot-air balloon on its cover.

It is not hard to see how the association came about. For the first time it was possible to slip 'the surly bonds of earth', to view the pattern of urban and rural landscapes and how they interconnected far below. Being literally able to rise above things made it possible to reconsider what had previously seemed immutable in the West: the Church, the State, hierarchies, even the natural world itself. This is not the place for evaluating the political or philosophical impact of Enlightenment ideas on Company policy, if indeed they did have an impact, but to examine how new thinking by individual Europeans led to tangible outcomes in India.

Early in April 1783, the newly knighted Sir William Jones was appointed judge at the Supreme Court in Calcutta. He arrived in the autumn of that year with his wife Anna and a reputation for being frighteningly clever as an orientalist, as well as a master of several languages including Greek, Latin and Arabic. At Harrow he had been known as the 'Great Scholar', and his reputation was enhanced by his degree from University College Oxford. He was elected a Fellow of the Royal Society in England. There seemed nothing that Jones was not interested in or involved with. He arranged to have Claude Martin (by now a colonel) collect as many seeds as possible to send to the botanist Sir George Young in the Caribbean, as part of a plan to transfer to 'the West Indies, the spicy forests of Asia'.[2] Music, astronomy, literature, languages, geography and local jurisprudence fascinated him. His learned interaction with Sanskrit scholars led to his nickname of Youns Uksfardi—'Jones of Oxford'.

When not at work in the Supreme Court, Jones spent time in his 'cottage' at Krishnagar, a simple two-storeyed, unglazed thatched building with a broad, covered veranda. This allowed him to visit the 'University of the Brahmins' at the nearby town of Nawadwip, which happily was also known as the Oxford of Bengal. The Krishnagar visits took place at the end of the rainy season. The hot months of April and May he spent at a Garden Reach villa on the banks of the Ganges ('that divine river', as he called it), where Lady Jones supervised a dairy farm which produced 'the best butter in India'. In spite of frequent illnesses experienced by both husband and wife, Jones' attitude to India was one of unbounded delight, curiosity and interest. He is remembered today for, among many other things, establishing the chronology of India's early forgotten dynasties, and for noting the similarity between certain words in Sanskrit and ancient Greek, which led to the proposition of a common Indo-European language.

Within 6 months of his arrival, Jones had called together a number of prominent European men and established the Asiatick Society, the first 'oriental' society in the world, which predates Britain's Royal Asiatic Society by nearly 4 decades. In an astute move, Jones invited the governor general Warren Hastings to lend his support to the Society. Hastings refused the post of president, and so the post went to Jones. He did, however, bring to the table his own oriental interests and of course his useful association with government. The aim of the Asiatick Society was, as Jones stated, simply to study 'man and nature, whatever is performed by the one, or produced by the other', specifically in India and adjoining countries.[3]

Nothing could more clearly reflect the enlightened, open approach of Jones and his colleagues, and the Society quickly became the major forum for learned lectures, debates and the publication of academic papers. The Society's journal, (which continues to this day), had as an early title page *Asiatick Researches: or, Transactions of the Society Instituted in Bengal, for Inquiring Into the History and Antiquities, the Arts, Sciences and Literature of Asia*. Articles in the 1792 volume, edited by Jones, included: 'On the musical mode of the Hindus', 'An Account of the Battle of Paniput', 'On the Nicobar Islands and the Fruit of the Mellori' and 'An account of the method of catching wild Elephants at Tipura'. The journal was sold to Society members as well as the public for 20 rupees (£2.4s). *Asiatick Researches* 'took Europe almost by storm'; a pirated edition was brought out, and it was translated into French.[4] The American Academy of Arts and Sciences, founded in 1780, contacted the Society for information about old Jewish settlements in Malabar.

The Society's meetings were held in a room at the Old Court House, Jones' workplace, and conveniently close to Writers' Building. Some familiar names are among the earliest members including John Farquhar of the Ishapur Gunpowder Factory; Reuben Burrow, the mathematician; Colonel Antoine-Louis Polier, engineer and architect; and the artists Ozias Humphry, Thomas Daniell and Johan Zoffany. The Society held weekly meetings, but when only six members turned up Jones doubted its survival, calling the Society 'sickly', so the success of *Asiatick Researches* was an important boost. However, the Society lost the support of Warren Hastings when he left Calcutta for England, where he was to face impeachment for supposed offences during his term in office. A more serious blow was the death of Jones himself in the Spring of 1794 from a liver complaint, at the age of forty-seven. His wife had returned earlier to England because of poor health. Sir John Shore, who had been appointed governor general a year before Jones' death, took over as president of the Society, and at Lady Jones' request wrote the first biography of her husband, *Memoirs of the Life, Writings, and Correspondence of Sir William Jones*.

Shore gathered together copies of as many of Jones' letters as he could find and added his own commentary to them. While appreciative of his former colleague, Shore defended the Britons who had worked in India before the Asiatick Society was formed. He complained that his 'fellow labourers in the East were reproached for a disinclination to explore the literature and antiquities of Hindustan' because they were too busy pursuing riches, 'which was supposed to be the sole object of the servants of the East-India Company, and to engross their whole attention'. No allowances, he said, had been made for the inevitable difficulties of newcomers, the tropical climate or the reserve of the natives: 'The reproach was unmerited; and long before the arrival of Sir William Jones in India, the talents of several persons there had been applied with considerable success, not only to investigations ... but to scientific researches, which he more effectually promoted.'[5]

Jones had acted as the focal point for discoveries and investigations that were already being made by Company officials, who were not all greedy men (or 'nabobs', as they were known with not a little envy by those in Britain). Shore also noted that in the 20 years since the Society was established, 'more accurate information of the history and antiquities, on the arts, sciences and literature of India, has been given to the world, than ever before appeared'.[6]

All this came at a price. The Society still had no permanent meeting place, nor funds to purchase one. Two years after Jones' death, the Society was actively soliciting manuscripts, books, 'curiosities' and coins, with the intention of setting up a museum and library, the first such dedicated place for oriental scholars in India. Membership fees were introduced—four gold mohurs per annum, equivalent to over £600 today—which debarred impecunious amateurs. At the turn of the century, 162 members were listed, including the botanist William Roxburgh, the artist William Devis, the engineer Colonel Alexander Kyd and the former surveyor (now general) Claude Martin. Indians were not allowed to become members until 1829, and in that same year the king of Awadh, Nasir-ud-din Haider, generously made a donation of 20,000 rupees to promote research into the literature and natural history of India, though he himself did not seek membership.

The question of why Indians were not admitted earlier to the Society has not been asked. William Jones relied heavily on his *pandits* to teach him Sanskrit and elucidate manuscripts. Indeed, his marble memorial in University College Chapel, Oxford shows him seated at a small writing desk, facing Indian scholars who are squatting on a low platform in front of him. The memorial, commissioned by Jones' widow Anna, was sculpted by John Flaxman, who had never been to India and therefore had to rely on her verbal accounts of Jones meeting the scholars at his Krishnagar home. Inevitably, it has attracted postcolonial criticism on the grounds that Jones is seated higher than the scholars and that he is wearing shoes while they are barefoot. This is to ignore the fact that both parties—the British judge, and the Indian *pandits*—were comfortable in their relative positions: Europeans were happier sitting in chairs with their shoes on, while Indians preferred to sit on the floor, having left their sandals at the door. The fruitful banana trees in the background of the memorial are a tribute to the sculptor's skill, but Jones and the scholars are likely to have been seated on the veranda of the Krishnagar 'cottage' rather than in the garden. A rational—in fact, an Enlightenment—view of the memorial and of Jones' decade-long governance of the Asiatick Society might conclude that Flaxman had correctly positioned the Indians and the British man in their appropriate spaces, each acknowledging the other's surroundings but without wishing to inhabit them. The Asiatick Society was a club for educated British men with the odd anglicised foreigner like Zoffany admitted. It would no more have thought of inviting Indians to join than of inviting women.

Following the increase in membership and donations of books, manuscripts and artefacts, the Society petitioned the government for a plot of land on which to build a permanent home. This was granted in 1805, and the Society was given a corner site on Chowringhee and Park Street which had previously housed a riding stables. The French-born watercolour artist Jean-Jacques Pichon was selected as architect, working with the engineer Captain Thomas Preston. The building was completed 3 years later and remains on its original site. It was a well-proportioned two-storey structure with an arched entrance, outside which sat a giant figure, probably a Buddha. Part of the façade is still visible today, although the grandeur of this early nineteenth-century building can best be appreciated from the interior, with a fine staircase leading to the first floor and its Ionic columns. Over time the garden surrounding the Society was nibbled away at, and today its Park Street façade has been completely changed by a large modern structure housing shops at a busy street level.

During its early years, *Asiatick Researches* published numerous articles on languages, the Hindu pantheon, antiquities and exploration. Among them was 'Narrative of a Journey to Sirinagur' by Captain Thomas Hardwicke, which appeared in Volume 6 in 1801. Hardwicke joined the Company in 1778 as a soldier, though his many interests overlapped with those of engineers, surveyors, meteorologists and naturalists. Having begun his career in south India, he was posted to Bengal in 1793 as Adjutant and Quartermaster of Artillery, possibly because he had been wounded earlier and these were less taxing or dangerous jobs. Even so, this didn't prevent him from taking leave to travel into Garhwal in the Himalayas for 2 months in the spring of 1796. It was a journey of exploration, with no other object than to report on what he found, with particular emphasis on the natural world.

The 'Narrative' was followed by a lengthy appendix entitled 'Enumeration of Plants noticed in the preceding Tour between Hurdwar and Sirinagur in the months of April and May'.[7] Hardwicke set off from Fatehgarh, the Company cantonment north of Cawnpore, in March. His journal, on which the article was based, is one of the first to describe the hilly, wooded country bordered by Tibet to the north. With his team of porters and guards, the party could only move forward with the permission of local rulers. As one of the first white men seen in the area, Hardwicke was the object of intense curiosity wherever he camped, with villagers crowding round his tent for a peep.

Hardwicke notes in meticulous detail the routes he took, estimating the mileage between towns, the number of dwelling houses, the climate and the terrain. He used the local pronunciation of Sirinagur, rather than the later, anglicised version of Srinagar. (This is not the better-known Srinagar in Kashmir, but the town of the same name on the River Alaknanda in today's Uttarakhand.) The great range of hills and forests extending from Hardwar through Rohilkhand and Awadh 'produced many kinds of valuable timber', he wrote, 'and an abundant store of plants, never yet, perhaps, brought under the systematical examination of the botanist'. And this is what Hardwicke attempted to do in an astonishingly short period of 2 months. Nearly forty pages of close-packed descriptions of trees, bushes, plants and flowers were written up in 'systematical' botanical terms. Here is his entry on an orchid-like plant (the lesser-flowered Lady's Slipper) that he discovered 'in the low grounds near Asophgurh, below Hurdwar':

> Gynandria Diandria. *Limodorem*. Bulbs solid, large, smooth, mostly triangular, the corners pointed, sending forth a few fibres; scape simple, from the middle of the bulb, columnar. Smooth; erect, about twelve inches high. Flowers scattered: petals oblong-linear, nearly equal: nectary three-cleft, the middle division much larger, rounded. It resembles *L Virens* of Dr Roxburgh.[8]

To a lay person this description would not mean very much, unless accompanied by an illustration. Hardwicke had taken with him at least one Indian artist to illustrate what he found and these paintings were subsequently published in the sixteen-volume *Plants of India*. Today Hardwicke is better known in zoological than botanical circles, but it is worth considering his Garhwal expedition and its implications for European thinking on the natural resources of India.

The Swedish botanist Carl Linnaeus had published *Systema Naturae* in 1735, one of the first, and ultimately the most successful, early categorizations of objects in the natural world of animal, vegetable and mineral. Twenty years later, by the time the book had gone into its 10th edition, nearly 8,000 species had been added and named according to the 'families' to which they belonged. Linnaeus developed the system of 'binomial nomenclature', which simply means giving two Latinised names to growing plants, flowers and trees. The first word, always capitalised, is the genus or family to which it belongs, and the second word refers to the specific item: so with *Tagetes erecta*, for example, *Tagetes* describes the marigold family and *erecta* describes the actual round, ball-like flower, commonly used for making ceremonial necklaces in India.

Few men can have seen such a rapid and universal uptake of their ideas in their own lifetime as Linnaeus did. His system was quickly adopted throughout the Western world, and by extension throughout the European colonies, until it was superseded by a more accurate classification. Linnaeus himself instructed his most promising students, whom he called his 'apostles', to go forth and spread the word. One of them, a botanist and physician named Johann Gerhard König, travelled to Tranquebar in southern India where he became 'naturalist' to the *nawab* of Arcot in 1774. A fraternity was established, a network of men who knew enough Latin to be able to discuss the newly bestowed names of plants and their characteristics, and who were often themselves active in exploration. Hardwicke had to consult his botanist colleagues in naming the many flowers and plants he found in Garhwal. He sent samples of dried specimens to Calcutta, together with paintings of them and precise written descriptions, as we can see from the Lady's Slipper extract above. Writing up his finds in such detail took much longer than the actual expedition to Sirinagur—years, in fact—given that he was also a serving officer in the Company's Bengal army.

Linnaeus' method of identifying plants and its later development is particularly characteristic of Enlightenment thinking: to see the natural world in a new and rational way, and then to catalogue it. There were many advantages to this approach, not least in that it encouraged the systematic enumeration of flora which Hardwicke and others had proposed, thus leading to an increased exploitation of plants for food, drink and medicinal purposes. Botanical gardens were established for the study of plants and trees, as we will see.

Seeds, specimens and illustrations travelled freely around the world, underpinned by a growing database that used Latin as its *lingua franca* (in one of the language's final appearances as such). It led to European collectors commissioning botanical paintings from Indian artists. This resulted in these artists developing a radical new way of looking at flowering plants, which became an important genre in the Company School of painting.[9]

But at the same time, it did something to India's flowers, plants and trees: it colonised them. Plants were listed, named in Latin (a language which was even more foreign than English) and painted in a new style, albeit by Indian artists who had 'gone British'. Somehow what had been taken for granted had now been taken over by foreigners. To name something is to stake a claim to ownership. If this sounds like an exaggeration, consider the opening statement made in an article published by the Society for the History of Natural History in 2008:

> 200 years ago the identification and classification of plants was at the forefront of scientific inquiry—underpinning botanical science's pre-eminence was the extension of European power around the world; the activities of plant collectors were intimately tied into colonial expansion, facilitating rule practically and ideologically.[10]

A few of the plant paintings in Hardwicke's collection and other collections of the same period have their native, original name, written at the top of the folio in Urdu. (This does not mean that the artists were Muslim, simply that the convention at the time when dealing with European patrons was to write in Urdu.) So a painting of a teak tree is labelled *saj derket mada*, which translates as the female *saj* tree, with the Linnean name of *Tectona grandis* at the bottom of the page. The fragrant frangipani tree, often found in old European cemeteries in India, is *champa* in the local dialect but *Plumeria acutifolia* in Latin, while the ubiquitous round marigold, noted above as *Tagetes erecta* is simply called *genda* or *gendi*, that is, ball-shaped.

There are no recorded objections from local people to the Europeans' collecting and classifying of India's flora. On the contrary, it led to work for the porters accompanying naturalists like Hardwicke and for the artists he employed. Hardwicke does not say whether he consulted local people about the plants and flowers he found or whether he relied entirely on their identification by his European colleagues in Calcutta and London. When the governor of Dutch Malabar, Hendrik van Rheede, compiled his twelve-volume treatise *Hortus Malabaricus* a century earlier, he had had the generous co-operation of Indian herbalists who advised on the medicinal properties of plants. Indeed, the earliest botanical gardens in England and Europe were established for medicinal purposes, such as the Chelsea Physic Garden in London set up by the Worshipful Society of Apothecaries.

By the time Colonel Robert Kyd proposed a botanic garden across the river from Calcutta, the emphasis had shifted from medicinal to commercial and economic considerations. Kyd had joined the corps of Bengal Engineers as a cadet in 1764 following an education in Scotland. He rose in rank to become Secretary to the Military Department of Inspection in Bengal while at the same time pursuing his love of horticulture. In 1786, he wrote to the Board of Control in Calcutta suggesting the establishment of:

> a Botanical Garden, not for the purpose of collecting rare Plants (altho' they also have their use) as things of mere curiosity or furnishing articles for the Gratification of Luxury, but for establishing a stock for disseminating such articles as may prove beneficial to the inhabitants as well as the natives of Great Britain and which ultimately may tend to the extension of the National Commerce and Riches ...[11]

Among the plants suggested were those producing cotton, tobacco, coffee and tea, as well as various other commercial products, and probably included indigo. Kyd had seen the devastation caused by the Bengal famine of 1769–71 and the later Chalisa famine of 1783, and he believed that the promotion of new crop varieties would help to avert future calamities: the awful desolation caused by 'famine and subsequent pestilence', as he described it. So there was a strong humanitarian argument for the creation of the botanical garden, as well as good commercial reasons. Kyd's idea was eagerly taken up, and a 1.5-mile-long tract of land, fronting the north bank of the Hooghly, was secured by the government for the garden. A number of villagers were described as 'squatting' at the northern end of the site, with no written proof of their right to do so, but they were nevertheless compensated by the government, and they moved out.

An attractive aspect of Kyd's proposal was that teak trees could be planted here which in time would supply Calcutta's expanding shipbuilding industry with timber. Sourcing lengths of straight timber suitable for the masts and yardarms of the Company's sailing ships was a particular concern. Initially fir trees were sent from Britain, but it was inconvenient and expensive to ship them. The Court of Directors ordered that timber should be obtained locally, and so an expedition set out for the Morang region in eastern Nepal, headed by the Scotsman William Mirtle. Mirtle was a Company employee who had been a timber collector in Bihar before exploring the lucrative fir tree trade further north. But he was murdered in Nepal, probably in 1769, so the Company appointed two further officers, Francis Peacock and James Christie, with strict instructions not to engage in trade nor interfere with the 'country government'. Rather, they were told to be: 'circumspect in their treatment of the natives and avoid all acts of oppression or violence'. Their sole purpose was to cut fir trees for shipbuilding as well as extract and refine pitch and tar, which makes one wonder what Mirtle had been doing.[12] It was a reminder that white-faced foreigners were not always treated with the courtesy and harmless curiosity that Hardwicke had encountered. But the project to grow teak trees in Calcutta had to be abandoned after three decades because the muddy soil of the Gangetic plain was found to be unsuitable. The 40-acre site where the failed experiment had taken place was given to Bishop's College, a Christian institution.

Kyd's enlightened beliefs were not shared by all his contemporaries. On falling fatally ill with an unidentified disease, he drew up his Will, which included his funeral arrangements: 'It is my further desire that I may be buried in my own garden without the attendance of offices of any priest whatever.' In a codicil written 9 days before his death on 27 May 1793, he trusted that his friend Captain Apsley would 'see my last remains committed to the ground in my own garden, on the west side of the pucka-walled tank near to where an alligator pear [avocado] tree now stands, and that my funeral expenses do not exceed 300 rupees'.

This was a step too far for his liberal friends. Captain Apsley may have tried to fulfil his friend's last wish, but Robert Kyd was interred in 'the old burial ground' in Calcutta. In compensation, a handsome memorial urn was commissioned from the English sculptor Thomas Banks and placed in the botanic garden where it still stands today. The column supporting the urn is covered with a leaf pattern in low relief, and cheerful pots of living marigolds (*genda*) surround the base. In addition to stipulations about his final resting place, Kyd had left further instructions in his Will about pensions for two Indian servants and 50 rupees each for two 'Orphans of the Garden', Boonchi and Chunnia, the former probably a little girl. Both are pet names for Bengali children.[13]

The theme of collecting, enumerating and cataloguing the natural world and its inhabitants runs strongly through the eighteenth-century Enlightenment. This was the case not only for terrestrial phenomena but for the oceans and heavens as well. Astronomical observations were common to all early societies and essential for seagoing sailors. Important medieval observatories included that at Samarkand, established in the early fifteenth century with later Mughal and Rajput sites at Jaipur, Delhi and Benares. The development of the telescope in seventeenth-century Europe changed the nature of observatories in India so that they were no longer outdoor sites filled with giant sundials, sextants and meridian arcs, but European-style domed buildings that housed astronomical instruments. Colonel Watson, Burrow's patron, had already flagged up the need for surveyors who could determine longitude and latitude, 'which useful Branch of Learning is more particularly necessary for the Corps of Engineers in this Country'. Until these simple co-ordinates could be established through astronomical observations, it was impossible to make accurate surveys and maps.

The Madras Observatory was not originally a Company initiative but had been established as a private venture in 1786 by William Petrie, an officer and amateur astronomer. On his departure for England 3 years later, the Company took over Petrie's house, where the observatory was housed, and appointed its own astronomer and marine surveyor, Michael Topping. A new and larger observatory was constructed nearby in 1792 on the bank of the River Cooum, described as India's 'Greenwich'. The building was a single, high-ceilinged room, more like a long hall, with a central granite pillar and a grandiose (and untrue) inscription in several Indian languages that read: 'Posterity may be informed a Thousand years hence of the period when the Mathematical Sciences were first planted by British liberality in Asia.' A granite step to the door of the library was used as a benchmark for the Great Trigonometrical Survey of India which began in 1802–3. 'Six very good telescopes' were ordered from Britain, and an inventory of 1812 shows that equipment included pocket chronometers, sextants, a microscope, thermometer, compass and a spirit level. Among the observatory's publications was a catalogue of 11,015 stars and their positions in the firmament in 1835.[14]

Observatories were expensive to set up, not so much for the actual building itself, which required a dome or 'folding roof', but for the expensive equipment inside. Reuben Burrow's plea for an observatory in Calcutta had been turned down on grounds of expense, as we have seen. The Company was therefore delighted when it learned that Nasir-ud-din Haider, the wealthy ruler of the kingdom of Awadh, proposed setting up his own observatory in Lucknow and meeting all its expenses too. But the reasons for this initiative had less to do with a genuine wish to further knowledge than with a complicated web of personal interests. Both the chief minister of Awadh, Hakim Mehndi, and the assistant British Resident to the Court, John Paton, had their own reasons for urging the king to fund an observatory 'not only as a means of establishing a series of observations of the heavenly bodies but more particularly as a school for the young courtiers in which some knowledge of Astronomy and general Physics might be taught'.[15]

It seemed such a noble intention—and an observatory in north India would be so useful—that the Company was willing to find and appoint a Bengal military engineer as superintendent: Captain Richard Wilcox. This talented man, then in his early thirties, already had a reputation as a surveyor and had spent 4 years in Assam exploring the source of the Brahmaputra. Although his findings were inconclusive, he was subsequently recruited to take part in the Great Trigonometrical Survey and had been put forward for the role of Deputy Surveyor General, but the post went to an older man. Wilcox published his *Memoir of a Survey of Asam and the Neighbouring*

Countries in *Asiatick Researches* in 1832 and was one of three men to apply for the post of Superintendent of the Royal Observatory at Lucknow. A previously appointed superintendent, Captain James Herbert, had died before much work could be carried out. Wilcox was in post by 1835, not initially as an astronomer, but as the engineer responsible for building the observatory.

There were numerous delays, and the building—called Tarawali Kothi (Starry House)—took 6 years to complete. This was not the fault of Wilcox, but of *durbar* politics. The death of King Nasir-ud-din Haider 2 years into the project had brought it to a halt, and his successor had to be persuaded by the Company that a Royal Observatory in Awadh would add lustre to the new king's name. The observatory was built under contract, and the Company had no direct control over its erection because the king was paying for it and had appointed his own contractor. Wilcox was in the difficult position of having to explain the delays, which were not of his making, to the British Resident at the Court of Awadh, who in turn had to plead for him with the Company's political secretary.[16] The drawings for the building had long been made by Wilcox, who was responsible for supervising the workmen himself, but he was at the mercy of the influential Raja Bukhtawar Singh, the contractor who had many other projects on the go. Wilcox complained that he had not been given authority for the actual execution of the observatory (although he seems to have been responsible for sourcing construction materials), writing 'that I have no control beyond that of merely directing what is to be done, and of furnishing plans'. Building stone from Chunar that he had ordered over a year earlier did not arrive, and even once he managed to get 'many large beams procured from a great distance expressly for the Observatory [they] have been suddenly carried away and applied to other purposes'. The same thing happened to the bamboo scaffolding, which after a long delay Wilcox finally got erected only to see it taken down and used elsewhere in the city for another building that the king was more anxious to see completed.

The Company brushed aside these genuine reasons for the slow construction of the Royal Observatory and threatened to dismiss Wilcox and appoint another engineer in his place. There is an increasingly anxious tone to the correspondence from Calcutta to the British Resident in Lucknow: 'It must be satisfactory to the authorities at Home as well as the Government here to know that British officers placed, as these officers are, for professional duties of high responsibility in a Native State, make a favourable and lasting impression of their acquirements and exertions.'[17]

The observatory finally opened in 1841. Equipment for it had been purchased nearly a decade earlier on the orders of the first superintendent Captain Herbert, which meant some of it had already been superseded by new discoveries. Nevertheless, the items made by Troughton & Simms in England, described as 'first class instruments', were installed in the Tarawali Kothi, where Wilcox used them for the remaining 8 years of his life. In fact, the Lucknow instruments were considered far superior to those in the Company's own Madras observatory, a fact which rankled with a later Surveyor General of India, General Andrew Scott Waugh. Following the closure of the Royal Observatory at Lucknow after Wilcox's death in 1848, Waugh suggested that it would be 'very acceptable' were the meteorological, magnetic and equatorial apparatus to be transferred to his own office. This did not happen, and the Lucknow observatory became a coveted private house, while the instruments disappeared. Wilcox had dutifully submitted six monthly reports to the Company, but they probably went no further than Writers' Building. The initial proposal for the observatory had included a printing press to publish its meteorological and astronomical observations—as this was the whole point of an observatory, to share and refine information among the scientific community— but it did not happen. Only one publication was ever issued—*The Lucknow Almanac*—which contained the ascensions and declinations of the sun and planets in 1849 as well as horoscopes for members of the East India Company, a clear confusion between astronomy and astrology.

What this episode demonstrates is that the Company's effort to save money by getting the Awadh kings to pay for an observatory backfired, leading to accusations that the kings were frivolous and had no interest in furthering the scientific advances that so gripped British officials at the time. Lack of control meant the Company could only put pressure on its own engineer, the unfortunate Wilcox. At the same time, it shows the versatility of the Bengal engineer in the early nineteenth century. Wilcox had explored and surveyed Assam; assisted in the Great Trigonometrical Survey that began in south India; designed and supervised the building of an observatory; and conscientiously carried out meteorological research by recording temperature, air pressure and other atmospheric phenomena, as well as scouring the skies with a giant telescope that poked through the roof's dome.

It was not only India's skies that were to be measured with European instruments, but its lands too. The Great Trigonometrical Survey which Wilcox worked on is usually referred to as the GTS, and was not actually named as such until 1817, when it was taken on by the government in Calcutta. The Survey, and associated mapping of India by the Company in the period under discussion, has roused more passions than almost any other non-military act— certainly far more than giving foreign names to Indian flora. But the Enlightenment philosophy that by following rational processes 'correct and certain archives of knowledge could be constructed' was initially undermined by flaws in cartographic technologies. Equipment was faulty, calculations were shaky or simply wrong and the belief that a single survey could neatly construct all empirical geographical knowledge into a coherent and truthful whole was unfeasible. Worse still, colonial mapmaking was described as 'an act of geographical violence through which every space in the world is explored, charted and finally brought under control'.[18] Historians were accused of romanticising the men who went out with their steel measuring chains, transit telescopes and theodolites, accompanied by their Indian assistants and armed *sepoys*.

James Rennell was one of the first mapmakers working in Bengal, but it was in Madras that the origins of the trigonometrical survey were laid by William Lambton, a grammar-school boy who was commissioned into a British regiment. He was posted to India in 1796 and had the good luck to meet Colonel Arthur Wellesley 2 years later. Wellesley, later the Duke of Wellington, shared his Madras home with Lambton and both fought in the final Anglo-Mysore War, which led to the death of Tipu Sultan at Seringapatam. The sultan's death meant that the Company now had more land from which to collect revenue, and it appointed a surveyor, the engineer Colonel Colin Mackenzie, to produce topographical maps of the area. Lambton's proposal, which was supported by Wellesley, was both more theoretical and more practical. Surveys had been carried out in France and Spain to establish the curvature of the earth in northern latitudes, and Lambton wanted to extend the survey to India. He planned to do so by plotting a giant grid of triangles in a straight line from Cape Comorin in the extreme south to Dehra Dun in the Himalayas, along what was called the Great Meridional Arc.

To the unscientific mind it sounded a mad venture, and to some extent it was. It was not completed until 1870, long after Lambton's death in 1823. Much of the triangulation had to be re-surveyed because it was inaccurate. There were a number of false starts, and work had begun with a second-hand set of instruments intended initially as a gift to the emperor of China. But the endeavour epitomises the Enlightenment view that everything could be measured, catalogued, counted, numbered and rationally explained.

The GTS could be seen purely as a vast scientific experiment, although Lambton also emphasised its practical value in establishing the geographical co-ordinates of towns and points of interest. In a series of articles in *Asiatick Researches*, he explains his intention to 'cross the peninsular of India' with trigonometrical operations, to connect Fort St George with Mangalore (he calculated a distance of 362 miles) and 'to ascertain certain positions on the Coromandel and Malabar coasts and affix the latitudes and longitudes of all the principle places in the interior country within the extent of the operations for connecting the two seas'.[19] Page after page lists his calculations, the names of the sites grouped into threes where triangulation took place marked by flags and the position of the pole star. Lambton summarised his findings for the 'general reader', who he said may not have had the time or inclination to follow his findings in detail, but in truth there can have been very few such people who could have understood his complex calculations and probably even fewer among Company officials. Yet the idea of being able to capture even a small part of the Indian peninsula and reduce it systematically to the printed page was attractive. Could this be applied to other areas of what often seemed like a vast and inchoate country in which the Company had only a tiny, but increasing, hold?

Lambton's work was continued by his former assistant and successor George Everest, who had been trained at the Woolwich Academy and arrived in India as a cadet. In spite of later poor health, Everest carried out a number of surveys in Bengal. After spending some time in England recuperating, he returned and brought with him more accurate measuring tools, including 'compensation bars', so called because they allowed and compensated for the expansion and contraction of metal measuring rods.

Apart from the charts and maps that were produced during the GTS, a physical reminder of the venture exists on the road from Calcutta to Barrackpore in the form of two remaining survey towers. Because this area is notably flat, it was not possible to establish a baseline to begin measurements. So the 75-foot-high towers were built and observations were taken from their rooftops. Unlike the round semaphore towers, with which they are sometimes confused, the survey towers are tapered square blocks with arrow-slit openings at intervals.

For 16 years the Madras Observatory ran a surveying school for orphaned European boys. Opened in 1794, the teenage boys were taught 'practical' surveying for land revenue collection purposes. This was quite different from Lambton's grand surveys but of equal, if not greater, importance to the Company, which depended on this form of taxation to administer the areas newly under its control. Colin Mackenzie's topographical survey of Mysore would have noted, among other things, the amount of fertile land; how it was irrigated; which areas had fruit-bearing trees like banana, coconut and mulberry; and how much land was covered with jungle. All these were factors relevant in determining the amount of revenue to be paid.

The boys did not collect the revenue themselves; this was carried out by local men with armed *sepoys*. The surveying school was open to Europeans only, with Indians not admitted. Even the most unenlightened Company official in Fort St George had heard the stories of Indian surveyors measuring 'rich people's lands short and poor people's long', with the obvious connotation of bribery. (Whether European boys could be bribed was not discussed.) By 1813, after the closure of the Madras surveying school, the use of *harkaras*, or 'native assistants', for survey work was banned, 'as

Government were anxious to prevent the Natives from obtaining, or being taught, any knowledge of the kind'.[20] However, it was soon found impracticable to attempt any kind of survey work without involving the people whose country was being surveyed. But the temporary restrictions, and tighter controls once they were lifted, meant that Company officials had to familiarise themselves with the local terms relating to land tenure and its complicated web of ownership, landholding, temporary grants of land (*jagirs*) and rents, systems that had developed during the Mughal period and in some cases even earlier.

It was not only for surveying and revenue purposes that a knowledge of the languages spoken on the subcontinent was useful. Training *sepoys* in the three Presidential armies required European officers who could speak direct to the men in their battalions, not only to issue commands on the parade ground but to respond to their concerns and complaints. Not surprisingly, the first books aimed at teaching Hindustani to English speakers were written by two Bengal army officers, Captain George Hadley and Captain James Fergusson. Published separately in 1772 and 1773 in London, they were *Grammatical Remarks on the Practical and Vulgar Dialect of the Indostan Language Commonly Called the Moors* and A *Dictionary of the Hindostan Language*. Hadley had been appointed to command a battalion of *sepoys* in 1764, and his book reflects the language that an officer would use, with limited interest for a civilian.

A better-known author of the language was John Borthwick Gilchrist, who published the first volume of his two-volume *Dictionary, English and Hindoostanee* in Calcutta in 1786, dedicated to Sir John Macpherson, the temporary governor general. Gilchrist had arrived in India as an assistant surgeon in 1784, but after the publication of his dictionary he became a full-time author and produced a number of language books, including *The Oriental Linguist; an easy and familiar introduction to the Hindoostanee, or grand popular language of Hindoostan (vulgarly, but improperly, called the Moors)*. Gilchrist began teaching 'Hindustani' to Company officials at the newly opened Fort William College in Calcutta in 1800, and on his retirement to England he taught briefly at the new East India College at Haileybury. He was an opinionated and passionate man who had a low opinion of most Indians he met, and he claimed to have lost a considerable sum of money in a court case that went against him.[21] Probably for this reason he insisted that it was essential for Europeans to learn the vernacular languages in order to understand the Indian system of justice and to administer it properly. During his first years in India, he quickly discovered that Persian, the official language of northern India, was little used, and he compared it to 'Norman French' in Britain: an archaic language but held in esteem for formal events and correspondence. He noticed that Englishwomen in India often spoke vernacular languages better than their husbands because they were in closer touch with their servants and particularly their *ayahs* (nannies), who taught their young children Indian nursery rhymes and stories.

The success of Gilchrist's first book inspired the publication in London of *The Indian Vocabulary to Which Is Prefixed the Forms of Impeachment* (1788). The author is unknown,[22] and the book aimed to exploit the huge interest surrounding the impeachment of Warren Hastings, which began in February of that year. In order to understand the many charges Hastings faced, a dictionary of Indian terms defining people and places was useful. Chowdry, a common family name today, was defined as: 'A Landholder or Farmer. Properly he is above the Zemindar in rank; but according to the present custom of Bengal, he is deemed the next to the Zemindar. Most commonly used as the principal purveyor of the markets in towns or camps.' Oude [Awadh], which figured large in the impeachment, was described as: 'A suba or province, also the capital of that province. The revenues of this suba are supposed to amount to two crores of rupees per annum.' There is much else of interest, and clearly the author was familiar with India and particularly its legal and revenue administration.

Indian philology (the study of the subcontinent's languages) has led to a specific field of study, examining not just the languages themselves and their construction, but the extent to which British writers and teachers may have influenced them by codifying and capturing something which had not been captured before. Gilchrist was in no doubt about the importance of defining and learning Hindustani, the *lingua franca* of northern India: 'Power, permanent power has been the grand source of information in this [language] and the other branches of Indian lore.'[23] After Clive was granted the right to collect revenue and administer Bengal, Bihar and Orissa for the Company, he wrote: 'it is evident that the language of the East became an important, and desirable acquisition to all [its] servants, particularly those who were ambitious of distinguishing themselves, in the opening dawn of future glory and fortune'.

It was this quite naked admission that was later to lead to much critical examination, in particular by the American anthropologist Bernard Cohn, who writing in the 1980s used the phrase 'the language of command and command of language' in a series of influential essays under the title *Colonialism and Its Forms of Knowledge*.[24] Less dramatic than the accusation of 'geographical violence' flung at the survey of India, the acquisition and use of the vernacular languages by the British was a more subtle but equally important element of control.

The fight for control of knowledge of a different kind began in Calcutta, when the Irishman James Augustus Hicky started the subcontinent's first newspaper, *The Bengal Gazette*. The history of the printing press in India is not a smooth progression, more a series of jumps and halts. Early Portuguese settlers in India brought printing with them in the sixteenth century, and for almost two centuries it was associated mainly with Jesuits and missionaries. It was not until 1779 that the Company imported a press to print pictures and illustrations and taught Indian craftsmen the art of aquatint engraving. A second press was taken by river to Malda in Bengal, where *A Compendious Vocabulary [of] English and Persian ... Compiled for the Use of the Honourable East India Company* by Francis Gladwin was printed in 1780.

It was while James Hicky was imprisoned in a Calcutta jail for debt that he came across a 'treatise' on printing which gave him enough information to try his hand as a printer after his release. Hicky's lawyer, William Hickey, who had got the debt cancelled, takes up the story: 'By indefatigable attention and unremitting labour he [James Hicky] succeeded in cutting a rough set of types which answered very well for hand-bills and common advertisements ... having scraped together by this means a few hundred rupees he sent to England for a regular and proper set of materials for printing.' Hickey further described his client as 'a most eccentric creature apparently possessed of considerable natural talents, but entirely uncultivated. Never before had I beheld a mortal who so completely came up to what I had often heard described as "a wild Irishman!"[25]

The Bengal Gazette or the Original Calcutta General Advertiser was first published by James Hicky in January 1780 and lasted for only 2 years, its chief virtue being that it questioned the Company's administration, in particular that of the governor general Warren Hastings. As an independent Irishman of his time, Hicky could view the English East India Company objectively. He had been apprenticed to a London printer in his youth, giving him an advantage when it came to dealing with the technical side of publishing. *The Bengal Gazette* was a weekly newspaper priced at One Rupee, with a circulation of around 400. It carried short reports from Europe and India as well as local advertisements and long editorials criticising the Company's earlier actions, and its abuse of power. Hicky particularly embraced Enlightenment ideas circulating in Europe about the right to liberty and the pursuit of happiness. But by the end of that year the establishment had struck back, and *The India Gazette*, the mouthpiece of the Company, supported by Hastings, was being circulated in Calcutta as a freesheet, without postal charges.

As he became bolder in his criticism of Hastings; the Supreme Court Chief Justice Sir Elijah Impey; and the head of the Protestant Mission, Hicky was re-arrested and tried for libel, and he wound up serving a further prison sentence. There is something curiously modern about his treatment: an editor jailed for publishing uncomfortable information and a government prepared to silence him, first with a rival publication and then by imprisonment. Hicky continued to direct publication from jail, and when Warren Hastings banned the nascent postal system from carrying *The Bengal Gazette* to subscribers, Hicky arranged for it to be delivered to them by *harkaras* (messengers). He was unable to keep this up for long, and the paper closed down in 1782 when its printing press was seized and transferred to the offices of the government's *India Gazette*.[26] Two years later, Francis Gladwin (who had published the Malda *Vocabulary*) founded the *Calcutta Gazette*, which became a useful channel for public announcements as well as much entertaining gossip. However, it didn't have the sharp satirical and critical edge of Hicky's paper. Printing remained mainly in European hands until the Bengali language weekly *Samarchar Darpan* (*News Mirror*) appeared in 1818, based in the Danish settlement of Serampore and edited by the British missionary John Clark Marshman. The first Hindi language paper, *Udant Martand* (*The Rising Sun*) appeared in 1826, based in Calcutta and edited by Pandit Jugal Kishore Shukla, who had been born in the Company cantonment at Cawnpore.

There was a disjuncture between Enlightenment ideas that had travelled from Europe to India and the Company's attempted control of knowledge, not to mention its stance on free speech. This was exacerbated not only by the time it took for orders to travel from London to Calcutta but also by the lack of an ethical framework anywhere in between. It took a certain kind of man to become a successful Company officer, and a moral compass was not always part of an officer's kit. This is why it can be hard to explain Company policy and its actions at times. But to see the Company as an unchanging monolithic block is to ignore the many parts that made it up, as well as the passage of time which saw its makeup change from merchants to soldiers to governors. It was quite possible to hold several conflicting ideas at the same time. Sir William Jones, the epitome of a rational Enlightenment figure, kept a number of little slave boys, among whom his favourite was called Otho.[27] Claude Martin, another man of the Enlightenment, had at least three African slaves who were granted their freedom on his death, but not during his lifetime. So we have to balance the Company's sometimes questionable actions (as seen from today's perspective), with its seemingly altruistic gestures, although there was often a pragmatic reason behind them.

Where the Company did manifest its Enlightenment views in practical terms, this was to result in physical changes to the landscape in the form of new public buildings housing activities that had previously been largely private or non-existent. These included colleges, poorhouses, hospitals, lunatic asylums, libraries and museums. Some of these had of course been present in pre-Company days, usually attached to places of worship and funded by local rulers as a pious gesture. Local landowners sometimes made donations of land towards charitable purposes, and there are examples of land being allocated by Indian owners for Christian cemeteries. St John's Church, Calcutta stands on land given by Maharaja Nabakrishna Deb, the wealthy pro-British aristocrat from Shobha Bazaar.

It has been suggested that when the Company established a Muslim *madrasa* in Calcutta in 1780 and a Sanskrit College in Benares 10 years later, this was a device to get Muslims and Hindus to collect and study 'traditional information' which could then be passed on to the British. English was not taught in either *madrasa* or college, and this venture has been called the 'moonshee phase' where the tutors would learn more than their students.[28] However, it would be more accurate to see these establishments as 'centres of research' producing qualified administrators to assist Company officials. The Calcutta *madrasa* trained young men in Persian, Arabic and Muslim law who could then be appointed to minor judicial posts. It was established at the initiative of Warren Hastings and subsequently run by the government of Bengal. The Sanskrit College was founded by the British Resident, Jonathan Duncan, for 'the preservation and cultivation of the laws, literature and religion' of the Hindus, with the same intention of training young men to support British administrators, who were always too few in number to deal with the Company's newly acquired territories and large populations.

So while both *madrasa* and college were ultimately for the Company's benefit (they would not have been financially supported by the Company otherwise), there was also an important new element here. Neither institution was attached to a place of worship, and by physically moving education away from the mosque or temple and into the public domain, a separation had been made that would ultimately lead to secular teaching along modern European lines. But there was a long way to go. The Company's hesitation in promoting education for Indians has been noted with the short-lived Madras Observatory surveying school, and there was a reluctance to extend English-language teaching and technological education at any meaningful level to most Indians until well into the nineteenth century, despite the success of further colleges at Agra and Delhi set up in 1824 and 1825 respectively.

No objections were raised to private English-language schools, and two of Calcutta's best-known educational institutions were established by Company officers backed by influential Hindus. One was the Hindu (later Presidency) College, set up in 1817 at the instigation of the Chief Justice of the Supreme Court, Sir Edward Hyde East. It was generously supported by wealthy members of the Hindu community who wanted to give their sons a liberal, English-medium education. The college committee was headed by the prominent reformer Raja Ram Mohun Roy. A similar initiative for a girls' school was proposed by the British lawyer John Bethune, a lawyer and member of the Supreme Council. With the support of Dakshinaranjan Mukherjee and the social reformer Ishwar Chandra Vidyasagar, Bethune started the Hindu Female School which opened in 1849. It later became Bethune College, the first formal place of education for women in India, although small, private, fee-paying schools for both girls and boys were advertising for pupils at the end of the eighteenth century in Bengal.

Following the renewal by the government of the Company's charter in 1813, missionary societies were allowed into British India, and they quickly set up the English-medium schools that the Company had been reluctant to provide. The movement of the previous 30 years to de-secularise the education of Hindu and Muslim pupils now took a sharp U-turn. There is a distinct change from the late eighteenth-century liberalism as the influence of the Evangelical movement spread rapidly. Clearly the missionaries' aim was to promote Christianity, but this didn't prevent them from providing a solid and practical education for poor children of any caste or religion. The status of these missionary schools was enhanced in 1818 when a wealthy Hindu businessman in Benares, Jai Narain, donated £5,000 and a building to Daniel Corrie of the Church Missionary Society so that 'the poorest classes of his countrymen might receive education'.[29] By the mid-nineteenth century, English-language schools were being established by religious bodies for upper-class Indian and English pupils. These emphasised the Company's failure, possibly its most serious, to provide education where it was both needed and wanted. St George's School, Mussoorie is a case in point: established in the foothills of the Himalayas in 1853 by the Catholic Capuchin Fathers, it soon attracted paying pupils and is today one of India's best-known institutions. The fact that similar schools remain so popular today show that the Company had grossly underestimated the desire for education among the people it governed.

The idea that not all Britons in India were wealthy is hard to dispel and even harder to argue. Studies of poverty during the period under discussion inevitably focus on the poverty of many indigenous people, which was real enough. The Company was not going to advertise the fact that Britons could suffer too, although many of them did. This lack of statistical evidence has led to generalisations and assumptions that, apart from the high mortality rate among Europeans, their lives in the Presidency towns could be comparatively comfortable and profitable in an almost exclusively masculine world. Only a few recent authors have questioned this cosy picture, and there is hard evidence available that has not yet been fully utilised.

The deaths of urban Britons were recorded by chaplains or senior officials and forwarded quarterly to Company headquarters in London. These records are called the Ecclesiastical Returns and are available today in the British Library on microfilm. The cause of death and the burial place is sometimes, but not always, given, and it is estimated that around 70 per cent of the Returns are present. Other registers were lost at sea or are simply missing. However, the burial registers for Europeans held in Indian churches and cemeteries are often more detailed. An analysis of the registers from Bhowanipore Cemetery in Calcutta for the 2 years 1818 and 1819 has been made, and although this gives only a snapshot, it provides important data.[30] 'The rank/profession' of the deceased is given, which includes 'invalid', 'pensioner', 'orphan', 'widow', 'pauper' and so on, as well as the expected 'seaman', 'Private' and the occasional band-master, or bazar sergeant. Where married women or daughters are recorded, their husband's or father's name is given.

The total number of deaths noted in 1818 was 378, and of these 9.2 per cent were recorded as paupers. The proportion is higher the following year: total deaths 326 of which 12.2 per cent were paupers. The average age of death for adults and children over 5 years of age was 30 years in 1818 and 31 years in 1819. About a third of the names noted during both years are female, including infant daughters. The places from where the corpses came for burial are also recorded. The majority came from the General Hospital and others from the Regimental Hospital. A number of deaths occurred in Fort William itself, and others came from the Lower Orphan Asylum. (The terms Upper and Lower Asylum refer not to the inmate's age, but whether the orphan's father was an officer or private soldier.) The greatest number of deaths in both years were among soldiers and seamen. Burial registers survive from at least two other Calcutta churches: St Andrew's Kirk, for the Scottish cemetery, and St John's Church, which included South Park Street Cemetery. Although tombstones can give useful details, particularly of other family members, the majority of burials in Bhowanipore Cemetery are not going to have any memorials. A pauper's grave meant just that: a hole in the ground marked by a flimsy wooden cross that soon vanished.

There were an increasing number of poor white and Eurasian orphans appearing in the Presidency cities and cantonments. The majority were the result of liaisons between British men, often private soldiers, and Indian women. Being an orphan didn't necessarily mean that the parents had died; children were classed as orphans if their parents could not keep them, and there were also 'regimental orphans' where the father was a serving soldier posted away from his base or who had died and the mother could not provide for the child. Of the 276 male orphans listed in the Military Orphanage, 159 had 'fathers living'. From a total of 368 female orphans, no less than 216 had 'fathers living', and in both cases the fathers would have been European.[31]

It is difficult to differentiate between white and Eurasian children, because the latter were normally given their father's surname and a Christian forename. In the Bhowanipore burial register for 1819, both Mary Rayner and Elizabeth Bruce are listed as 'native women' from Fort William. There is no doubt that these 'orphan' children and young adults, whether poor white or Eurasian, were seen as a source of embarrassment by Company officials and others. This was in part because Eurasians were clearly the product of miscegenation— which was increasingly frowned upon—and secondly because the majority of them were working class, which was almost as bad. The generosity of spirit (and the French Revolution) which at the end of the eighteenth century had, for a brief period, seen all men as equal had quickly vanished. The Revd Bishop Heber who toured the Upper Provinces in the 1820s commented on 'the increase of the half-caste population as a great source of the present mischief and future danger to the tranquillity of the Colony.'[32] It is estimated that by 1830 the number of Eurasians, both children and adults, was greater than that of British civilians.

This was not a new problem. A charity school for indigent European boys had been established as early as the 1720s in Calcutta. It was funded by public subscription and would later become known as the Free School. It was the first attempt to deal with the growing problem of poor whites and was followed by a number of measures, both private and official. Charitable organisations were set up, including the Bombay Society for the Education of the Poor and the Bengal Military Orphan Society. Captain William Kirkpatrick of the Bengal Infantry, a member of the Bengal Society, had taken over a large and handsome building at Howrah, facing Calcutta across the river. Here 500 orphan children were housed for 8 years until they were separated according to their fathers' ranks, with the officers' children sent to a mansion in south Calcutta, supported by contributions from fellow officers. The Howrah house was renamed the Lower Military Orphanage and was funded by the Company.

By 1824, in Bengal alone there was the Government Chinsurah Schools, the Calcutta School Book Society, the Female Juvenile Society, the Ladies' Society for Native Female Education in Calcutta and Its Vicinity, the Benevolent Institution for the Instruction of Indigent Children, the Bengal Military Widows' Fund, the King's Military Fund, the Marine Pension Fund, the Bengal Mariners' and General Widows Fund, the United Charity and Free School, the Charitable Fund for the Relief of Distressed Europeans and Others, and the European female Orphan Asylum. Even with all these institutions, not everyone could be accommodated, and the Calcutta Free School frequently had to reject twenty or thirty 'deserving subjects' at a single meeting.[33] Those pupils who were accepted were taught gender-based subjects: needlework and housekeeping for the girls and military training for the boys, some of whom became regimental musicians as drummers, pipers and band-masters.[34] Printing was another male career option, and the Bengal Military

Orphan Society started its own Company-funded *Government Gazette* with official notifications and public advertisements.

The General Hospital, from which so many of the dead came to Bhowanipore Cemetery, was transferred to the military department in 1786. The majority of its patients were soldiers, some newly arrived from Britain who would subsequently be moved to regimental hospitals if they survived. There were also soldiers from both the Company's army and the Royal (King's) Army stationed in India. Seamen were admitted too, together with 'European paupers' and other Europeans. For those who could pay, a fee of 1 rupee per day was levied. It was pointed out, in delicate terms, that Europeans of a certain class who found themselves in the General Hospital might prefer something of an 'improved and distinct' nature, rather than being subjected to the 'promiscuous intercourse of a crowded ward'.[35] Crowded or not, this was a hospital for Europeans only, and it was funded by the Company.

A quarter of a century later, the Native Hospital opened, established by subscriptions from the governor general, his councillors, the wealthy *nawab wazir* of Awadh and two of his ministers. Indians working for the Company were eligible for admittance, as well as staff working at the Calcutta *madrasa*. Patients were placed in wards according to whether they were Hindu or Muslim, and the chief medical officers and surgeons were European. It is not clear whether the treatments offered were based on European or Indian (that is, ayurvedic or unani) medical practice. A return prepared for the year 1805–6 by the superintendent Dr Robert Wilson showed that by far the most numerous complaints and the reason for admittance were 'wounds', followed by fractures, ulcers and sores, contusions and fever.[36] A separate department for cataract operations was subsequently set up. Treatment here was free, and it continued to be supported by charitable donations. Patient numbers grew year on year, owing not so much to an increase in population but to the 'wider promulgation of the benefits of the Establishment, to the attention which is given to the habits and prejudices of the natives, and to their confidence in the tenderness and superior ability with which their ailments are treated'.[37] Similar hospitals were established in Murshidabad and Dacca, funded by public donations, including those from 'wealthy natives'.

Calcutta's first General Hospital had been opened in 1707 'at a convenient spot close to the Burial ground' of St John's churchyard, where Job Charnock rests today. The Company had provided Rs2,000, and the remainder of the cost was met from public subscriptions. As the town developed, this area became congested, and by 1770 the hospital had been relocated to the southern end of the Lower Circular Road. Here it was housed in a spacious new building, 'airy and healthy', with land around it where additional wings and houses for residential medical staff could be built. By contrast, the Native Hospital was at Durrumtollah in 'a thoroughfare frequented by multitudes of natives'.[38] The argument that fresh air circulating around free-standing buildings was healthy is of course to imply that crowded native streets and dwellings were not, an important theme that directed much Company thinking when fashioning India for British occupation.

The same pattern was followed when the European Lunatic Asylum was opened in 1817 at Bhowanipore, then on the outskirts of Calcutta. It covered a site of more than two acres and included numerous wards, a sizeable water tank and two large, but separate, gardens for female and male patients. There was a central administrative block for staff, with a library.[39] With its spacious layout, garden walks and its own water supply, the Bhowanipore Asylum anticipates the county asylums to be built in England in the 1840s with their large, walled gardens, dairies and farms.[40]

The number of patients at Bhowanipore seems to have been comparatively small, an average of around a hundred inmates per annum. By contrast, the Hospital for Native Insanes, as it was called, already had double that number by the 1820s. It too had been erected by the Company at Russapuglah, south of Calcutta, but had 'for a long time exhibited numerous glaring defects' which are not stated. Attitudes towards mental illness were changing, and institutions which had previously been 'merely receptacles for the detention of individuals dangerous to the peace of Society' now provided 'for the tender care and recovery of a class of persons for the most part innocent' but suffering from severe affliction.[41] Long before these urban initiatives, a small hospital for 'insane native soldiers' had been set up at the Company fort of Monghyr in 1795 at the recommendation of the commander-in-chief. The relationship between European officers and their Indian *sepoys* was by necessity close, particularly in small, isolated garrisons and where the men were often far from home.

One of the reasons for the discrepancy in patient numbers between the two hospitals is that many of the mentally ill European patients were repatriated to Britain. It was not a good look for the Company to have disturbed staff, civilian or military, remaining in India for too long. By 1818, the Company had arranged to send them to Pembroke House in Hackney, east London. There they were lodged under the care of a doctor who was paid £40 per annum for the care of minor civil servants, soldiers and sailors, and £100 per annum for officers and senior civil servants.[42]

The generosity of private donors, British and Indian, to the colleges, hospitals and lunatic asylums, not only in Bengal but throughout British India, cannot be underestimated. The cash-strapped Company had initiated the establishment of these institutions in the expectation that private money would turn its proposals into reality, and in most cases it did. The amount of lobbying and arm-twisting that went on to raise funds will never be fully known, but the Company gambled correctly on the prediction that necessity and fear would induce many to offer generous sums. The law-courts and other civil bodies needed educated Indians to fill administrative posts, and the growing number of poor, uneducated Eurasian children who would grow into uneducated teenagers posed a potential threat of delinquency. Decent healthcare provision for officers, if not always for private soldiers, was essential to maintain the Presidency armies. Both Britons and Indians who wanted to maintain the status quo were prepared to help pay for it where they could.

Money was raised in a variety of ways, including balls and theatrical performances. 'The Tragedy of the Fair Penitent' was performed to a full house early in 1786 as a benefit performance for the Orphan Society, and the newly established *Calcutta Gazette* commented that the size of the audience did credit to 'the liberal sentiments and humane feelings of the Settlement' (as Calcutta frequently referred to itself). The Society 'has for its object the preservation of a numerous train of helpless children, the offspring of our European Soldiers, who, before this establishment, were for the most part suffered to lead lives of ignorance and vice in the Barracks'. They were now being educated to become useful members of the State instead of a disgrace to the English name.

It wasn't just funding for philanthropic purposes like schools, hospitals and orphanages that got the good people of Calcutta digging into their pockets. The governor general Lord Wellesley had set up an 'Improvement Fund', which in 1814 was transferred to the Lottery Commissioners, who were empowered to raise money by lotteries for municipal improvements. St John's Church, built on land charitably donated, as we have seen, was largely funded by a special Lottery Commission, and this was noted on its foundation stone which read in part: 'Raised by the liberal and voluntary subscription of British subjects and others.' Most of the improvements were to do with improving the roads and drainage in Calcutta, which had grown too rapidly for its infrastructure. A Lottery Committee succeeded the Commissioners in 1817 and took over the balance of seventeen different lotteries, which amounted to four and a half lakhs of rupees.[43] But by 1836, public opinion in England had swung against the idea of raising money through gambling, which in effect a lottery was.

An under-researched element of funding for good causes is that of freemasonry. Not surprisingly for a secret society, detailed records are hard to find, although there was little secrecy about who was a mason in India. Most of the governors general were, including Lord Cornwallis and Warren Hastings, together with other prominent Company officials, lawyers (William Hickey) and churchmen like the Reverend William Johnson, vicar of St John's Church. The first lodge, the masons' meeting place, was at Fort William in 1729 and was named the East India Arms. It was followed by Lodge Star in the East and Lodge Industry and Perseverance, the latter also known as Labore et Constantia. By 1788, there were eighty-six members of the Calcutta Lodge Star who were described as being 'in honourable situations in life, and inspired with an earnest desire to support the credit of their Lodge'.[44] Cornwallis was the Grand Master of the Calcutta Lodges and took part in a procession and ball held to raise money for a new Orphan House for Girls in Madras in 1787.

Freemasonry had benefits both for its members and for the good causes it supported. A British mason from the Lodge Industry had the misfortune to be captured in 1783 during the Anglo-French war on the Isle de Bourbon in the Indian Ocean, but his captors received him 'with great civility and kindness' because they were masons too. On his release, a letter of thanks was sent from his Calcutta Lodge to the French Lodge, noting 'the true principle of Masonry at work'.[45] French freemasons fighting in India gained a reputation for their good care of captured British masons, and a number of otherwise unexpected promotions in the Company hierarchy may also have been influenced by the camaraderie of freemasonry. Lodges were promoted in the Presidency armies, and cantonments like Cawnpore had a choice of three Lodges.

Some prominent Indians were invited to become masons, including the Nana Sahib of Bithur and the *nawab wazir* Saadat Ali Khan of Awadh. The usual name for a masonic lodge—*jadu-ghar*, or 'house of magic'—reflected the ordinary Indian view. Wealth rather than class was a determining feature in who became a mason. There was a monthly subscription of Rs10 and clearly more donations were forthcoming, in fact so much so that the Bengal Lodges were able to send money to London where the Grand Lodge was being built on Great Queen Street. The Patna and Burdwan Lodges each contributed 20 gold mohurs, equivalent to over £4,000 today. Money and influence went hand in hand, and many of the institutions for which the Company took the credit were funded in part by freemasons' money. This was reflected in the Government Sanskrit College, Calcutta which was inaugurated in February 1824: 'The foundation stone of this Edifice ... was laid by John Pascal Larkins Esq. Provincial Grand Master of the Fraternity of Free Masons in Bengal. Amidst the Acclamations of all ranks of the Native population of this City In the presence of a numerous Assembly of the Fraternity.'[46] The same wording appeared on the foundation stone of the Government Mahommedan College which was opened 6 months later. Freemasonry, with its Enlightenment ethos and its foundation in medieval stonemasons' guilds, is an important and under-explored facet of the built environment during the Company period.

4

JOINING THE PARTS TOGETHER

In the Library of the Royal Academy of Arts in London is a simple, hand-drawn sketch map made in 1786 for the artist Ozias Humphry. Annotated in Persian, it shows the area between Benares and Delhi (Shahjahanpur) following the course of the Rivers Ganges and Jumna. The map is a small panorama—only 4 ½ inches tall but 18 inches long—and made from one, or possibly two, pieces of paper pasted together. It has been folded, not rolled, so it would have sat in a small bag, or more likely the pocket of an eighteenth-century traveller. Part pictographic, the map depicts the ancient city of Allahabad as a square and named Qila (Fort) Illahabad. The fort, which still stands today on the riverbank, was built by the Mughal Emperor Akbar in 1583 and was already a venerable landmark when Humphry passed by. Compass points are helpfully indicated on his map: *teraf shimal* (north direction), *teraf janub* (south direction), *teraf marush* (east direction) and *teraf magrib* (west direction).

This is a map prepared by someone familiar with the route between Benares and Delhi. There is a certain authority in the placing of the rivers, the fort and the various towns en route. The cartographer is likely to have been an agent who dealt with ferrying passengers and goods across the region. The existing map shows only a small section of the journey undertaken by Humphry. Other sections, now missing, might have been pasted on at each end to show the complete route from Calcutta, the Presidency capital of the East India Company, to Delhi, the Mughal capital.

Unlike the survey maps discussed later in this chapter, Humphry's map is an unique piece of ephemera. Dozens of such maps must have been carried by travellers unfamiliar with their intended route, which they then discarded like used train tickets at the end of a journey. Luckily for us, the artist was a methodical man, keeping a diary during his visit to Lucknow (although not while travelling). The map was probably tucked inside the pages of his diary at some point as a souvenir of the journey. There are no helpful arrows on the map to indicate in which direction Humphry was travelling, whether to Lucknow—where he arrived on 20 February—or back to Calcutta, setting out on a borrowed elephant in early August. A Lucknow acquaintance, the former surveyor Colonel Claude Martin, had generously loaned him the elephant, and because a letter from Martin is part of this small collection at the Royal Academy, there is a good chance the map was drawn in Lucknow for the journey back.[1] Humphry himself was unable to read the map's Persian annotations; it had been made for the literate man who accompanied him and who made the travelling arrangements on land and water.

Indian cartography before the arrival of the Europeans seems particularly elusive, even non-existent. The outline of the subcontinent appears on medieval maps of the world in more or less correct form, but its interior, the distance between its towns and the course of its great rivers, remained almost uncharted—although not unknown—until the middle of the eighteenth century. The 'Mughal' maps carefully documented by Susan Gole are in fact maps that the Frenchman Jean-Baptiste-Joseph Gentil commissioned while he was agent for the French government at Awadh, one of the breakaway provinces from the Mughal Empire.[2] We can speculate why pre-colonial maps of India have not been found: they were not needed while the majority of the population kept to a limited circuit of markets and places of worship; land revenue records were based on the names of landholders, not visual records of their holdings; lack of printing technology before the 1670s meant that hand-drawn maps could not be reproduced or widely circulated. But the contrast between medieval mapping in Britain, where credible maps were being produced by the thirteenth century, and India's cartographical silence is striking. And the implications of agreeing or even actively encouraging foreigners to survey and map your own country provides an important clue to the successful colonisation of that country.

If there are no known land maps until Europeans began surveying the subcontinent, this doesn't mean that 'personal' maps like Humphry's didn't exist, or maps for pilgrimage routes. It may simply mean that they haven't survived. The work of the Austrian Jesuit, Father Joseph Tieffenthaler, who arrived in India in 1740 provides the link between hand-drawn maps for travellers (*desi* maps) and the surveys begun under James Rennell for the East India Company. Although often linked together in accounts of early European cartography in India, the two men were very different in their approaches. Tieffenthaler, who spoke Hindustani and Persian, consulted with and used the work of Indian mapmakers. Rennell employed European surveyors who worked with Indian assistants using Western equipment and methods.

One of Tieffenthaler's most important contributions is his map entitled 'A General Chart of the Course of the Ganges and the Gagra', published in Paris in 1784, a year before his death at Lucknow.[3] Measuring 29 inches by 23, the 'General Chart' is made up of six separate maps, four of which are by unnamed Indian cartographers. Running through the map is Tieffenthaler's own partial survey of the two great rivers, the Ganges and the Gogra (Ghaghara), from their source in the Himalayas. Tieffenthaler had begun his survey 20 years earlier in the mid-1760s, when Calcutta was recovering from the damage caused by Siraj-ud-daula's attack, and it is correctly recorded in Tieffenthaler's map as one place-name among many others along the busy banks of the Ganges. A number of sacred sites in India were and still are the focus of regular pilgrimages by Hindus, Jains and Buddhists. The 'General Chart' has at its centre the lake of Mansarovar in the Himalayas, believed to be the abode of Lord Shiva. Tieffenthaler does not record visiting the lake and the adjoining Mount Kailash, so it follows that his map of the area would have come from an Indian source, from people familiar with the route who recorded it for other pilgrims, and this makes it a rare indigenous survival, preserved by a European.

It is Tieffenthaler's town maps that provide the clearest indication that he was using Indian sources and Indian draughtsmen too. Look at his panoramic maps of Laknao (Lucknow) and Maxvdabad (Murshidabad), both situated on rivers.[4] There is a sense of movement in the depictions of survey boats travelling upriver, but most striking is the way some drawn elevations of the buildings lining the banks are flung flat on their backs. The west bank of the Murshidabad map, the area called Mahinagar, presents a pleasant view of trees and buildings in conventional form. But you have to turn the map upside down to see the east bank in similar fashion, and here the great Katra Masjid appears in its own enclosure as a separate elevation which can be viewed by turning the map 90 degrees. The Lucknow map is similarly idiosyncratic, viewed from the north bank with the Macchi Bhawan fort gates and the Aurangzeb Mosque elevations aligned flat to the right while adjoining buildings remain horizontal. Neither map has compass points, although the directional flow of both rivers is correctly shown, and it would be reasonably easy to navigate one's way through these attractive towns with their distinctive buildings. This is the nearest we are going to get to the lost *desi* maps of pre-colonial India unless a hidden cache turns up.

Part of Humphry's map covers the Sarak-e-Azam, the Great Road, also known as Badshahi Sarak (Royal Road) and Uttarapatha (Northern Road). It lost its Indian names early in the nineteenth century to become the Grand Trunk Road, and today it is simply called GT Road. First established during the third century BCE, it runs for approximately 1,500 miles across the subcontinent from Bangladesh to Kabul and was the trade route that linked India to Central Asia. A sparse network of other roads zigzagged across the subcontinent during the Mughal era, providing trade and pilgrimage routes. An important road ran from Agra, via Jaipur, and Ajmer, leading south through Ahmadabad to the western port of Surat. But, as Jean Deloche reminds us in his definitive study of *Transport and Communications in India Prior to Steam Locomotion*, roads do not have an independent existence separate from human settlement, and they could fall in and out of favour depending on political and economic circumstances. [5] While the road between Delhi and Agra allowed the Mughal capital to shift comfortably between the two cities, the road to Surat dwindled in significance as power shifted to the developing port of Bombay. An extreme example of this is the old, pre-Mughal capital of Gaur in Bengal: once one of the most populated cities in the subcontinent, it was deserted when the Ganges changed course and is now only approachable by a single track.

Along a number of Mughal roads, particularly in northern India, the route was marked by a series of structures called *kos minar*. The *kos* is an ancient measure of distance, equivalent in Bengal to just under 2 miles, and *minar* is a pillar or tower (as in minaret), so this is a marker like the English milestone. Of the thousand or so *kos minars* constructed from the reign of Akbar onwards, just over a hundred remain today. They were built of stone, where it was available, or more frequently of brick covered with stucco, and they stand like giant pepper pots with rounded tops along the old roads.[6] A curiosity of the *kos* was that it differed in length through the subcontinent, stretching to almost 4 miles in the south of the country and contracting to about 1 mile as it approached Afghanistan. Along the routes were *serais*, or lodging places for travellers and their animals. (The term 'caravanserai' indicates that people preferred to travel in convoy for security.) The remains of Badli-ki-Serai a few miles north of old Delhi give a good indication of the size of a major *serai*, though unfortunately only its two giant gateways remain today. Inside its vanished walls were individual cells where travellers could rest, get stabling and fodder for their animals, and find a canteen for their own meals. All this had to be paid for, of course, but the safety of a well-organised *serai* was greatly preferable to pitching tents off the main road. Caravanserais are mainly associated today with the Islamic world, where many fine examples remain.

To move across India away from its main roads was dangerous, difficult and time-consuming, particularly for single travellers or small groups. Unpaved tracks between villages and small towns ran through areas called *jangal*, a Sanskrit-derived word meaning uncultivated land, but not necessarily thick forest as the term implies today. Snakes lurked in the long grass, particularly after the monsoon. Tigers did not hesitate to attack lone pedestrians or riders, and the malarial mosquito enjoyed swampy, shady areas. *Dacoits*, or highway thieves, were another peril, along with the thugs, who practised murder as well as robbery. Recent studies of thugee (*thagi*) have examined the claims of Company officials that thugee was a common practice which affected Indian travellers. It was Sir William Sleeman who was credited with putting an end to this practice, but it has been questioned if the thugee menace existed at all, and whether its supposed cessation was not simply an attempt by the East India Company to show itself as the guardian of law and order.[7] This academic argument would have been of little comfort to Indian travellers who fell victim to gangs who robbed and sometimes murdered them. Foreign travellers like Humphry were not targeted by *dacoits* or thugs, because they did not carry large sums of money or expensive goods with them, as Indian merchants did. When Company officials needed to move substantial sums of specie across the land, they were accompanied by units of armed *sepoys*, which deterred potential robbers. It was the Indian merchants and travellers who suffered most from the actions of their criminal fellow countrymen.

During the eighteenth century, as Mughal administration faltered, the roads deteriorated. Maintenance was not kept up, and the ever-present jungle rapidly advanced. The Political Agent James Tod, travelling in Rajputana in 1822, noted that part of what had been the major road from Agra to Ahmadabad now ran through a forest so thick that the path had to be cleared with axes. He wrote that 'No better proof can be given of the abandoned condition of this country ... than this relapse of civilisation into a state of nature.'[8] Other travellers reported that the number of *kos minars* along major routes had declined, as over time these masonry structures had fallen or were demolished for their bricks.

The increasingly poor condition of the Mughal roads limited the kind of transport that could be used. Although English-made sprung carriages were exported for sale to India, they could only be driven in the centre of towns, where a few roads had been 'metalled' with crushed stone embedded in tar and rolled flat. But such roads were so infrequent that travellers usually viewed them as curiosities. Elephants with or without attached *howdahs*, as Humphry had used on his journey, were the elite method of travel, followed by horses and then bullock carts for those who could not ride. Palanquins required at least four men to carry them, and unlike the Western sedan chair, where the passenger sat upright, they required a half-lying, half-sitting position, wedged in with cushions. And of course they could only go as fast as the palki-bearers, as they were called, could stride.

One senses the relish with which James Rennell began the work of bringing order to the geography of the Company's newly acquired territories. Rennell had been appointed surveyor general in Bengal by the governor general Robert Clive shortly before the latter's departure for England. As we have seen, Clive had got the *diwani* of Bengal, Bihar and Orissa, which meant he possessed the right to collect land revenue in the three provinces. So accurate surveys were necessary not only to establish land holdings but for military purposes too. Officers had to know where they were leading their troops in pursuit of *zamindars* who were reluctant to pay their new landlords, to settle boundary disputes and to escort sums of money to the Company's Treasury. Rennell's instructions from the Council in Calcutta were clear: he was 'to form one general chart from those already made' and 'to set about forming a general map of Bengall with all Expedition'. In forwarding maps to Calcutta from his base in Dacca, Rennell was also given permission to publish and sell his own books, which he began to do on his return to England in 1777.

The subtitle of the *Bengal Atlas* published in 1780—'Maps of the Theatre of War and Commerce on That Side of Hindustan'—lays out the intention of Rennell's work, and makes a clear statement of the Company's priorities. But more interesting is the preface to his book *A Description of the Roads in Bengal and Bahar*, published 2 years earlier. Rennell listed Calcutta (the seat of government), Murshidabad, Patna and Dacca 'as centres from whence all the great roads issue'. There were also about twenty-eight stations, 'either the seats of provincial councils, or of collectors, subordinate military stations, or factories; or places, which for their situation are likely to become military posts in time of invasion'. This was where the *Description of the Roads* would prove so useful:

> The utility of such a work in *any* country must strike every one: much more so in a country where the people employed by Government are sojourners, and from the want of local knowledge must depend upon the information of Guides ... at best those guides know only the most frequented roads; so that in crossing the country no information whatever can be derived from them: and as for the peasantry, or ryots, they cannot be supposed to know the roads beyond the circle of the markets which they frequent.[9]

Rennell's comment on the lack of knowledge, or indeed curiosity, of the guides was echoed by the surveyor Samuel Showers, who was offered such men by a landholder but then found it necessary to change them every 2 miles, as their local knowledge did not extend any further.[10] And surveying was not simply about measuring distances and mapping roads, as Rennell told his mapmakers. He insisted that 'a perfect knowledge of the Country may be of the greatest Consequence to the Hon'ble Company' and that they were to record 'the Properties of the Water, and the means of Procuring it; the Nature of the Soils, their Produce, with their effects on the health of Animals, and the salubrity or un-wholesomeness of the Air'. Maps were also to show 'village sites and names, salt works, roads, creeks, protective embankments, tree symbols and elevated land.'[11]

The climate had to be considered too, such as the fact that rivers and *nullahs* (streams) which could be crossed in the dry season turned into torrents during the monsoon. This meant in practical terms that fords could only be used between December and June, which clearly had military implications. If not quite the Bengali Domesday Book that some have claimed, then the *Bengal Atlas* was certainly the most comprehensive land survey undertaken so far, and it facilitated the Company's penetration into areas where Europeans had not been seen before.

During his long years of retirement in England, Rennell was able to update the information he had gathered in India in his *Memoir of a Map of Hindoostan or the Mogul Empire*, published in 1788 and dedicated to Sir Joseph Banks, President of the Royal Society. (A third edition was published in 1793.) This was an 'attempt to improve the Geography of India and the neighbouring countries' and was an holistic examination of the geography of the subcontinent, not just of Bengal, from a European perspective. During his long career, Rennell had seen a substantial and rapid increase in the material needed to update earlier maps:

> Considering the vast extent of India, and how little its interior parts have been visited by Europeans, till the latter part of the last century, it ought rather to surprise us that so much geographical matter should be collected during so short a period; especially where so little has been contributed towards it by the natives

themselves, as in the present case. Indeed, we must not go much farther back then thirty-five years, for the matter that forms the basis of this Map.[12]

Rennell explained the rationale behind the various boundary lines drawn on his map. In northern India he had kept the *subahs*, the provinces established during the Mughal era, as a permanent feature. Perceptively, he had found that the idea of boundaries were 'impressed on the minds of the natives by tradition' as well as being detailed in the *Ain-i-Akbari*, which contained administrative reports from the reign of Akbar. But the old *subah* boundaries were not drawn consistently over the whole country. In the Deccan, for example, Rennell had used 'modern divisions', made following the territorial struggles between England and France and the defeat of Tipu Sultan of Mysore, which 'has produced much new geographical material'.

Since the Mughal Empire had been dismembered and new divisions of its provinces had taken place under new, autonomous rulers—in particular Awadh and Hyderabad—these areas showed both the old *subahs* and the new provinces. These distinctions were indicated by different colours on Rennell's map: British possessions—red; British allies—yellow; Mahratta states—green (the largest area); Seiks—blue and so on. Rennell used information from many different sources in compiling the map, including the French governor general Bussy's marches in the Deccan; descriptions from travellers like the Englishman George Forster and the Jesuit Father and spy Padre Wendell as well as the earlier maps of French geographer M. D'Anville. But there were still untapped sources, Rennell noted, including a 'vast fund of geographical knowledge' from the public records in Portuguese-held Goa, and probably much more 'in the hands of people who are ignorant of its value'—a common complaint of the dedicated researcher.[13]

While the Company recognised the importance of mapping India, it was reluctant to change the country's topography by building new roads. Sir George Chesney, looking back on the start of his career as a Bengal engineer in 1848, claimed that:

The Court of Directors did not recognise the prosecution of public works as a necessary part of their policy. The construction of a road or canal was regarded by them much in the same light that a war would be—as a necessary evil, to be undertaken only when it could not be postponed any longer, and not, if possible, to be repeated.[14]

The impatience of the young engineer is clear, but there were reasons why the Company did not begin a programme of road building until near the end of its existence. Cost was an important factor: not only the cost of materials and labour, but the amount of compensation due to the landholder as well. If a local ruler could be persuaded to pay for a new or improved road, or if he requested one, then he would be lent military engineers from the Company but would be charged for labour and materials. The area under direct Company rule was still limited, and new roads petered out a few miles from the Presidency towns. The 16-mile-long road between Calcutta and Barrackpore, the summer residence of the governor general, remained the longest stretch of Company-built road for many years, with the exception of the 'new military road' that ran between Calcutta and Benares. This opened in 1781, shaving some 200 miles off the old route which had meandered along the bank of the Ganges.

Conveniently, the new road passed mainly through Company territory until it reached the *zamindari* of Benares, which had been attached to the *nawabi* state of Awadh but was now leased to the Company. This meant that there had been no need for negotiations with local rulers, and the road was soon busy with traffic. Only the Raja of Benares, Chait Singh, objected, rebelling against the Company's financial demands and threatening the governor general Warren Hastings. The neatly finished road striding into the Raja's city from the British capital must have been an added aggravation.

The lack of decent roads led the Company to explore an ingenious method of communication. During the early nineteenth century, there was a short-lived attempt to use semaphore, or the 'visual telegraph', as it was called. Around 45 semaphore towers were erected between Calcutta and Chunar, over a distance of nearly 400 miles. The towers were substantial, brick-built structures, fitted with an interior staircase and standing in a straight line at varying distances—in some cases 9 miles apart, in others

13 miles—depending on the terrain. Where the land was flat, the towers were four-storeyed so that the moveable wooden arms or paddles at the top would be visible. For towers on the hills, two storeys were sufficient.

Semaphore towers had been developed in France during the Revolution and were adopted in England, specifically between London and Portsmouth, so that news about the arrival and departure of shipping could be swiftly known in the capital. In 1817, the Bengal Council asked surveyor George Everest to advise on the route to Chunar, and shortly afterwards construction of the towers began. Chunar may seem an unlikely place to deserve this kind of attention. Its fort stood at the top of a tall natural spur of rock that thrust itself into the Ganges. After it was ceded by Chait Singh to the Company, it was used as a depot for the artillery and as a store for ammunition. By itself it was not of prime strategic importance, but it lay only 14 miles from Benares, which was. Once built, the towers were manned by two or more men with telescopes who 'read' the signals from the neighbouring tower and passed them on. When everything was working well and there was no mist or fog to obstruct the view, messages could be sent from Fort William to Chunar in under an hour. However, by 1828 the scheme had been abandoned because it was not considered economically viable.[15] All that effort in building the towers and training the men to read semaphore signals was lost. Today some of the towers still stand, 200 years after their construction, and there is a particularly well-preserved example at Barrackpore.

After the defeat of Tipu Sultan in south India, and with the French confined to Pondicherry, it was not thought necessary to build new roads at all. A robust attitude prevailed, and George Chesney claimed that the 'want of roads taught Indian armies how to do without them ... on the breaking out of war, nothing had to be improvised, and the troops took the field without difficulty and confusion'.[16] Rennell's military routes that had added to geographical knowledge were simply routes, not roads. Changes in Company policy towards road building came very slowly even as more territory was conquered or annexed. Roads were built on an ad hoc basis, as and when needed, like the roads to the newly developed hill stations at the foot of the Himalayas. And although the Mughal capital Delhi had been seized by the Company in 1803, it would be another 30 years before a metalled road from the British capital of Calcutta was started under the governorship of William Bentinck. Repairs and extensions to the Grand Trunk Road were made by metalling only part of it, and at a huge cost which soared towards an estimated £35,000 per annum by the 1840s.

One of the reasons cited (apart from expense) for the Company's lack of road building was the difficulty of bridging India's huge rivers. Engineers trained in Britain with its docile rivers were faced with the great Ganges, the Jumna and the Brahmaputra, among others, miles wide and simply unbridgeable with the technology of the late eighteenth and early nineteenth century. Of course, rivers had to be crossed, and this was done mainly by ferry or pontoon bridge, the latter being a series of anchored boats supporting a rigid walkway that carried people and animals. In the mountains there were scary rope bridges that could only be used by people crossing in single file. On the plains there were a number of Mughal-era bridges built of stone and brick, but these were relatively uncommon. The Comte de Modave, a Frenchman travelling from Calcutta to Delhi in the 1770s, noted that he had found only 'three or four [bridges] that merited attention'. The Hooghly at Calcutta had no bridge at all until the 1870s, when a fixed pontoon was put in place, and its cantilever bridge built on caissons sunk into the river was not opened until 1943, though it had long been planned.

Despite Rennell's maps, his atlas and his *Description of the Roads*, the traveller still faced a good deal of uncertainty during an overland journey. Would water be available from the wells or tanks along the route? Would villagers have spare food to sell? Would there be fodder for the animals? Would there be safe places to lodge overnight? It was uncertainties like these that made river travel the preferred method for most, both Indian and European. As we have seen in Tieffenthaler's chart of the Ganges and the Gogra, in the mid-eighteenth century the population of India had far more knowledge about the subcontinent's great rivers than its interior.

The change from water-borne travel to road and later rail, was profound and irreversible. It was perhaps one of the most significant effects of European intervention in the subcontinent, but one of the least studied. The extent to which India's rivers were used for trade, travel and pleasure can only be appreciated today from miniatures by its own artists, as well as European painters like Frans Balthazar Solvyns, a Belgian artist who spent a decade in Bengal at the turn of the eighteenth century.

There was a rich and considerable variety of boats, some distinguished by their construction methods and materials and others by their functions. The *mugachara*, a vessel with a lightly thatched roof, carried wedding parties and festive processions to their destinations. Statues of the gods and goddesses were similarly transported by boat, either to new temples or for *darshan* (the viewing of a holy image or person) when the devout would line the banks to catch a glimpse of the boat and its sacred cargo. There was the *woolock* or baggage boat that accompanied soldiers and their equipment; the flat-bottomed *pattello*; the *jeelea dingi* for inland lakes; the *budgerow* where cabins with windows took up two-thirds of the boat and the simple mat-roofed fishing boat. There were special boats for different goods: the salt boats, the wood boats and the betel leaf boats, among others. For rulers and the aristocracy there were the elegant rowing boats with animal prows: the *morpunkhi* (peacock-head) and the *feelchara* (elephant-head). On the River Gomti which runs through Lucknow there was a three-masted schooner, *The Sultan of Oude*, a pleasure boat fitted out incongruously with eighteen cannon, as well as a steam-powered, fish-shaped boat made from gilded wickerwork.

But the epitome of luxury was the *Soonamookee*, the state barge commissioned and built for the governor general and commander-in-chief, the Marquess of Hastings, in 1813. The following year, he embarked on an extensive river and land tour of northern India, from Calcutta to Delhi and back. The purpose of the tour was for the newly appointed Hastings to inspect British possessions along the route and meet Indian rulers. In keeping with the idea promoted by the former governor general, Lord Wellesley, that the Company was the successor to the Mughal Empire, this had to be done in some style to create the right impression. Emily Shakespear, who accompanied her civil servant husband and Hastings' large party upcountry, described the 'golden-faced' barge in detail:

Its exterior is painted a deep green & is richly ornamented with Gold. The apartments which consist of a Drawing room, bed rooms & two Dressing Rooms with Marble Baths attached to each, are white & gold, and are handsomely fitted up with green Morocco Furniture. Another Pinnace of equal Dimensions & almost equal beauty with the Soonamookee is appropriated to the use of His Lordship's Children & their Governess, & a third for a Banqueting & audience boat. A splendid Barge for the reception of the band, a Feelchara or State Barge & a large Vessel fitted up with all the conveniences of a kitchen are also in attendance the whole of them painted Green with gilt mouldings to match the State Pinnace. The fleet consists of about 400 Boats ...[17]

The Indian-built *Soonamookee* and its accompanying flotilla were sailing boats with oarsmen, dependent on the wind and the tides (the Hooghly is a tidal river). A decade after the *Soonamookee* was commissioned, the first steamship was launched in Calcutta, an innovation that brought considerable change to river travel in India, although not always for the better. The *Diana* was a steam paddle vessel—a boat with a circular paddle powered by a steam engine that pushed it forwards or backwards. The *Diana*'s wooden frame had been built at the Kidderpore Docks in Calcutta, and the engine was imported from Henry Maudslay of Lambeth.

Steamboats (which are smaller than steamships) were first used as tugs to tow large sailing ships bound for Calcutta as far upriver as they could reach. As the East Indiamen grew bigger to accommodate more goods, they became too large to navigate the Hooghly and had to dock at Kedgeree or Culpee at the mouth of the Ganges. Here passengers and goods would disembark and continue the last 50 miles to Calcutta in smaller, pilot-guided boats. Then, in August 1828, the government's new steamer *Hooghly* chugged along the Ganges from Calcutta to Allahabad on an 'experimental voyage', a journey of nearly 1,000 miles along the river's very meandering route. Although the journey by road was only half the distance, being some 500 miles, steamboats quickly became popular. At top speed they could reach a dizzying 7 miles per hour. The *Hooghly*, on its first journey, took 20 days to reach Allahabad, with 12 hours of daily steaming 'labouring under the disadvantage of a defect either of construction or in her rudder'. The return journey took 14 days, with a 2-day delay at Benares. Initially, passengers were towed along behind in an 'accommodation barge' or 'flat' while the steamer carried goods.

There were drawbacks, as a British Parliamentary Enquiry had established. The insurance on goods shipped by river was very costly, in fact as expensive as transport to England. The River Insurance Company's rates from Calcutta to Allahabad were 3½ per cent. From Calcutta to London, they were between 3 to 4 per cent. There were hidden dangers along the Ganges too, including the currents, the winds, sandbanks and sunken trees.[18] But the main recommendations of the Enquiry, which drew heavily on a report prepared by a senior Company officer, Henry Prinsep, Secretary to Council, at the specific request of the new governor general William Bentinck, was positive.

Given that the Company's main concern at the time was to turn a profit for its shareholders, Prinsep argued that there were pragmatic reasons for introducing steamers into India. The cost of transporting 'treasure'—a term for specie, or actual coins—was high. A loan of thirty-eight lakhs of rupees from the princely state of Gwalior to the Company had needed an 'entire battalion' to escort it from Agra to Calcutta in 1831. A steamer would not have required such a great extent of valuable manpower, and the rapid transmission of 'treasure' from Benares to be recoined in Calcutta could potentially render superfluous the proposed Mint at Benares, thus saving another large sum of money.

Transporting officers and men of the Company's Bengal Presidency Army upcountry would become cheaper too. Every army officer got a 'boat allowance' paid per annum, the allowance from Calcutta to Allahabad being for 3 months, the estimated journey time by sailing ship. So to transport a regiment like HM 31st Foot upcountry to the cantonment at Cawnpore cost Rs46,000, equivalent today to nearly a quarter of a million pounds. A steamer was estimated to take only a month, and it was reported that 'junior officers would prefer to have a speedy passage on board a steamer' while newly arrived cadets could be sent up straight away.[19] The argument for steam travel was strong: the regiment could be transported with 'security, comfort and healthiness to the men' together with their accompanying children, followers, hospital and commissariat. His Majesty's regiments in India did not travel lightly.

More arguments in favour of the steamers were given. Depots along the river route would not need to be so fully stocked because supplies could now be provided within a month. Four expensive boats had been kept in a state of constant readiness to transport written orders from Calcutta to various upcountry stations, but these could now be dispensed with. Most important of all, argued Prinsep, steamers carried their own fuel and could travel for nearly a week without needing to replenish the coal used to produce the steam for the engines, so coaling stations would only be needed every 120 miles, or one coal relay. Among places named as coaling stations en route were Rajmahal, Mongyr, Dinapore, Ghazipur and Benares. Cawnpore, the 'principal station of the army of Hindustan is doubtless a most important place to be reached by steam', which could be done by extending the steamer route from Allahabad.

Both the *Hooghly* and her sistership *Burhampootur* were built in India following technical drawings sent from England. They were fitted with 25 horsepower engines supplied again by 'Mr Maudsley [sic], one of the first machinists of England'. They cost respectively Rs85,000 and Rs65,000, but modifications had to be made immediately: the rudder of the *Hooghly* was adapted for shallow water (when it was raised) and deeper water (when it was lowered). Although well-constructed, both steamboats were considered defective, with far less accommodation for officers than planned and a draught exceeding 3 feet, which meant that on its second voyage from Calcutta in March 1829 the *Hooghly* could not go further than Benares, where the pre-monsoon Ganges became too shallow to continue.

There were all kind of considerations, including the climate, the fugitive sandbanks, the lack of experienced pilots, the construction of the steamers themselves (they were designed in England, not India) and the unanticipated obstacles created by local fishermen. Describing a voyage through eastern Bengal, a passenger, A.P. Wall, wrote:

> In passing through the Modomutty [Madhumati], a remarkably broad and deep river, offering in itself no impediment to the

navigation of vessels of any description, I found it in four different places ... strongly staked with fishing stakes completely across the river, leaving only a small boat passage of about 20 feet wide, in passing through which the 'Hooghly's' paddle wheels were greatly endangered.

The stakes also impeded the current, so sand had built up around them. On the return journey, negotiating a passage through a number of large country boats, it was found that the fishermen had moved their stakes, but 'a number of other bamboos, stuck in different parts of the channel' presented the greatest difficulty.[20] Nevertheless, by 1833 a regular steamer service along the Ganges was established, its paddle wheels now protected against concealed stumps and roots by iron guard rails. Envious eyes were cast far afield. 'The Americans of the Mississippi have this advantage in the economical construction of their steam vessels that the forests from which they procure their timber are up the stream which it is wished to navigate, and their fuel, whether wood or coal, likewise found near its banks,' reported the engineer Captain Thomas Prinsep, adding that it would be a long time before the Ganges became as profitable as the Mississippi.[21] Detailed records were kept of freight carried up- and downriver, of the price paid to transport it and of the number and sorts of passengers. By 1840, the Ganges steamers had been further modified and were now iron-hulled instead of constructed entirely of timber. Freight was calculated in terms of cubic feet, the amount of room needed on board for the goods, and was charged accordingly. The public paid Rs2.10.10 per foot, while the preferential government charge was less than half that amount at Rs1.8.0. During the year 1840–1, nearly 400 passengers were carried upcountry from Calcutta, with 150 on the return journey downstream. A detailed report by the civil engineer Rowland Macdonald Stephenson, published in 1844, carried the following exchanges in question and answer form:

Q. Have natives proceeded as passengers in the iron boats, and if so, to what extent, and at what rates of passage money?

A. No natives, excepting some of the higher ranks, have been passengers in the boats; these have engaged cabins, and paid the established rates. Deck passengers are charged one anna per mile, but very few avail themselves of the steamers.

Q. Do native traders, and natives of other descriptions, shew a disposition to take advantage of the steamers on the Ganges, and do they fully appreciate the saving of time they occasion?

A. Native merchants are the principal shippers. When freights are high they send valuable goods, but seldom accompany them. They fully appreciate the saving of time and insurance, etc.[22]

One 'native' who would certainly have engaged a cabin was Dwarkanath Tagore, the Calcutta-born entrepreneur and businessman who travelled by steamboat to Allahabad and quickly realised its potential. Tagore became involved with private and government steamboat companies through his own company, Carr, Tagore & Co., which dealt under licence in the opium trade with China. It also shipped Chinese tea bushes to Upper Assam and, significantly, purchased the large coalfields at Raniganj in upper Bengal. East India Company officials had discovered coal here in 1774, but it was not until Carr, Tagore & Co.'s purchase that mining became systematic and profitable. Coal had not previously been needed in India as fuel for heating or cooking purposes because the countryside was then still so well-wooded, but the arrival of steam engines both facilitated mining and greedily demanded its produce.

Stationary steam engines had been in use in England throughout the eighteenth century, although it was not until 1775, when James Watt took out a twenty-five-year patent for an improved engine, that they became more widely used. Watt was a partner with Matthew Boulton at the Soho engineering works in Birmingham, and, while the company exported steam engines to Europe and Russia, only two are known to have gone to India, and those to a private buyer.[23] Steam engines were used primarily to pump water out of tin mines in Cornwall and coal mines throughout the rest of Britain. So the synchronicity of the steam engine and its preferred fuel coming together in eastern India in the early nineteenth century marked a radical step forward in the Company's plan 'to join the parts together', and Bentinck spoke enthusiastically about 'this grand invention upon the rivers of India'. He himself had travelled in the *Hooghly* from Monghyr to Calcutta in only 8 days.

While the Ganges and the Brahmaputra rivers were amenable to steamboats, the great Indus river, originating in the Himalayas and flowing westwards into the Arabian sea, was not. As the historian Clive Dewey has shown in his book *Steamboats on the Indus* (with its telling subtitle *The Limits of Western Technological Superiority in South Asia*), years of experimentation and huge sums of money failed to offer the benefits that the governor general had praised. The Bombay Flotilla, operating between 1839 and 1862, was the first of four companies which for over three decades struggled to provide a viable method of shipping goods and troops upcountry to the Punjab and the north-west frontier along the Indus and its five tributaries. Here we are mainly concerned with the ecological effect, as the Indus steamboats gobbled up the forests, a trend accelerated by the Company's annexation of Sindh in 1843 and the Punjab 6 years later.

Unlike eastern India, there were no viable coalfields within the Indus basin. Hopes were raised, then dashed. Samples of coal sent to Calcutta for testing seemed promising, 'But somehow the coal was never available in commercial quantities. When it came to setting up a colliery, there was always a fatal flaw.'[24] Major Henry Pottinger, Resident at Cutch, reported in 1827 that two shallow shafts had been sunk at a local coal mine, both of which had filled with 'about 7 feet of water'. He added that a well in the Residency grounds itself had more than 50 feet of water in it and that a man had fallen in and drowned several years earlier. An attempt to drain the well had been unsuccessful: 'After employing 4 sets of bullocks at it, besides people bailing it with buckets from sunrise to sunset, it had only decreased five feet and had attained its usual level the following morning.'

Pottinger had deputed Lieutenant Clark to drain the coal mine shafts, but after working a whole day at it with 'two sets of bullocks and the usual apparatus, and had also set a number of men drawing with a large cask; that he could not get one of the shafts clear before dark, and this is again accumulated during the night'. It was suggested to Pottinger that a steam engine could be used to pump out the water, to which the major replied that he was 'quite ignorant of the power of steam, when used for raising water, or other similar purposes', but was willing to receive two steam engines. However, he insisted that it was 'indispensably necessary that a proper person shall be sent with the Engineer to direct their application'.[25] From this exchange, we can see that it took time, energy, money, personnel and training to get steam engines from England to India and then to get them set up and working successfully in mines and ships.

Coal was by far the most efficient fuel for steam engines, with one ton producing as much steam as two tons of wood, but it was hard to come by and ridiculously expensive—around £7 for a ton of coal, while a ton of wood was 8 shillings, in today's terms approximately £735 to £42. There was coal available at Karachi, but it had been imported *from* Newcastle, so it had to be mainly wood for the Indus steamers, but not any kind of wood: some trees burnt better than others. Mangrove in particular was a good burner, but it only grew in certain salt-water swamps where steamers could not travel, which meant much labour had to be expended in gathering and transporting it. Processing the cut wood was also labour-intensive: it had to be chopped into logs of a certain size, dried for 6 months and stacked in standard solid blocks of 15 square feet, and each reckoned to weigh 100 maunds. But contractors could cheat the purchasers by presenting seemingly solid blocks with poor, unsuitable wood concealed at the centre.

Then there was the problem of getting the logs onto the steamers from the wood stations along the riverbanks. Ideally, the stations would be situated on 'a well-defined high bank with deep water alongside' where a steamer could tie up and a human chain could load the wood. But, as Dewey points out, deep water along a high bank meant the river was cutting into the land, sometimes quite rapidly, and piles of carefully prepared fuel could simply be washed away.[26] The steamers' logbooks reported that there were occasions when crews, Indian and European, would have to disembark to seek wood, delaying their journey for hours, if not days. The attrition to the forests was tremendous. By the 1860s, over 20,000 tons of wood was being burnt in steamers annually in the Punjab alone, and this figure doubled with the introduction of steam trains as the railway reached Lahore.

The introduction of railways into India lagged considerably behind Britain for a number of reasons. While the first passenger and freight journey between Liverpool and Manchester had taken place in 1830, it was not until 1853 that the first passenger train ran between Bombay and Thane. The primary reason was again financial. It cost an extraordinary amount of money to build a railway in England: a pair of double rails alone was estimated at £5,000 per mile, and the 30-mile line between Liverpool and Manchester was estimated at £25,000 per mile. It was not just the rails and the trains that were so costly, but the price of the land itself over which the railway was to run, which included the fencing, embankments, cuttings, viaducts and bridges, as well as the parliamentary and law proceedings necessary to secure the sites.

It was argued in a series of Parliamentary Papers that the difficulties of such work in India:

> would not be greater than those that have been met with in England, and that they are not such as the Natives under European superintendence (or without it, if the nature of the works was explained to them), could not overcome, [it] is perfectly evident from the vast embankments, irrigating canals etc. which have been executed both before and since the Europeans have established themselves in the country.[27]

In fact, the initial proposal was not for railways with steam-driven trains, but for railroads, which involved the laying of parallel rails along which wagons could be hauled by animals. The advantages of this halfway measure, which had initially been used in England with wooden rails, was that it would conserve the 'precious water' required to produce steam and that public works could be undertaken without the need for the intensive manpower required for real trains. Rhetorical questions were posed by men who had clearly never been in India: 'What would be said if men were employed carrying earth on their heads in baskets in England and why should it not be equally ridiculous and absurd in India?'

It was asserted that 'a prodigious saving' could have been made on the construction of a new bulwark in Madras. Rather than transporting 500,000 tons of stones by having men and women carry them on their heads for over eight miles, horses with wagons carrying the stones could have been drawn along rails; this would have saved nearly Rs400,000. It was also noted that when Indian labourers had been taught how to use wheelbarrows, 'after a few hours practice, they preferred them greatly to baskets' carried on their heads.[28] Like many innovations, there were compromise steps along the way.

It was again the engineer Macdonald Stephenson whose persistence led to the construction of the first railway line in eastern India, from Howrah to the coalfields at Raniganj. He had been secretary of the East India Steam Navigation Company, the organisation that planned steamship journeys between England and India, but, having failed to obtain a royal charter, he decided instead to concentrate on railway development in the subcontinent. Stephenson travelled to India in 1843 and in the following year published his *Report Upon the Practicability and Advantages of the Introduction of Railways into British India*, a seventy-seven-page booklet which included 'full statistical data on existing trade'. He wrote to everyone who might support his cause, including Dwarkanath Tagore and other Indian businessmen, as well as British engineers, surveyors, civil architects, merchant houses and the Military Board. He obtained statistics on roads, animal transport, the cost of excavation, the salt trade, the coal trade, the sugar trade, customs duties, timber specimens and public works. For a snapshot of traffic and trade in Eastern India in the early 1840s, there is no better compilation.

During one winter month alone, the British-built military road between Calcutta and Benares saw nearly 2,000 bullock carts, 84 wheeled carriages, 118 palanquins carrying passengers and about 780 people on foot. Troops, elephants and horses added to the traffic. On the river, huge quantities of merchandise were shipped down the Hooghly to Calcutta, the bulk being saltpetre (34 per cent) followed by sugar (29 per cent), cotton (24 per cent) and smaller quantities of indigo and rock salt. The annual number of river passengers was over 26,000. Macdonald Stephenson travelled back and forth to India, setting up a joint-stock company in England, the East Indian Railway Company (EIR), whose board of directors included bankers, engineers, and shipping managers. A portion of shares was allocated in India through the EIR Bengal local committee. It took time for Macdonald Stephenson to negotiate details with the East India Company, and at one point he had to appeal directly to the liberal Prime Minister Lord John Russell, whose intervention secured an agreement. The East India Company conceded that it would guarantee a limited rate of interest to shareholders for a period of 20 years. Much of the initial outlay by the railway company was expended in England on the rails, the fabric for bridges and girders and the rolling stock (that is, the trains themselves and the steam engines). Nearly everything that furnished the first Indian railways was imported from Britain, with little or no attempt to engage local manufactories.

A similar move was taking place in western India, where the Great India Peninsular Railway Company (GIPR) had formed an alliance with the East India Company and had begun building the 21-mile line from Bombay's Bori Bunder station to Thane. The inaugural rail journey saw fourteen carriages hauled by three steam locomotives from the site of today's Chhatrapati Shivaji Terminus (formerly Victoria Terminus). Lord Dalhousie, the governor general who took up his post in 1848, had previously been president at the Board of Trade in England when 'railway mania' was at its height, and he arrived in India both knowledgeable and enthusiastic about railways. It was Dalhousie who ordered that the meter gauge of 5 feet 6 inches be used throughout India (with certain exceptions), and this ruling enabled single lines to be joined up with others to create a rail network. By 1860, eight railway companies including the EIR and the GIPR had been established, covering Bengal, the Madras Presidency, Bombay to Baroda and Central India.

A civil servant, Charles Lushington, was appointed Railway Commissioner in Bengal to oversee the acquisition of land for the EIR line from Howrah to Raniganj. His chief duty, he was told by the financial department of the East India Company, was to prevent 'extortion and jobbing' on the part of the *zamindars* whose land would be taken up for the line.[29] It all seemed quite clear at first. The surveyors drew up the plan showing where the line would run and Lushington worked out the amount of compensation for the landholders. Then he drew up bills of exchange from the treasury and the government purchased the land. There would be objections, as there had been from landlords in England where land had been compulsorily purchased, but Lushington thought that the surveyors' plans would be as accurate as those in England and 'that the boundaries of each holding, however small, would be clearly and distinctly defined'. 'With such plans,' he wrote, 'and a list of the proprietors before me, there could be no difficulty in determining the claims, either by private bargain or by arbitration in the usual course of law.'

It was not that simple, of course. Nothing in India to do with land and property ever is. Lushington found himself having to explain the delay to the Bengal Government officials, comfortably housed in Writers' Building:

> I suggest a walk through any of the thick plantations in the immediate neighbourhood of Calcutta ... they will then be able to appreciate the difficulties that had to be encountered. They will see huts, houses, bamboos, and trees of every description mixed up together, without any boundaries to mark the division of the properties or anything of any description, beyond proximity to huts or houses to give a clue to the parties to whom the trees may belong.[30]

The Court of Directors in London had argued that 'wherever railways have been introduced, they had added greatly to the value of the land through which they pass not only by offering great facilities for its improvement and cultivation but also by affording an easy and cheap access to market for the produce', and so compensation should be on 'much more moderate terms' than that suggested by the government of Bengal. But persuading Bengali villagers of these advantages by taking away their land, their huts and houses and their trees was not easy, and it was agreed that 'full compensation' had to be paid. It was also ordered that only 100 yards, on both sides, measured from the centre of the proposed line, was to be taken for earthworks, bunds, viaducts and bridges.

Small groups of Indian civil officers were sent out headed by the Deputy Collectors accompanied by an *aumeen* (supervisor), with two *moharirs* (writers)—one to take notes, the second to prepare the legal documents for purchase—and one *burkandaz*, an armed policeman. They carried with them 30-foot-long chains with which to measure the land, which was divided into plots. Notices were posted up (to a largely illiterate population), and a drummer marched along the line of the land to be taken, beating out the route. Trees were to be measured and their ages and produce estimated;

huts were measured and their condition and value noted; where brick-built houses existed, each room was measured, its doors and windows counted and valued. Claims were made by the owners or occupiers which the Deputy Commissioners had to reconcile with their own measurements, and where disputes occurred buildings had to be measured again. Then there was the problem of whether the occupier was in temporary or permanent possession of the dwelling. Owners were allowed to take away felled trees, but the value of the timber would be offset against their claims. Once a fair price had been fixed, the government purchased the land and everything on it, including houses, trees and bamboos and any stone that could be used for construction. The government then made all this over to the newly formed Railway Company who employed Messrs Burn & Co. with its working parties to clear the land in preparation for tracks to be laid.

In fact, the Railway Company was so keen for work to start that it began without permission from the chief engineer, cutting down trees and throwing up earthworks. There was a local difficulty at the French-held enclave of Chandernagore when the magistrate, M. Vignette, disputed the land to be taken and imprisoned twelve of the railway coolies. The matter went to arbitration, with the French huffing about jurisdiction, but after the Railway Company agreed to alter the line of the railway and pay generous compensation, the magistrate approved the site for the new station. The Grand Trunk Road had to be crossed and bridged with help and advice from the Military Board. It was the first time in the Company's history that land had been sequestered on this scale. Previously, the compulsory purchase of land had been 'confined to small tracts in the neighbourhood of Towns or Stations for the reception of buildings, or the construction of Docks', so this was something new and potentially unsettling, although there were no reports of physical opposition. Surveying work had begun at the start of the cold season in 1850, and by the following May, 33 miles had been wrested from the countryside and its inhabitants. But there were still nearly 90 more miles to Raniganj, which took another 2 seasons to reach.

Dalhousie was actively involved in siting the rail terminus at Howrah, on the west bank of the Hooghly, directly opposite the hub of Calcutta. Because the river could not at the time be bridged, this was the only practical site for the line that followed the river north through Barrackpore and Serampore before branching west to Raniganj. The west bank included the great Botanical Garden, the Seamen's Hospital and Dispensary and a number of English-owned bungalows situated in large gardens. There was also an extensive range of valuable light industrial buildings, including mills and a cotton screw (for compressing bales of cotton before shipment), so it was the bungalows that were compulsorily purchased, eleven in all and a number of huts. The first terminus was a modest affair: a single-storey, brick-built long shed, with a corrugated tin roof and a single platform.[31]

The station needed both a river frontage with a *ghat* (landing stage) and a wide road running parallel leading to the small town of Howrah. There were few, if any, facilities for passengers, because the bulk of traffic on the line was to be coal, brought down to Calcutta to feed the hungry steamboats. There was no need for warehouses, claimed the resident engineer, because the coal would not linger on its arrival but be utilised almost at once, enabling steam traffic on the Ganges to increase exponentially.

Although the introduction of railways into India is today considered one of Britain's notable achievements, its initial importance was by no means obvious in the early 1850s. There was a strong lobby that argued railways could not compete with road or river traffic, which is why the EIR line from Calcutta was initially regarded as merely a supplier of steamboat coal, rather than a new mode of transport in its own right. The line was originally planned to go from Calcutta to Delhi, but because of 'clamour' from opponents—including Colonel Arthur Cotton, the canal engineer—it was stopped at Raniganj.[32] There was a proposal that the line could wander off towards Rajmahal to connect there with steamboat traffic on the Upper Ganges, but this didn't happen.

However, there were more positive voices, including that of the influential *Spectator* magazine, which emphasised the importance of developing main lines throughout the country so that linking branch lines could reach iron and coal mines. This, it was said, would lead to the improvement of specific areas and:

to calling forth those enterprises in agriculture and mining which will render the district a source of wealth to the shareholders of the company, to the native population, to the Indian Government and we may say to all connected with India. It is most desirable, therefore, that while following the strict economy necessary in the present depressed state of Indian resources, the construction of the railway should be carried out with the utmost speed ...[33]

As news of the Uprising reached Britain, *The Times* with the benefit of hindsight wrote on 7 July 1857:

Had the East Indian Railway been complete from Calcutta to Delhi, as it ought to have been, instead of halting halfway, the late disastrous events at Meerut and Delhi would never have occurred, or within twenty hours troops would have been conveyed there, whereas it will now take about eighty days to march.

By 1856, about 4,000 miles had been surveyed across the country for the main lines, but building lagged behind. The engineer and economist Henry Hyde Clark, author of *Colonisation, Defence and Railways in Our Indian Empire* (1857), argued that 'the guarantee of the [British] Government has been very dearly purchased at the cost of Government interference in the control and management of these great undertakings'. He continued:

it is now eleven years since the two great lines in the Presidencies of Bengal and Bombay [the EIR and the GIPR] were set on foot and thanks to the paralysing influence of Government protection and interference, neither is yet completed but each 'like a wounded snake drags its slow length along'.[34]

The problem was mainly financial. Hyde Clark believed the British government's commitment to a guaranteed 5 per cent of profit to British shareholders was itself flawed and that profit, rather than the completion of the railway lines, was its main objective.

Despite the 'wounded snake' analogy, one thing no British commentator had foreseen was the eagerness with which Indians took to the railway. This simply had not been expected, which is why little provision for passengers had been factored in. At the Howrah terminus, for example, passengers had to buy their tickets at a booth set up at Armenian Ghat (on the east bank), then take the ferry across the Hooghly to the station. (The fare for the ferry ride was included in the ticket.) It demonstrated a complete lack of understanding on the part of the British of the Indian ambition to move forward, both literally and metaphorically. A close relationship doesn't necessarily mean a friendly one, but half a century earlier both nationalities had had a better understanding of what the other was thinking and feeling and could react appropriately. It was this severance of empathy that led to the British being taken by complete surprise at the Uprising of 1857. Had the Company held a more nuanced view of the introduction of railways, informed by the kind of detailed research that Macdonald Stephenson had carried out, it would not have been surprised at the enthusiasm ordinary Indians had for speedier travel, nor would it have scoffed at the idea that the railway would not attract poorer people too.

Figures are dry things that one falls back on to support an argument, but the information contained in the British government's *Statistical Abstract Relating to British India* is staggering.[35] The first EIR train from Howrah station to the old Portuguese capital of Hughli ran on 15 August 1854. The following year saw 383,744 people travelling on the trains. This brought in a passenger revenue of £24,000, while the freight traffic only generated £8,000. There were running costs, of course, but even taking these into account there was a healthy profit of over £20,000 during a single year. Three years later, over a million passengers were annually travelling the 121 miles to Raniganj and back. And this was not something peculiar to Bengal. In the Bombay Presidency, nearly half a million people travelled the 35 miles from Bombay to Thane in 1855, generating an equally large profit.

Why did Indians take so enthusiastically to rail travel? It was not a particularly comfortable way to move across country, although certainly speedier than a buffalo cart on a dodgy road. From the outset, trains were divided into three classes, following the British pattern: first class, second class and third class. The majority of passengers chose the last option; in fact, almost 86 per cent of travellers travelled in third class on the EIR in 1855. There were no facilities, no lavatories, no food and often no seats. Passengers stood in open carriages like cattle. But the fares were kept deliberately low to attract passengers: a quarter of an anna per mile for third class and 2 annas per mile for first class. Luggage, apart from a small carpet bag, was also charged for. As the number of passengers increased, the EIR did not raise fares, but they did cram more travellers into smaller spaces.[36]

The reasons why they were prepared to endure hours of moderate discomfort cannot be fully known. Some certainly found it convenient and cheaper to move goods by train rather than road, but the disparity between the number of passengers and the comparatively small amount of freight being moved would argue this was not the main object of travel. It was suggested that pilgrimages to holy sites and participation in religious festivals like Durga Puja were their motivation, and this is certainly plausible. Bengal is rich in Hindu shrines, including the Taraknath temple at Tarkashwar and the city of Durgapur, and the handsome *imambara* in the small town of Hughli was an attraction for Shi'a Muslims. Even so, this still leaves a large number of people who may simply have been travelling by train for the sheer novelty of being able to do so. And the novelty didn't wear off as the increasing number of passengers year on year shows. British advocates of railways in India made grandiose claims: it would break down the caste system by forcing people of different castes into close proximity, and it would act as 'the most persuasive missionary that ever preached in the East' as Indians were forced to re-evaluate the dynamic Christian beliefs of their rulers against the ancient wisdom of their own gods. But Edwin Arnold, whose missionary zeal had got the better of him, also thought (more accurately) that 'railways may do for India what dynasties have never done ... they may make India a nation'.[37]

Running alongside the new railway lines were the tall bamboo posts of the electric telegraph, with copper wires sheathed in iron and strung between them. Although the properties of electricity had been known during the eighteenth century and demonstrated at scientific gatherings like the Royal Society, it was not until 1837—the year of Queen Victoria's coronation—that its practical use in sending messages was applied. A patent was taken out by William Cooke and Charles Wheatstone for 'Improvements in Giving Signals and Sounding Alarms in Distant Places by Means of Electric Currents Transmitted Through Metallic Circuits'.[38] This neatly sums up the benefits of the early telegraph and the reason it was initially associated with railways, which was to communicate the movements of trains between stations. It was particularly useful on single-track lines, as the majority of the early railways were, to prevent accidents between two trains using the same line. Isambard Kingdom Brunel, chief engineer for the Great Western Railway, oversaw the laying of 13½ miles of telegraph from Paddington to West Drayton, running the insulated wires through an iron tube below ground at the side of the railway. It was completed in July 1839, at the cost of nearly £3,000, and became the first effective working telegraph put to daily use over a fairly long distance.

Two months earlier, an even longer line had been constructed in Calcutta by William O'Shaughnessy, an assistant surgeon in the Bengal army, professor of chemistry and joint secretary of the Asiatic Society of Bengal. He had read reports in periodicals about telegraphic experiments in England, Europe and America which seemed to him 'conclusive as to the perfect practicability of establishing, at a cheap rate, telegraphical communications, acting through electrical agencies'. He was assisted in his experiments by Dr Wallich, the superintendent of the Botanical Gardens in Calcutta, who allowed him to set up 42 rows of bamboo stakes, each 15 feet tall, driven into the earth of the Garden. Between the stakes were iron wires coated with 'tar varnish' and strung in continuous lines, each half a mile long. Copper wire would have been preferable, admitted O'Shaughnessy, but he was unable to obtain a sufficient quantity in Calcutta, nor would he have been able to afford it had it been available.[39]

Running along a large rectangular area in the Garden, the total circuit was 22 miles. Currents were successfully generated by an electromagnetic induction machine and a galvanometer which had been made in England. The pulsations, as O'Shaughnessy termed them, were connected to a pair of watches, which had been modified by Colesworthy Grant—the 'ingenious artist' then in Calcutta—so that the second hand swung round to the letters of the alphabet and the numbers 1 to 10. Further experiments were made by immersing one long wire in the Hooghly and a second on dry land, both of which terminated in the library of Dr Wallich's handsome house on the riverbank: 'ample proof of the great conducting power of water for this form of electric impulse', wrote O'Shaughnessy. Like

Brunel, O'Shaughnessy favoured an underground telegraph where the wires ran through split rattan canes wound with tarred yarn.

But this ingenious experiment which could have seen India advance in parallel with telegraphic developments in England was dismissed out of hand by Company officials and 'regarded generally with contemptuous scepticism'. It took 11 years before the Court of Directors in London stirred itself to ask the government of India for reports on O'Shaughnessy's work, which had been entirely self-funded. Not until December 1851 was an 'experimental' line, half-subterranean and half-overground, constructed between Diamond Harbour and Calcutta, a distance of 30 miles.[40] The telegraph line was inaugurated in November the following year when O'Shaughnessy's assistant Sib Chandra Nandy sent the first signal from Diamond Harbour to Fort William. Dalhousie appointed O'Shaughnessy the Chief Superintendent of Telegraphs and sent him to London to report to the Court of Directors and to purchase materials and stores.

Telegraph lines were proposed from Calcutta to Agra, Bombay, Peshawar and Madras. Nandy was appointed inspector of the Diamond Harbour line and tasked with training new signallers. After the Court of Directors had ignored the telegraph for so long, now all of a sudden O'Shaughnessy reported that 'such rapidity in the dispatch of an important measure is, perhaps without parallel in any department of Government. All subsequent steps were taken with proportionate speed'. Impetus was also given by the second Anglo-Burmese War when news of the capture of Rangoon was telegraphed to Calcutta within days and the announcement posted on the gates of the new telegraph office. Now sixty telegraph engineers were enlisted and trained, English and foreign telegraphs inspected, instruments collected, estimates and drawings submitted by December 1852. The materials included 5,600 miles of galvanised iron rod, *gutta percha*- (rubber) covered copper wire, oak brackets, stoneware insulators and electric clocks, all gathered together in great haste.[41]

O'Shaughnessy preferred the telegraph to run underground, as did Brunel, but the majority of the Indian lines were constructed overground, parallel with railway tracks and running along major highways. Although costs were comparable—and certainly from the aesthetic point of view it was better to bury the lines—the main argument for the overground telegraph was that faults and breaks could be speedily found and repaired. The picture of a linesman up a telegraph pole is much more familiar than someone rooting around through jungle-like growth looking for something they can't see. The overground lines worked well, including the line from Lucknow to Calcutta, newly installed after the kingdom of Awadh had been annexed by the Company in 1856. The Lucknow Electric Telegraph Office had been rapidly set up in the former banqueting hall of the British Residency complex, a large site in the centre of the old *nawabi* capital. Only a month after it was set up, the new governor general, Lord Canning, complained that excitable young officers in the Residency were using it to send messages to Calcutta 'upon matters of the smallest importance and of no urgency'.[42]

During the Uprising of 1857, the electric telegraph was one of the first things to be destroyed by those opposing Company rule. The line from Lucknow was cut early in June 1857 so that news of the massacres at Cawnpore and the subsequent efforts to rescue those trapped in the Residency had to be carried by *harkaras* (messengers). (In a return to an earlier technology, semaphores were rigged up on the roofs of British-held buildings to signal the advance of Sir Colin Campbell's relieving force.) The telegraph lines striding across the countryside were both a visible sign of foreign interference as well as something sinister which allowed the British to talk to each other through the air—a kind of malevolent magic. It was easy for determined men to dismantle the posts and wires, which were put to good use as 'extempore ordnance' during the fighting. The iron rods were melted down and refashioned into small cannon, while the copper wire was chopped up and used as shrapnel and the bamboo poles became firewood.

Similarly, the railway line—which was at last being extended from Raniganj at the beginning of 1857—was attacked and the newly built station works at Allahabad were destroyed, including the locomotive and carriage shops. Railway staff were targeted in Bihar, and EIR staff quickly formed themselves into a volunteer force to fight the rebels. In destroying telegraph lines, rail tracks and stations, Indian fighters were disrupting the enemy's communications, a classic tactical move in war. But perhaps something more radical is indicated. Was it Luddite behaviour or a calculated strike back at foreigners despoiling the countryside in the name of progress? We will probably never know, because those initiating the strikes were voiceless and illiterate. Nevertheless, it is an intriguing question.

The Company's policy on communications was patchy, to say the least. Progress, where it occurred, was often led by individuals who had to demonstrate the value of their discoveries to sceptical officials both in India and at home. There were imaginative appointments during that fertile period in the late eighteenth and early nineteenth centuries, like that of James Rennell, who was selected by Clive to be surveyor general. But the last decades of Company rule were characterised by excessive caution, an unwillingness to entertain new ideas and the inevitable arguments about cost. The Company and its employees saw Indians as characters in an antique, unchanging landscape, and it ignored entrepreneurs like Tagore. It was completely taken by surprise at the enthusiasm with which Indians welcomed steamboats and rail travel in spite of the initial discomforts and expense. Joining the parts of India together for the Company's convenience had also begun to join the country together for its own people.

CANTONMENTS, COUNTRY HOUSES AND HILL STATIONS

More than half the battlefield of Plassey has been washed away by a change in the course of the River Bhagirathi. What remains today is a large, flat area of wheat fields, approached down a steep bund that leads from the road. At the top of the bund are two monuments: one is a plain obelisk on a black base erected by the East India Company in one of its final acts. Exactly 100 years after the battle of Plassey on 23 June 1757, the British placed their memorial here just as the Great Uprising swept across northern India and swept the Company away too. The second monument, put up in 2007, is a bust of Siraj-ud-daula, *nawab* of Bengal, who fought here against Robert Clive's army and lost. In the middle of the wheat field is a third monument: three square, brick-built pillars commemorating the *nawab*'s officers who fell. One of these was Mir Madan, shot dead at about 3.00 pm and whose death demoralised his men. Shortly afterwards, the *nawab* fled back to Murshidabad where he was to meet his death the following year. The hunting lodge where Clive and his officers sheltered from a monsoon downpour and kept their powder dry has also disappeared. The village of Palasi lies nearby. There was another memorial too. On his return to England in 1767, Robert Clive bought a country estate in Shropshire from the impoverished Walcot family. In its extensive grounds he planted saplings that spelled out the word 'Plassey'. He did not live long enough to see them grow to maturity, but they flourished as the Plassey Wood and remained there until the Second World War, when they were cut down to prevent Nazi aircraft from identifying the area.

Plassey was both a victory for the Company and revenge for the sack of Calcutta the previous year, although the battle of Buxar, which took place 7 years later in October 1764, was of much greater political significance. Here in Bihar, under the command of Sir Hector Munro, the Company army defeated the combined forces of the Mughal Emperor, Shah Alam; the new *nawab* of Bengal, Mir Qasim; and the *nawab wazir* of Awadh, Shuja-ud-daula. Perhaps not surprisingly, the battle memorial at Buxar is today poorly maintained, with its marble steps chipped away and the stucco peeling from a tall brick pillar. Buxar was a defeat that led to the Treaty of Allahabad the following year when the Company was awarded the *diwani*. It marked the beginning of Company rule and ultimately British government in India.

There were many implications following the award, but the one that most affected the landscape was the establishment of cantonments in the newly acquired provinces. These were permanent military bases, a new word and a new concept. From the French 'canton', a defined district, which indicates its European origin, the word could also be used as a verb (e.g., 'to canton soldiers'), and its earliest use seems to occur during the Anglo-French conflicts in south India during the 1750s. Today, the cantonment area of towns is often the most pleasant, with wide, tree-lined streets, substantial bungalows in large compounds and a church and Christian cemetery in the background. Some are now entirely civilian, others have restricted military areas run by cantonment boards. The transition over 250 years from thatched barracks to favoured residential area has not been well-documented, though it is surely one of the most significant reminders of British rule.

The idea of maintaining a standing army in its own accommodation was foreign to the Mughal rulers and provincial governors, who relied on their nobles and other chiefs to provide men when needed for warfare or hunting. It was a carefully graded system in which a man who could summon 5,000 soldiers was known as a *mansabdar*, with other titles for those with fewer soldiers. There was a small number of permanent household troops for the palaces and forts of the emperor and his provincial governors, together with bodyguards, but the majority of fighting men came together and lived under canvas while on the battle or hunting field. This ad hoc arrangement meant there was no regimental system and that armed men might not actually meet their commanders or fellow soldiers until they were on the battlefield. Cavalry troops formed the bulk of the Mughal fighting forces, a reminder of their Central Asian origins, and they had to provide their own horses, with the preferred ratio of two horses to one soldier. Foot soldiers or infantrymen were often delegated to logistical tasks like drawing up the cannons and organising supplies of ammunition. Because rations were generally not supplied, troops had to forage for their own food and for their animals' foodstuffs too. This did not make them popular in the countryside, where huge hunting parties the size of small towns could settle for weeks. A prolonged siege of a particular fort could have the same effect. So the idea of fixed accommodation with stabling, food, fodder and a parade ground for regimental drill was novel. The Company *sepoys* would also receive weapons, uniforms, a small pension and medical care. The importance of infantry soldiers, long recognised in European armies, meant that a different class of men now joined the Company's three Presidency armies: men who could not necessarily provide their own horses or weapons, but who wanted a career in soldiering.

Building on the Company's successes at Plassey, Buxar and the Allahabad Treaty, Robert Clive announced to the Select Committee of Fort William in July 1765 that:

> our earliest considerations ought to be to station and canton the forces in such a manner as will best serve to defend the country and preserve the lives of men. Patna & Boianpore [*sic* Berhampore] plain near Cossimbuzar, are, in my opinion the two fittest places to answer these purposes. At the former there are already Cantonments. At Boianpore there are none. It will be proper therefore without loss of time to send Captain [Fleming] Martin the Chief Engineer to Boianpore with orders to make the necessary Survey of the Plain, & to lay before you as soon as possible a plan & Calculation of the Expense of building Cantonments for at least twelve hundred Europeans and five thousand sepoys. Although the greatest economy should be observed in erecting these buildings, yet those for the Europeans should I think be strong, durable, and convenient since we may reasonably expect that the Company's influence and power in this country will be lasting and rather

increase than diminish ... Those for the sepoys may be more slight because from Diet, Temperance & Constitution, these People are enabled to struggle with the inconveniences of the Climate much better than the Europeans.[1]

This was an important statement not only because it set in motion the chain of cantonments, initially across Bengal and Bihar, but because it emphasised from the outset that the *sepoys'* quarters were to be 'more slight' than those of British soldiers, a distinction which was to remain throughout the following century.

The early cantonments followed the course of the Ganges, from Calcutta to Allahabad, so men and equipment could be transported by water where roads were poor or non-existent. With one exception—Monghyr—newly acquired land was laid out in a pattern not previously seen before. As with the Commercolli silk filature, the regular, brick-built terraces stretching in straight lines— some of them two storeys high—was a new and foreign concept. There are competing claims for the first purpose-built cantonment between Berhampore and Barrackpore, the latter some 15 miles north of Calcutta and an early site for a permanent concentration of soldiers outside Fort William itself. As the name implies, it was initially simply a settlement (*pore/pur*) of barracks, easily accessible by road and river and which could have been quickly erected during a single season. Berhampore, which is described later in this chapter, was a more elaborate and important construct.

The fluid political situation in the early 1760s meant that chronologically speaking Monghyr was the first cantonment, although this has to be qualified, because it was not technically a new site but the adaptation of an already existing fort belonging to the *nawab* of Bengal, Mir Qasim. Immediately following his defeat at Buxar, the Company's 1st Bengal Brigade moved into the large, ancient fortress, which contained a saint's tomb, a small palace, a temple in a wooded garden and an arsenal. The fort is on a small hill, not as dramatically high as it appears in some Company paintings, but certainly standing proud of the river. Rectangular in shape, it was surrounded by a wide moat with three drawbridges and a watergate. Its chief attraction was its strategic placement: Murshidabad, which was to remain the capital of Bengal for at least another decade, was downriver; Patna, an important trading crossroads, was upriver; and Allahabad, further upriver, reached into the borders of Awadh, changing hands several times between the Company and the *nawab wazirs*.

The 1st Bengal Brigade, one of three newly created units, following Clive's reorganisation of the army in 1765, numbered about 7,400 men: Indian *sepoys* commanded by European officers. This included a small unit (118 horsemen) of Mughal native calvary, a poignant reminder of the great medieval army of the emperors. Each brigade had roughly the same number of troops, so the entire Bengal army now had a strength of some 22,200 men. In addition, there was auxiliary staff which included surgeons, interpreters, bandsmen and 'a large but indefinite number of lascars' to assist the artillery.[2] This was by far the largest number of people, in a single occupation, to be employed by the Company. It was much greater than the number of civilian officials throughout the whole of India, and this imbalance was to continue for as long as the British remained in India. Active recruitment had started immediately after the Company's victory at Buxar, when the London-based Court of Directors had authorised six European captains to recruit 200 men each. They had done so satisfactorily (no doubt paid a consideration for each man), and this continued until the requisite number of men were enrolled. Although none of the three contestants defeated at Buxar—the Mughal, Awadhi and Bengali rulers—were deprived of their armies, restrictions by the Company were now put in place, including the stationing of battalions in Awadh, ostensibly to protect the province from invasion, for which the *nawab* had to pay.

Clearly, the entire 1st Bengal Brigade could not move into the Monghyr Fort—it simply wasn't large enough—so some men were stationed in temporary tented accommodation outside while other units were deployed across the Company's new territories. Much has been written on the Presidency armies, which later merged to become the Indian army, but there are few studies of their peace-time impact on the landscape, or of the employment opportunities that building and repairing army quarters provided for engineers, labourers and brick-makers.

Monghyr was not a happy cantonment. It was here that the 'White Mutiny' broke out in 1766, so-called because a number of European officers protested about the withdrawal of *batta*, an extra allowance for soldiers on active duty. It was reported that the secret meetings held by officers to plan the protest were disguised as masonic events. The revolt became so serious that Clive had to leave Calcutta and travel to Monghyr himself. The Brigade's commander, Colonel Robert Fletcher, was court-martialled and a number of white officers were due to be deported from India, although this ruling seems subsequently to have been modified.[3] Whether the physical conditions in the Monghyr Fort exacerbated the soldiers' feelings of resentment has not been examined, but the small, extra allowance would have bought some much-needed comforts as well as status. A damning report 6 years later showed that the place was a mess and had been for some years.

Colonel Archibald Campbell had been appointed chief engineer in Bengal in 1768 and was asked by Warren Hastings to recommend improvements at the fort and at Patna. Campbell was a polymath of a man, with an exciting past as a soldier and a notable future as governor of Madras. He had directed work on the second Fort William and was a man to be taken seriously. His lengthy report on Monghyr noted that its fortifications had been originally built:

> of very bad materials and from a want of constant and timely repairs have suffered greatly by the Rains. At this period there are about 20 Breaches in the Walls, three of which are become so unacceptable, that they are now made use of, as common passages in and out of the Garrison.[4]

There was much else. The gateways needed repairing, the interior of the fort was thick with weeds and undergrowth, and the area assigned to the European troops as a hospital was ruinous, not large enough and backed up on one side with an earthen wall, which excluded fresh air and caused 'a nauseous dampness'. The artillerymen were lodged under a very bad thatched shed, and the barracks for the European men and officers were 'in a most ruinous state, and seem already, to have undergone every kind of repair, which art was master of'. The thatched bungalows for the Indian officers were in very bad condition, with some of them completely caved in. Everything was buttressed, both the interior and exterior walls, to stop the whole thing falling down. The powder magazine, part of Mir Qasim's arsenal, was in 'tolerable repair' but was not bombproof, so if something went wrong it could have blown the whole fort up.

Nevertheless, part of Campbell's brief was not only to report on the current state of the fort but to suggest how it could be improved. Its location was its chief asset. 'As a Central position, and from the Security of its preferred Situation on the Banks of the Ganges, it is certainly the best adapted of any, as a Grand Magazine to our Army on the Frontier'.[5] Practical measures were suggested: for the breaches in the walls to be stopped up and the walls themselves repaired; for proper gates to be fitted; for 'a few pieces of Cannon [to] be deposed along the several fronts of the Fort'; and for the ramparts and the interior to be cleared of weeds. Roofs were to be renewed on the existing barracks and their interior partitions removed so air could circulate freely. A hospital bungalow was needed, as well as sheds to house the field artillery, improved quarters for the officers, and for the unsatisfactory powder magazine to be converted to a granary and a new magazine built capable of housing 10,000 barrels of powder.

Assessing the fort with a professional eye, Campbell added that if the repairs he suggested were carried out, then Monghyr would be 'secure against any attack which may be expected from the Country powers' that is, from local rulers. With three *sepoy* battalions garrisoned here, 'it will be capable of a very formidable resistance against such an attack as may be expected from the united powers of Indostan'. On the other hand, because of the nature of its construction and the 'injudicious disposition of its parts for defence it would not be able to withstand the efforts of an European force'. Campbell doesn't state which European force he had in mind. France had been the only European country to offer a serious threat to the English Company's ambitions in India, and, with its surrender of Pondicherry in 1761, French power in the south had been virtually quashed. The French enclave of Chandernagore in Bengal had suffered the demolition of its Fort d'Orleans by Robert Clive 3 months before his victory at Plassey as part of the Seven Years War, which had been fought vicariously in India and concluded by the Treaty of Paris in 1763. The *Compagnie des Indes* had been effectively dissolved in 1769, so Campbell, writing in 1772, is unlikely to have imagined a renewed threat from France. But his belief that the fort could stand up to an attack by Indian forces reflects the sense of confidence that the victories of Plassey and Buxar had given the Company, victories achieved in the face of astonishing odds. (The estimated joint Indian forces at Buxar numbered 40,000 against the Company's 7,072 troops.)

It was this confidence, together with the three new Brigades, that made the cantonments at Berhampore and Dinapur viable, although their construction was not without problems. Plans for Berhampore were drawn up by the engineer Captain Henry Watson (the same man who was later to promote Reuben Burrow). There are earlier references to 'Berrampore Farm', and the site, lying conveniently just south of Cossimbazar where the Company already had a factory, was on flat ground on the east bank of the Bhagirathi. Although it was to be a showcase cantonment, the usual strictures about expense were applied. Things went wrong from the beginning. The existing Committee of Works sourced a contractor to supply bricks—sixty lakhs of bricks during the first season of building in 1767—but this fell short because twelve lakhs had been rejected as unfit by temporary inspectors. In fact, there was nothing wrong with these bricks, and they were sold 'to private persons first', no doubt resulting in a nice profit for the inspectors.[6]

The Court of Directors blamed the Committee of Works for not appointing 'regular inspectors', that is, men who could not be bribed (or at least not bribed very much). Captain Fleming Martin from the Corps of Engineers was in charge of construction, with Thomas Forbes as contractor for the supplies of bricks and George Williamson for timbers. Both of these contractors sold bricks and timbers to the Company, and it was here that the largest profits were made by the corrupt Company men. The financial part of the project was supposed to be managed by Francis Sykes, then the Chief of Cossimbazar. The Directors found an 'enormous excess of expence' had been incurred which could have been avoided if Sykes had done his job as accountant properly; Sykes claimed he was too busy to give his full attention to Berhampore. Other people were also blamed and found 'guilty of notorious negligence or great unfaithfulness when they audited and approved accounts so very fraudulent'. The Indian staff were blamed too, in particular the *bakhshis* or paymasters, some of whom had been with the Company for a long time. Over-charging was rife and at least Rs2 lakhs had been lost during the first year of construction. But this sum was trivial when compared to the enormous costs that were eventually racked up. It is a familiar story today.

When the proposal for the Berhampore cantonment had been approved by Robert Clive and the Council, it was agreed that the cost of the whole site should not exceed Rs3 lakhs 'at the most'. In fact, the eventual bill was estimated at Rs22 lakhs. Halfway through construction, alterations were made to enlarge the site, meaning some of the work already done had to be demolished. Fleming Martin resigned his commission and Thomas Forbes was allowed to return to England, citing poor health. Francis Sykes, the negligent accountant for the project, went on to become one of the richest *nabobs* of the period, returning to England with a fortune. The most serious miscalculation, and one that was to have long-lasting effects, was that accommodation for the Indian soldiers had to be scrapped. The Court in London was outraged by this, expressing astonishment that while fifteen sets of apartments for European subalterns had been built—superfluous apartments, as it turned out—there was nothing for the *sepoys*: 'Had the expense incurred by building those supernumerary officers' apartments been frugally applied towards providing comfortable shelter for the poor sepoys, less apology would have been necessary for venturing to exceed the sum so expressly fixed by Lord Clive and Council.'[7]

This set an unfortunate precedent. Various excuses were made, including the claim that for caste reasons the *sepoys* preferred to build their own accommodation. Whether they did actually prefer to or not, this is what they ended up doing. Unlike the smooth, sophisticated quarters for European officers with their white, stuccoed walls and flat roofs, the *sepoys'* quarters were thatched huts made with unbaked bricks. The Hindustani word for cantonment is *cha'oni*, which means thatching, a clear indication of how these military sites were seen by Indians. The proportion of *sepoy* housing would always be far greater to that of the European officers' and men's quarters, with some distance separating each block.

Having said this, when the Berhampore cantonment was completed late in 1767, it was magnificent. Artists drew and painted its long, sleek terraces, fronting on three sides the great, grassed parade ground called Barrack Square. Most officers were lodged overlooking the Square, with soldiers' quarters to the rear of the terraces. The senior officers and administrative staff were initially in a block overlooking the Lal Dighi, an artificial tank at the rear of the complex, which later became the European barracks. Architecturally, Berhampore must have had the same impact on European building in India as Corbusier's buildings were to have in twentieth-century Europe: its design was modern and built for a specific purpose, 'a machine for living in', unlike Monghyr, which had developed haphazardly over the centuries.

A striking feature of the new cantonments was their lack of defensive ramparts, moats and curtain walls around the site. This was not an area that expected to be attacked, a belief that held good even during the Uprising. The cantonment was initially unwalled, but 5 years after its completion there was a pained exchange between the Court of Directors and the Committee of Works:

> We are greatly surprized to find that notwithstanding the enormous sums which have already been expended on the cantonments of Burrumpore and that the same are still incompleat, you should entertain a thought of involving us in an additional expense for the erection of a wall round those extensive works in order, as is alleged, to keep the soldiery with in proper bounds, or to prevent their being intoxicated by the spirituous liquors which may be introduced into the said cantonments.[8]

The Court added piously that if the officers took 'proper care and vigilance' then the private European soldiers 'might be hindered from such immoderate use of spirituous liquors as would otherwise prove destructive to their health or prejudicial to the service'.

It was an age-old problem, trying to separate soldiers from alcohol, or at least the wrong kind of alcohol. While the officers drank costly imported claret, madeira and cherry brandy, their men were experimenting with locally produced drinks, based on sugar cane (arrack) and palm tree sap (toddy), with a high alcoholic content. It was not until the 1820s that the first European distillery was established at Kasauli in the Himalayas, producing beer and whisky, which made it easier to supply the men and ration their supplies.

At Dinapore a few miles west of Patna, a second cantonment was established, similar though not identical to that at Berhampore. Initially it was called Bankipore, which has led to confusion over whether there were in fact two separate cantonments, but this was not the case, although there were Company buildings at Bankipore. Dinapore was built almost simultaneously with Berhampore, with a large central square while here the officers' quarters lay to the west in their own site, with auxiliary areas like stables and prison cells around the periphery.

Neither Berhampore and Dinapore were self-sufficient and, unlike Monghyr, could not have withstood a siege of any length. The soldiers who moved into their new quarters needed food, drink, clothing, water and entertainment, while their horses needed fodder. Lucrative army contracts were given to Company officials who subcontracted them to local suppliers. Uniforms, saltpetre, grain and bullocks were among the items brought into the cantonments, and bazaars were quickly established outside providing auxiliary goods and services, including prostitutes. This was something else that was frowned upon, not so much on moral grounds but because the venereal diseases inevitably contracted were difficult to cure; until well into the nineteenth century, mercury was the only recognised, if ineffective, treatment. The Court of Directors' criticism of 'spirituous liquors' could equally well have applied to the soldiers' sexual behaviour as 'destructive to their health or prejudicial to the service'.

There were many causes of death among Europeans in eighteenth-century India, just as there were among the local population, although information on the former is more readily available through burial records, as we have seen. One of the first sites to be established outside every cantonment was a Christian cemetery. Unlike burial grounds in Britain at the time, these cemeteries were not attached to a church. In some cases, churches were erected much later; at Dinapore, for example, St Luke's Church was completed more than 60 years after the cantonment was established, and there is no adjoining church at Berhampore. The idea of unattached cemeteries was radical and not accepted in Britain until the 1840s, so there was no precedent for the cantonment cemeteries in Bengal, Bihar and later across other parts of India. Unlike the civilian cemeteries in major cities like Calcutta and Madras, cantonment cemeteries were originally simple, low-walled enclosures with barrel or box tombs inside. The majority were of course for soldiers, with a few graves for the families of officers and the odd European merchant or mercenary who had died during their travels.[9] Not all cantonment cemeteries could be consecrated immediately—this could only be done by a visiting bishop—and several years could elapse between establishing a cemetery and having it sanctified.

In and around the cantonments, more facilities were added, including leisure areas, although it is likely that the use of the fives court and the racquet court was restricted to officers. Although there is no specific information, the men probably enjoyed playing football. Small libraries were established for them, where the choice of books was initially didactic or religious, and supervised by army chaplains.[10] When the catalogue was broadened and fiction introduced, it was discovered that Sir Walter Scott's *Waverley* novels were among the most popular books.

Not every cantonment could be built along the same lines as Berhampore, the first and ideal prototype. Expediency and the fluid political situation in late eighteenth-century India meant the Company could not choose its own sites in some cases or develop them as it wished. Monghyr, as we have seen, was in a ruinous condition when it was occupied by the First Brigade, but following Campbell's damning report and a devastating storm 9 years later— when the 'Matt Bungaloes' for the *sepoy* officers and the verandas of the infantry officers were blown down—a considerable amount was spent on improving the interior of the fort.[11] A new hospital with adjoining bungalows was erected for the brigade's surgeons, barracks were repaired and outhouses built. A team of carpenters, bricklayers, smiths and coolies was assembled, and materials including timber, bamboos, iron and *chunam* were employed to renovate the officers' quarters, while the commander's new house was given sophisticated wooden venetian blinds and window frames.

The Treaty of Allahabad in 1765 which had led to the Company's occupation of Monghyr also led indirectly to the establishment of its cantonment at Cawnpore 5 years later. Although the *nawab wazir* of Awadh, Shuja-ud-daula, had been one of the three losing contestants at the battle of Buxar a year earlier, Robert Clive, the newly appointed commander-in-chief, was told by the Select Committee at Fort William that for the sake of trade—which, after all, was the Company's main concern at the time, it would be better to reconcile with the *nawab wazir*. The Marathas presented the chief threat to peaceful trading (although the Rohillas and Jats were also contenders), so it was politic for the Company to align with Shuja-ud-daula and defend both Awadh and Bengal against their mutual enemies. Clive considered this could best be done by stationing a Company unit in the *subah* of Awadh at Cawnpore, a small village on the west bank of the Ganges. At the same time, it would be useful to have an outpost here to keep an eye on the *nawab wazir*, whose recent allegiance to the Company was in question, particularly when it was learnt he had sent an envoy to the Marathas on the pretext of buying horses from them. Loyalties could be quickly transferred in the period that came to be known as 'the great anarchy', when yesterday's ally could become today's enemy.

It was a very different situation to that in Bengal, where the administration and revenue collection had been handed to the Company. Now, 8 years later, Clive seemed anxious for another fight, and this time in Awadh. The Select Committee at Fort William was more conciliatory and more rational too. It argued that the idea of gaining additional territory through warfare would place an unnecessary burden on the Company, unless 'it proposed one day to resume the thought of extending [its] Dominions', which was something that the Court of Directors was firmly against at the time.[12] Instead, Clive was urged to seek permission to carry on free trade in Awadh 'with the privilege of establishing Factories wherever we think proper—to which shall be annexed contiguous lands and districts as may be found necessary to the convenience and support of the settlements'.

The idea of strongholds 'and protecting our Commerce by Military power' was something that could be worked out later as expedient. In fact, the Company had set up just such a factory a century earlier in Lucknow to trade in textiles, indigo and sugar. A house and 'factory' had been hired in 1647 near the Chowk and the large sum of Rs70,000 remitted to the factors there for the 'cloth investment'.[13] Goods were sent for export via Surat, on the west coast, because this was before the Company had a base in Bengal. But transport was scarce and expensive, so the factory was closed after 6 years. The area retained its name of Farangi Mahal (the foreigners' house) and the whole venture was seemingly forgotten, although it matched almost exactly the idea now put forward by Fort William. Trade was still a priority for the Company, and the annexation of land which it would then have to defend and administer was regarded as a burden. So the outpost at Cawnpore did not mean an inevitable advance of the Company from its Bengal headquarters, and the ad hoc nature of the cantonment reflects this.

The site at Cawnpore was chosen because it was far enough outside the ambit of Bithur, a town some 30 miles upriver that had been captured by the Marathas. Cawnpore village was conveniently near the ancient settlement of Jajmau, where the Ganges was bridged and which had been the site of the peace talks between the Company and the *nawab wazir*. The first settlement here was made by a detachment of the *nawab wazir*'s troops in 1770. They were joined by the 3rd Bengal Brigade commanded by General Sir Robert Barker, whom we last met working as a reluctant engineer in Calcutta. The Maratha threat meant that earthworks and defensive ditches had to be quickly put in place, built on rising ground outside the village. Because the settlement was planned to be temporary, and only for as long as the *nawab wazir* required protection, there was no proper shelter at first. Both the arsenal of weapons and the hospital for sick and wounded men were accommodated in flat-bottomed boats moored in the river.[14] Only the brick-built magazine holding gunpowder supplies had been erected; the officers and men of the brigade had to make do with tents, while the camp followers settled some distance away and set up small bazaars.

However, the perceived need for defence did not diminish, and more troops were needed until an estimated 10,000 were encamped in the vicinity. Thatched huts were erected for, and often by, the *sepoys*, with barracks for the European men. Officers had to find their own lodgings, and a number of them got their own bungalows built along the riverbank with their own large compounds. Because there was no overall plan, buildings were dotted around at random; the bullock and camel sheds were next to the rum *godown* (warehouse) and near the soldiers' cemetery which adjoined the new water tank. The quarters for the *lascars* (workmen) stood in front of the foot artillery lines, and the hospital had been moved from the boats into a new building. By 1778, it was acknowledged that the settlement was in fact a permanent cantonment, growing after 1857 to be the largest in India.

A later commander-in-chief, Giles Stibbert, wrote to the governor general, Warren Hastings, regretting that proper barracks had not been built earlier. It would have been a considerable saving, General Stibbert said, if small brick ranges had been erected, with terraced roofs (based on the Berhampore model). As it was, the 'temporary' barracks needed annual repairs. If a decision had been made sooner about whether Cawnpore was a cantonment or not, then expenses could have been kept down.[15] There was no wall around the site, which sprawled inelegantly for several miles along the riverbank. The isolated bungalows were at risk from thieves and animals too: a sentry had been killed when he was attacked by a pack of wolves.

Political and military expediency had led to the birth of the Cawnpore cantonment. The same pattern was repeated on a smaller scale at the Mariaon cantonment near Lucknow, the city which became the capital of Awadh in 1775. Here, again, the Company could not dictate what it wanted, because it was on 'foreign' soil that belonged to the wealthy *nawab wazirs*. The two battalions stationed here for Shuja-ud-daula's protection were initially encamped on the north bank of the Gomti, which was known as the 'English side' of the river. This became a well-furnished cantonment with quarters for the officers, barracks for the European men, artillery sheds, an arsenal, powder magazine and guard rooms. Repairs were carried out promptly as needed, and the wages of auxiliary staff— including watchmen, messengers and 'artificiers'—were all met by the successor *nawab*, Asaf-ud-daula.

By 1806, the British Resident at the Lucknow Court suggested that additional buildings were needed including storerooms, a hospital, stabling for cattle and 'private stabling' for officers who kept their own horses.[16] After much correspondence, a site was chosen: again on the north bank, but this time some four miles from the city. It was not ideal because it put a considerable distance between the military quarters and the civilian Europeans housed in the Residency on the south bank. But it was all the Company was going to get, and the new *nawab*, Saadat Ali Khan, laid down strict conditions too. Only British troops were permitted to live at Mariaon in bungalows and barracks, and no bazaar was to be erected there, because it would take away custom from the city traders. No fortified buildings were allowed, no 'delinquents' to be given sanctuary and no moneylenders to settle there without special permission. There was to be a ditch dug around the whole 4-mile perimeter site, with no encroachments beyond, and masonry pillars to be erected around the ditch as added markers.

Clearly the *nawab* was trying to exercise control over the new cantonment, which seemed reasonable as he was paying for it and the officers' salaries too. A description from an English traveller, Thomas Lumsden, in 1817 commended the Mariaon cantonment and noted that the officers' bungalows were built in the 'cottage style, very well adapted for the climate, and each having a garden around it, with a range of out offices, consisting of a kitchen, stables and servants' houses'.[17] It sounded ideal, and for many years it was. A bandstand was set up in a large garden where Europeans could enjoy an evening walk after the heat of the day had diminished. Later, British Residents had their own 'country house' in the cantonment, and the last chaplain found he could grow strawberries in the garden surrounding his bungalow. Once the Uprising of 1857 began, rebellious *sepoys* shot flaming arrows into the thatched roofs of the bungalows and murdered a number of British officers. Families fled to the comparative safety of the city Residency, where they were to endure a prolonged siege. The whole cantonment was subsequently demolished, and only the cemetery remains today, surrounded by new buildings.

There was considerable variation in the cantonments that spread westwards from Bengal, but the common factor was that they were all foreign military bases: some off-limits to civilians, others a mixture of military and residential accommodation and each providing employment for large numbers of people to service them and support the troops on campaigns. During the first Anglo-Maratha War, the Company's fighting force of 6,700 officers and men required an enormous entourage of 19,000 servants plus 12,000 bazaar staff to provision them on the march.[18] With these figures, we can see how each cantonment would attract a sizeable workforce around it, and in peacetime too there were considerable employment opportunities.

Following the formal abolition of the East India Company in November 1858, its cantonments were seamlessly absorbed by the new British government. In some cases they were rebuilt, as was the case with the destroyed Mariaon cantonment, which was relocated nearer Lucknow and renamed Dilkusha. In 1947, the cantonments passed into the hands of the Indian and Pakistani armies and are maintained today by the military cantonment boards. While the location and layout of some cantonments has been questioned, their utility has not; they remain among the most successful of the Company's constructions. Berhampore was an exception, demilitarised in the early twentieth century in Lord Kitchener's army reforms.

It was the establishment of Berhampore that accelerated the development of a cluster of European-style country houses at Maidapur, 3 miles east of the cantonment and on the road that runs between Murshidabad and Calcutta. Because none of these grand houses remain standing today and are only known through paintings, their importance has been largely ignored. However, it is clear they present a significant example of how unlimited financial resources allied to a high administrative position were exploited by Company officials in eighteenth-century Bengal. 'Moidapore House', as it was called, was already in existence before 1757, and it was here that Robert Clive encamped 2 days after his victory at Plassey when he was on his way to Murshidabad. It was described as the East India Company's principal house in Bengal and would have acted as an embassy between Murshidabad and Fort William before Calcutta became the de facto capital of Bengal. It was also conveniently near Cossimbazar, which had been a Company trading post for almost a century. Moidapore House was a rambling, two-storeyed, stucco-covered building with a pitched roof over a central hall and two adjoining redbrick structures for stabling and staff. It was a handsome enough house but nothing in comparison with Afzalbagh, which subsequently became the official British Residency to the Court of Murshidabad, a largely nominal post after 1772 when Bengal's administrative functions had moved from the old capital.

Sir John Hadley d'Oyly was the British Resident from 1779 to 1785, and it is unclear whether he had Afzalbagh (described as a magnificent mansion) built or whether he merely rented it. Its name means the 'Most Excellent Garden', and it became even more magnificent after Robert Pott 'bought' the post of Resident from d'Oyly. Pott, who had lived for a time in Lucknow manufacturing and dealing in armaments, had been nominated Resident to Murshidabad by the Court of Directors in London. But, on returning to India to take up his position, he learned that d'Oyly planned to retain his job as Resident for several more years. However, he 'persuaded' d'Oyly to resign immediately after the two men negotiated a huge bribe of Rs3 lakhs (£35,000 at the time, equivalent today to nearly £4 million).

As part of the deal, Pott was forced to buy 'a parcel of trumpery old furniture' in the Afzalbagh mansion for another Rs90,000. He was prepared to pay these enormous sums because the perquisites of the Murshidabad Resident were even larger. William Hickey says quite frankly that the salary allowed by the Company to the *nawab* was 'passing through such Resident's hands, in which channel a considerable portion of it always stuck to his fingers'.[19] The Resident also purchased and paid for every European item that the *nawab* wanted, and in doing so collected the Customs duties for Murshidabad and Cossimbazar. D'Oyly was estimated to have returned to England with a fortune of £100,000.

When Pott got possession of Afzalbagh, he immediately threw out the old furniture he had been forced to buy and began work on extending the Residency. He altered the whole plan, 'laying two rooms into one, building several additional apartments and creating an entire new staircase, making it altogether by far the most splendid thing in India'.[20] There was a cluster of other European houses nearby, not as grand as Afzalbagh but still pretty spectacular by the standards of the flat Bengal landscape where a simple thatched hut was the norm. Thomas Pattle, a senior judge, lived at Champapoka House, which had earlier been called Felicity Hall. The Cossimbazar Factory House where the superintendent of the cloth investment lived was a large, two-storeyed mansion with a *godown* to the side for storing bales of fabric, and the engineer Colonel James Parlby had a large bungalow surrounded by deep verandas.[21]

None of these houses had any kind of defensive walls around them, for none were needed. It was the tranquillity and security of this part of Bengal that allowed these English country houses to be built, together with the cheapness of labour and materials, and the fortunes made in bribes and commissions. But the political situation that had led to the creation of the exclusive Maidapur enclave was changing. As Calcutta became the new capital of Bengal, so Murshidabad declined, accelerated by a severe famine. By the end of the eighteenth century, its outskirts lay in ruins as the jungle advanced. There was still *nawabi* money around as the construction of the Hazarduari Palace and later palaces shows, but there was no longer any real power. So Maidapur lost its raison d'être, and one by one the grand houses were sold and demolished. By 1833, Afzalbagh had passed through several hands since Robert Pott's departure some 40 years earlier. It had been sold to the Bengal *nawab* Ali Jah, who gave it as a gift (and something of a white elephant) to a favourite eunuch, but 'the house has been utterly neglected' and was in a ruinous state, with the surrounding land leased to farmers who ploughed it up.[22]

Today, nothing of the house remains. Indians found no use for large, isolated mansions out in the countryside, and the site is now only identifiable by the lake that fronted it and the raised, flat plain where it stood, which is now a mango grove filled with monkeys. It wasn't only Company houses that suffered the fate of Maidapur either. A building to rival or even surpass Afzalbagh was Ghiretty House, the country retreat of officials from the French enclave of Chandernagore. Again, it is only from illustrations that we know this large, two-storeyed mansion with an octagon tower. The most poignant image, by an unknown Indian artist, shows Ghiretty in decline. Trees and bushes are growing too near it, the rooftop parapet is broken and cows are foraging in the overgrown grounds. The gateposts, often the last things to go, remained long enough to be photographed in the 1860s.

It was the Anglo-Nepalese War that led indirectly to the establishment of India's first hill stations, which were to flourish during and after British rule. The Treaty of Sagauli, signed in 1816, acknowledged the Nepalese defeat and ceded to the Company the areas of Garhwal, Kumaon and, importantly, Dehra Dun, lying in the low foothills of the Himalayas. The Company declared:

It would be impracticable for us to abandon the country on the expulsion of the enemy as the government had desired; on the contrary, in order to maintain our guarantee of protection not only against the foreign enemy, but retaining [in] their ancient principalities the chiefs whom we had restored, it would be necessary for us, however averse to territorial acquisition within the hills to retain such portions of the country as appeared best adapted for military positions and also calculated to indemnify the Government for the expenses of the military force it was forced to retain in the hills.[23]

At first sight, this statement looks like a masterpiece of expediency. A similar tactic had been put in place after the Treaty of Allahabad half a century earlier, when the *nawab wazir* of Awadh was 'persuaded' to accept two battalions of Company troops for his own protection (and of course at his own expense). After Sagauli, the Company, reluctant though it was, nobly agreed to accept some land for hill cantonments in order to ensure no further Nepalese incursions as well as to support several 'ancient principalities'.

Although the Company hoped that the little town of Dehra, tucked under the foothills of the Himalayas, might act as a new trading post with its links into Tibet, the Treaty of Sagauli was more concerned with military than commercial matters. There was, at the time, no fixed border between Nepal and its neighbour Awadh, putting the latter potentially at risk of a Gurkha invasion. The heavily wooded hills of Garhwal and Kumaon, nominally under the rule of rajas and local chiefs, were not great revenue-producing areas, like Bengal. So on the face of it the Company had not made a particularly good deal. However, within a couple of decades this reluctant 'territorial acquisition' was to become the site for highly popular summer resorts. Unlike later hill-stations, Shimla was not developed simultaneously with a cantonment but came under the protection of the Subathu garrison, 24 miles away. It was established almost entirely on the initiative of one man, Captain Charles Pratt Kennedy, an officer in the Bengal Artillery who was appointed Assistant Superintendent of Sikh and Hill Affairs. Around 1820, he built the first permanent residence in Shimla and named it Kennedy House. It stood among a cluster of tribal huts, in an area known as Shyamala after the goddess of a local temple. The name was later anglicised to Simla, though the correct pronunciation is Shimla. For the construction of Kennedy House, 'hundreds' of local people were summoned, who felled the trees on the selected site, 'squared them rudely' and, together with workmen from the plains, erected a spacious house within a month.[24] When it was finished, it resembled a Swiss chalet, with its sharply pitched roofs and chimneys.

Some of the land here belonged to local hill chiefs, but the bulk of it was owned by the maharajahs of Patiala and Keonthal. Negotiations were carried out to persuade the maharajahs to exchange their Shimla *parganas* with those the Company had acquired elsewhere in the hills. Once this was agreed, Shimla developed at an astonishing rate: 'a considerable village has risen, as it were, by enchantment' wrote a French visitor in 1830.[25] 'Many hundreds of mountain labourers and coolies were employed, cutting timber, raising stone and erecting several buildings; the material for which are close at hand in excellent firs of the forest and the fine flaky stones which abound here.'[26] The first European cemetery was opened in 1828 on an empty hillside and closed a decade later because of the encroaching town. Twenty years after Kennedy House was built, there were well over a hundred new houses, and their names are an indication of how quickly and thoroughly this remote area had become anglicised: Stirling Castle, Annandale Lodge, Primrose Hill, Prospect House, Bellevue, Kenilworth and Richmond Villa are among many similar evocations of 'Home'.

The temperate climate of the hills was the chief attraction that compensated for all the other inconveniences, including getting there, which in the early days meant being carried up in a palanquin, or risking travel by camel. Bullock carts brought up heavy luggage, including furniture and pianos, while monthly supplies of wine, poultry, mangoes and plantains arrived from the plains (tropical fruit could not be grown in the hills). Even in July, the hottest month of the year, the temperature seldom rose beyond 80 degrees Fahrenheit, and in winter there was snow and picturesque walks among the fir trees. There was something about the climate that brought out a long-concealed sense of fun among British officials. The military staff attached to a commander-in-chief, Sir Harry Fane, who were lodged in Shimla during one winter 'had not seen snow for 40 years [and] were half crazy with delight, charging out of their houses to make snowballs'.[27]

Lord Amherst was the first governor general to visit Shimla in 1827, and he spent 2 months at Kennedy House. The following year, the commander-in-chief Lord Combermere stayed for 5 months in the same house, but his staff and entourage had to shift for themselves, and consequently 'the leisure hours of many of his officers were employed in building their houses and afterwards in enlarging and beautifying them'.[28] Combermere's aide-de-camp, Captain Godfrey Mundy, described the noise of axes and hammers as the men constructed their houses, which were scattered promiscuously over every level area or gentle slope, joined by narrow roads. Little attempt was made at planning, apart from the Mall, the main street, which ran along an upper ridge, while the bazaar ran parallel on a lower ridge. Many of the houses were built of locally sourced materials, including blocks of a slate-like stone, which were held in place by pine beams inserted at regular intervals. Roofs were either flat and covered with beaten clay or pitched with wooden rafters and covered with slate from nearby quarries. Letting these houses to summer visitors became a useful source of income for their owners who were able to charge high rents: anything between Rs400 and Rs1,500 per annum.

By 1844, the construction of Christ Church had begun, designed by the Bengal engineer Colonel John Boileau. It was funded, like other churches in India, by subscription, but it ran into financial problems when the local quarry, that had been expected to provide sufficient stone for the project, became exhausted. This meant that bricks had to be used (and brought up from the plains), which increased costs. With some reluctance, the Company provided a loan, to be repaid from the rents of the pews, which was a common practice in Anglican churches at the time. The delay meant that the church was not consecrated until 1857. There had also been another unfortunate holdup when the donation of a stained-glass window led to an arcane dispute. The window depicted animals representing the four evangelists, including a lion, a calf and an eagle, and the church committee voiced its unease that this could lead 'to the most serious misconceptions in the native mind as to the nature and extent of our worship as Christians ... [and] will be naturally led to conclude that these figures are the objects of our reverence and worship'.[29] The committee initially refused the donation, but, since the window had already been commissioned and delivered, the Bishop of Calcutta agreed that it could be erected. However, he added that it might be an idea to darken 'the more prominent figures, if possible by a wire gauze fastened on the interior, or in any other way'.

The 'season' in the hills, when Europeans left the plains, could run from March to November. When Shimla became the official summer capital of British India in 1864, the viceroy and the majority of his staff left the heat of Calcutta and governed the country from the hills for several months each year. Provincial governments had their own hill stations too. In spite of the geographical absurdity of locating a capital, even temporarily, at the very periphery of the subcontinent, the annual pilgrimage continued into the twentieth century and only ceased on the construction of New Delhi, where electricity was used to power fans and refrigerators.

Shimla was the earliest hill station to be established; others followed rapidly. Mussoorie, 70 miles south-east of Shimla, developed from a single house built on the Camel's Back as a shooting lodge in 1823. Lieutenant Frederick Young, leading a party of Bengal artillery troops, had been captured during the Anglo-Nepalese War by Gurkha troops. When he was released unharmed, his commanding officer, Sir David Ochterlony, ordered him to recruit some of the Gurkha prisoners of war who had been captured and imprisoned in the Doon Valley. These men later formed the Sirmur battalion, the first Gurkha unit in the Company's Bengal army. Young became friendly with the Anglo-Indian John Shore, a Political Agent and magistrate, and the two used the shooting lodge until their own houses were built. (It was unusual for an Anglo-Indian to be appointed to these posts, but Shore was the son of Lord Teignmouth, a former governor general, and an Indian *bibi*, so in this case rank overcame prejudice.)

Mussoorie is adjacent to the cantonment of Landour, and both lie on the mountain plateau that rises almost vertically from the town of Dehra. By 1828, Landour was also a convalescent home, 'a depot of European invalids' who were living in tents while waiting for new bungalows and the hospital to be roofed over before the summer rains. Many of those sick were already recovering, it was reported, thanks to 'the effects of the delightful climate', and there was a welcome financial benefit too: 'the establishment of this station, so convenient for the invalids of Meerut and other great northern cantonments, will be a great saving to government, who were obliged before its creation to send their sick servants to the Cape of Good Hope, or at least to sea.'[30] Ten years later, when the author Fanny Parkes spent a summer there, the bazaar's 'Europe' shop was stocked with pâté de fois gras, champagne and other luxuries. Mr Webb had set up an hotel with a ballroom and five billiard tables. A church had been built and there was a small botanical garden where tea plants were being cultivated.

Further hill stations were rapidly developed, including Darjeeling, which had initially been rented from the raja of Sikkim for £300 per annum until he was persuaded to present the site to the Company in 1835. It had already been earmarked as a suitable site for a military garrison and another sanitorium for British soldiers. Subsequently, Dr Archibald Campbell of the Indian Medical Service was appointed as the first superintendent of Darjeeling, and along with the Bengal engineer Robert Napier he began to lay out a plan for houses and hospital buildings. Patients had to be carried up from the plains in palanquins until a road was constructed 4 years later.

Shimla, Mussoorie and Darjeeling are only three among the many hill stations established between 1818 and 1860. It is estimated that some sixty-five stations were built in this period, the majority of them in the 1830s and 1840s.[31] In some cases, stations were developed immediately after the defeat of a local ruler. In others, it took time to realise and exploit newly gained territory. Ootacamund, for example, was not established until 1819, 20 years after the death of Tipu Sultan. Again, it was one man's enthusiasm that led to the creation of this particular station. John Sullivan, the Collector of Coimbatore, said the area in the middle of Toda territory reminded him of Switzerland, and the hilly site began with a single house. The origins of Mount Abu in Rajputana are less clear, but it became the summer residence of the British Political Agent to the governor general in 1845. The owner of the land, the Rao Sheo Singh of Sirohi, laid down strict conditions for the formation

HE FORMED A DIGEST OF HINDU AND MOHAMMEDAN LAWS

13. Memorial to Sir William Jones in University College Chapel, Oxford.

14. The Madras Observatory in 1827.

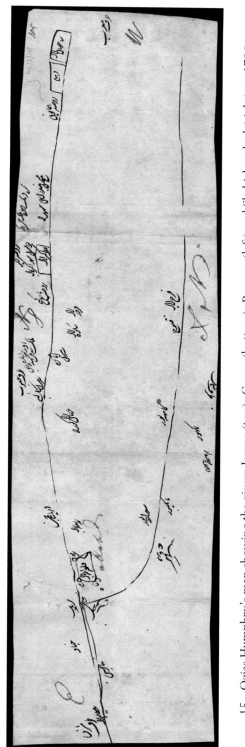

15. Ozias Humphry's map showing the rivers Jamna (top), Ganga (bottom), Benares (left) and Shahjahanabad (right), c. 1786.

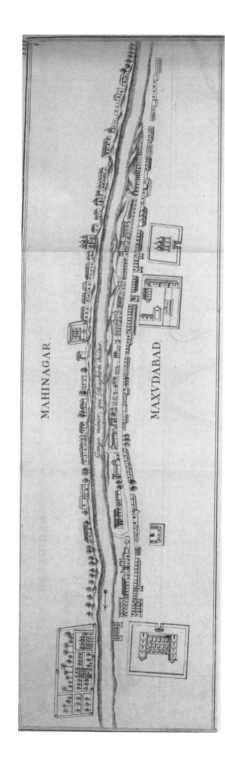

16. Murshidabad map by Joseph Tieffenthaler, Plate 29 from *Description historique et géographique de l'Inde*, Berlin, 1786—8. The Katra mosque, bottom left, in a box.

17. 'Barrackpore House', c. 1816 by Colonel Robert Smith. The semaphore tower is in the foreground.

18. 'Ind: State Railway Engine - Engine & Tender in one - Suited to reverse work', early 1860s.

AN INDIAN RAILWAY STATION.— SEE PRECEDING PAGE.

19. 'An Indian Railway station' on the Bombay to Thana line in 1854 from *The Illustrated London News*.

20. Unconventional travel: using *mussacks* (inflated buffalo skins) to propel a charpoy across a ford. Late 19th century.

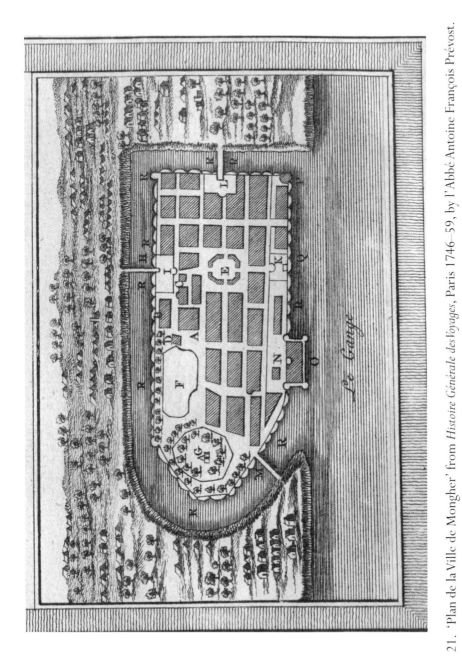

21. 'Plan de la Ville de Mongher' from *Histoire Générale des Voyages*, Paris 1746–59, by l'Abbé Antoine François Prévost.

22. 'Berhampore cantonment', c. 1795, from *The Louisa Parlby Album*.

23. 'Afzalbagh House Maidapur', c. 1795, from *The Louisa Parlby Album.*

24. Captain John Foote in native dress, oil by Sir Joshua Reynolds, 1765.

of a sanatorium. British soldiers, presumably recovering invalids, were forbidden from going into nearby villages and molesting the inhabitants or dishonouring the local women. Nor were they allowed to kill cattle or import beef into the sanitorium, and trees were not to be felled without permission.[32]

Murree, now in Pakistan, was developed straight after the annexation of the Punjab in 1849. The site, lying to the west of the Himalayas, was particularly suitable for a hill station, located as it was some 7,400 feet above sea level. (The preferred height was between 6,000 to 7,500 feet.) The site was now Company territory, but, unlike Shimla, it was already populated by eleven hamlets. Negotiations with the villagers took place and a financial settlement was reached, with the Company undertaking to pay Rs50 per annum in perpetuity as a lease. Again, with astonishing rapidity, fifty bungalows were completed in the year following the annexation of Murree, with permanent barracks for the British soldiers constructed by 1853.[33] A sanatorium for a hundred men and a 'convalescent depot' were soon added. Stone was plentiful and was used for building the foundations and walls, topped by steeply pitched timber roofs covered with slate or shingles. The Himalayan hill stations were similar in appearance, since they were constructed of the same materials and were, by definition, built on hills, their layout organised so that the bungalows clung to the slopes while the Mall and the church occupied the upper ridge and the local bazaar ran along a lower ridge. By the 1850s, 'European' shops were becoming more sophisticated, run by men from the plains, including enterprising Parsi shopkeepers.

Although much has been written on India's hill stations—as individual stations, and as sanitoria—there has been little analysis of their role in the Company's defensive strategy during the final half-century of its existence. A chain of military garrisons had been flung across the foothills of the Himalayas and other temperate regions of India with little, or no, opposition. Geographically and politically, this was as significant for the expansion of the Company as the grant of the *diwani*. A hill station had its own cantonment, sometimes tucked away out of sight behind a convenient escarpment and often catering for invalid soldiers too, but it was still a military base. This element has been played down in written descriptions for three likely reasons; firstly, the cantonments were often not immediately visible to visitors and have therefore not been so frequently described in accounts. Jutogh, for example—which was not constructed until 1840, when a further exchange of land with Patiala took place—was 3½ miles away from Shimla. Secondly, many cantonments had a substantial number of recuperating invalids (although, as we have seen at Mount Abu, there were prohibitions against the recovering soldiers molesting local women). This meant that the hospitals and sanitoria were generally not on the tourist map for fear of visitors contracting infection. Thirdly, there was also a general need for secrecy; these were military bases, after all, and not all troop movements and arrangements were to be publicised. These factors meant that the military significance of the hill cantonments has not been fully appreciated or explored.

These were considered 'soft' cantonments, where commanding officers lived in comfortable bungalows surrounded by garden compounds and where soldiers enjoyed the temperate climate without the rowdy distractions or dangers of the plains. They were also regarded as suitable areas in which to develop schools for British and Anglo-Indian children. Sir Henry Lawrence, who was British Resident in Kathmandu in the 1840s, wanted to establish 'hill schools' for the children and orphans of private British soldiers, who had been brought up in barracks in the plains. Lawrence and his wife Honoria persevered in the face of initial indifference, and in 1847 the first school, named the Lawrence Military Asylum, was opened at Sanawar, near Shimla. A similar asylum was established at Mount Abu a few years later, and two posthumous asylums, in memory of Lawrence, who was killed at Lucknow during the Uprising, were built at Lovedale near Ootacamund, and Ghora Gali near Murree. Lawrence's aim was to create an asylum:

> [free] from the debilitating effects of the tropical climate, and the demoralizing influence of Barrack-life; wherein they may obtain the benefits of a bracing climate, a healthy moral atmosphere, and a plain, useful, and above all religious education, adapted to fit them for employment suited to their position in life.[34]

Both girls and boys, strictly segregated, were given a boarding school education 'that stressed discipline, obedience, piety, respectability, and acquiescence to a future of limited opportunity'. The boys wore military-style uniforms, and some were subsequently recruited into the army, while others found employment with the railways or the telegraph offices. Influenced by the growing Evangelical movement in the West, the idea was promoted that a temperate climate produced a healthy moral atmosphere, or at least less opportunity for immoral behaviour, than that of the plains. Few of the hill cantonments were threatened during the 1857 Uprising, although there was an unfortunate misunderstanding at Shimla where (unfounded) rumours of an uprising among a Gurkha battalion stationed at Jutogh led to European women, children and their *ayahs* sheltering in a local Bank, while the men of the station armed themselves.

The distinction between the hills and the plains, although obvious to us today, was not so clear to Europeans living in the Presidency cities and towns in the 1820s. Geographical knowledge of India was limited, and the Great Trigonometrical Survey had another half-century to run before it concluded at Dehra Dun. The army officers who pitched their tents, and later built their houses in the foothills of the Himalayas, were exploring newly acquired territory, ceded by conquest or negotiation. Once a hill base had been established, its rationale followed—an army garrison to ensure that the treaty held, a militarily protected site for a hospital and convalescent quarters, followed by residential accommodation once senior Company officials were adventurous enough to visit their new territory. The idea of 'them and us', the hill stations and the plains, was to develop far beyond the geographical realities into something much more metaphorical, certainly for the British who began creating a facsimile of Home, 5,000 miles away from the real thing.

The initial impact of hill stations on the Indian landscape has been largely overshadowed by their later development. There were both positive and negative outcomes in the years leading up to 1860. Descriptions of 'hundreds' of labourers building the first British bungalows meant that hill tribes were recruited from their villages, many of them meeting Europeans for the first time and some receiving wages in cash for the first time too. The hill people were described as 'simple-minded, orderly people, quiet and submissive to authority and peaceful in their pursuits'.[35] Agriculture and trade formed their economy: wheat, barley, opium poppies and cannabis were the main crops, the latter of which was exported as *charas*, a labour-intensive but lucrative hallucinogenic. The majority of the hill people were Hindu, apart from a colony of Kashmiri Muslim weavers who had settled at Subathu and produced shawls made with traded wool brought in from Tibet.

There is little evidence that these docile people became a domestic workforce for the foreign visitors, who brought their own servants with them. Emily Eden, sister to the governor general Lord Auckland and who visited Mussoorie and Shimla with him in 1838, writes that her Bengali servants who accompanied the tour party were 'very miserable ... and were starved with the cold, and were so afraid of the precipices that they could not even go to the bazaar to buy food'.[36] Eden was sympathetic enough to realise that for people who had lived all their lives on a flat plain, 'these mountains must be terrific'. She was not the first to comment on the mental adjustment needed for plains-dwellers visiting the hills for the first time, but no one seems to have remarked on the physical adjustment to the high altitude which makes newcomers out of breath for the first few days. Nevertheless, there was no thought of hiring local people except as palanquin bearers, woodcutters and porters. Language was another barrier; the hill people spoke Pahari, which is allied to Nepali but was not familiar to most people in Bengal or the rest of India.

The hill tribes would soon see two of the most fundamental changes to the Himalayan foothills: the decimation of its wildlife and uncontrolled deforestation. All of this was instigated by the British, some of them employed by the Company, who recruited local labour in their own search for profits. The widespread hunting of animals for their skins or for food is not recorded in the sparse, early accounts of the foothills.[37] Left to their own devices, the hill tribes, mainly Hindu or Buddhist vegetarians, ate what they could grow. They were described as living 'almost entirely on the precarious fruits of a not very productive soil', and when Captain Kennedy began distributing seed potatoes (tubers) around his Shimla district, the villagers were reportedly 'not a little grateful for this useful addition to their provisions'.[38] At the beginning of the nineteenth century, before British settlement in the hills, the only animals the hill tribes deliberately sought out and killed were male musk deer for their musk pods, a valuable trading item, and bears for their grease. As a result, wildlife was plentiful around the new hill station districts and largely unafraid of man. All this was to change rapidly in the 1820s. The early European hunters used rifle-shells to kill animals, shells that exploded inside the body like the later Dum-Dum bullets developed near Calcutta for use on humans.

Captain Mundy, describing the Dehra home of John Shore in 1828, wrote: 'The verandah and rooms of this active persecutor of the wild animals of the forest are adorned with the grim skulls and stuffed skins of tigers, bears, boars, monkeys and other characteristic drawing-room furniture.' However, Mundy himself was no animal lover, as he later describes shooting a female tiger and her cubs.[39] *Hunting in the Himalaya* by Robert Dunlop, published in 1860, was only one of a particular genre of books and prints detailing the killing of animals. Dunlop writes with unconscious irony about elephants that 'have been known, in mere wanton cruelty, to chase and kill the government letter-carriers without the least provocation'. Since the majority of the hunted animals were not shot for food, a trade in taxidermy developed in the hill stations which stimulated the Victorian craze for stuffed animals and birds.

At Landour, a Mr Morrow, described as the steward of the hospital, set up a 'menagerie-cum-shop of a plumassier' (someone who dealt with ornamental plumes and feathers).[40] Morrow's daughter, Ann, married into the Corbett family, though she was not a direct ancestor of the twentieth-century hunter Jim Corbett. His shop sold stuffed and mounted birds that had been killed in the surrounding forests, the most popular being the monal, or blue pheasant. Mrs Theodore, who ran an hotel at Rajpur, a few miles from the hill station, also traded in birds, plumes and stuffed beasts, charging Rs1,600 for 'a complete set', a considerable sum of money which didn't include the fee for transport in packing cases.

During the first half of the nineteenth century, hill tribes were not recorded as owning or using firearms, so the slaughter of large animals—including tigers, leopards, bears and elephants—was carried out primarily by European hunters, and occasionally by hill rajas armed with imported rifles. Once the hill people learnt that

Europeans would pay for dead birds, they began killing them with sling shots. They roughly prepared the birds, stripping their innards and stuffing their skins with moss before bringing them down to the hill station taxidermists. Here the taxidermists removed the moss and applied arsenical soap, which halted decomposition and insect infestation. Not all animals could be stuffed, wired and mounted. Wild elephants, which frequented the Doon Valley, were a particular challenge, so often only the head would be preserved and mounted on a wooden plaque as a wall ornament. Elephant-foot umbrella stands also became a popular item of furniture in Victorian Britain.

On her departure from Mussoorie, Fanny Parkes purchased 'only a few specimens' from Mr Morrow's large collection, including one golden eagle, one black eagle and a number of red and blue pheasants. She added another couple of eagles, explaining that, although they were rather large birds to carry, she had so much luggage that another few cases would not matter.[41] Parkes also obtained a hawk, some small birds and four heads and horns of the goral, 'the small wild deer of the Hills'. These were carried down to Meerut, together with her butterfly collection. Parkes should not be singled out for her animal and bird purchases; her detailed descriptions of them are useful in recording what was being killed. However, if other visitors to the hill stations came away with similar souvenirs for more than a century, then it is easy to see how the widespread slaughter of wildlife to feed the tourist trade has led to its near extinction today.

The story of Frederick Wilson, known as 'Pahari' Wilson, serves as an example of how much damage one man could do. He had joined HM 11th Dragoons as a private soldier in 1834 and was stationed 2 years later in Meerut. Here he fell ill and was sent to Rajpur to recover, which was where he met Morrow and visited his shop. Wilson returned to England, where he was discharged from the army as being unfit for service. He was back in India around 1840 with few possessions apart from a double-barrelled percussion gun and a few rupees. He started hunting, killing birds for their plumage as well as musk deer and bears, from which he was able to make a living. He began employing local men to set snares. Wilson became well-known as a man of the hills, hence his nickname, and he was hired to accompany wealthy Europeans on shooting expeditions, including Prince Waldemar of Prussia. Wilson was literate and contributed papers on Himalayan birds and animals to the *Calcutta Sporting Review*. By the 1850s, he was selling skins in Mussoorie as well as exporting them to England from his own taxidermy workshops. Bharals, a species of goat-antelope, were a particular favourite.

As Wilson grew older, he turned his attention from hunting to logging, supplying timber to the railway contractors. For this he had to petition the raja of Garhwal for permission, which was granted. Wilson and a European colleague signed a five-year contract, paying the raja Rs6,000 per annum. 'The deodar was being decimated in the Bhagirathi valley—mainly Wilson's handiwork as a logger and forest contractor,' [42] and he neatly solved the problem of getting the timber to the plains by floating the logs downriver to Hardwar. After securing a collection point for a nominal rent, Wilson was in business. He was later able to float his timber on rafts as far as Cawnpore, where the railway was being rapidly constructed after the Uprising. Initially, wooden sleepers had been imported, but this was expensive so different kinds of local wood were tried, including *sal* and *sissu*, although both had their disadvantages. The deodar was the answer, a tree that was easy to work, resistant to termites, and did not need creosoting to prevent dry rot. It was extensively exploited, and Wilson renewed his contract with the raja for another 4 years.

The contract was transferred to the government in 1864, but Wilson was still involved in felling trees and sending them downstream. He employed a considerable workforce, including woodcutters, bill-hookers, 'rollers and floaters', as well as clerks and watchmen. He is credited with being the first European to plant an apple orchard near his newly built house at Hursil, where he also set up a bakery and watermill to grind wheat. It was at this point that he started issuing copper tokens in lieu of cash. These are simple, well-stamped discs, with a starburst pattern on the reverse and the wording 'F. Wilson. One rupee. Hursil' on the obverse. By the end of his life, in 1883, Wilson was a property owner, a director of the Himalaya Bank in Mussoorie and a very wealthy man. His fulsome obituaries emphasised his humble origins and his fame as a *shikari* (hunter).

The British impact changed the Himalayan foothills forever. True, it had not been a pre-lapsarian paradise before their arrival, although some early British visitors did describe it as such. The hill tribes had previously been ruled by rajas who demanded forced labour from them during the dry season; their diet was sparse and monotonous and leprosy and syphilis were common among them. As Company officials and other foreigners began to exploit the area, new opportunities for employment arose; leper asylums and other medical facilities were established, and American missionaries settling in Subathu in 1837 started schools for the hill children. Today, the hill stations attract such large numbers of tourists from other parts of India that pollution and water shortages are now chief concerns. At the same time, Indian visitors express an odd 'nostalgia for the Raj' as well as an acknowledgement of the British foreigners' half-timbered fantasies of home.

6

THE PASSAGE OF TIME

Historians should be better qualified than most to record changing attitudes over time, yet some histories of the East India Company offer the picture of a static but malevolent organisation occupying the subcontinent until its abolition in 1858. This unnuanced view is to ignore political trends at home and abroad; the empiricism of the Enlightenment; the rise of the Evangelical movement; changing attitudes to race, sex, slavery, corruption and native dress; as well as scientific advances which included photography, introduced in the 1840s. For the first time, photographers were able to capture the built environment, past and present, as well as archaeological sites, tribespeople and the British in India at leisure. And it would be wrong to imagine that, because communications were different in the eighteenth and early nineteenth centuries, Company officials were somehow immune to ideas that were shaping other parts of the world. The mortality rate alone meant there was constant recruitment of Britons to fill civilian and military posts in India, who brought with them modern ideas, new policies and new prejudices. Not only do organisations change and grow, the people within them do too. How these overt developments affected India before 1860 has been the theme of this book together with a more subtle colonisation resulting from foreign occupation over a very long period of time.

Europeans who were employed by the Company, particularly in engineering, had brought different ideas that emphasised the lack of training for their counterparts in Britain. Company policy in the mid-eighteenth century was dictated as much by external events as it was by orders from its Court of Directors in London.

As we have seen, the distinction between merchants and soldiers was a thin and wavering line which took decades to resolve, and the role of the early, often untrained, engineers was to support both categories with defensive urban buildings and temporary structures on the battlefield. By the mid-nineteenth century, a substantive alteration had taken place. While there had been no major changes in construction techniques (the use of iron and steel in buildings was still some way off), the role of the engineer had become defined and professionalised. And this was led in part by events in northern India.

The Anglo-Nepalese Wars of the early nineteenth century had resulted in the rapid creation of the hill stations, as we have seen, and the Anglo-Sikh Wars of the mid-century meant that a huge area of the Punjab—almost as large as the entire United Kingdom—now had to be reckoned with. Writing in 1851, Sir James Thomason, the lieutenant governor of the north-western provinces, laid out the work to be done in a precise blueprint:

> A tract of country about 78,000 square miles was then added to the British Empire in Hindoostan. Throughout the whole of this Territory the work of improvement has been commenced with much energy. Already plans are matured and in progress for the accurate survey of all this extensive area. The Trigonometrical Surveyor is casting his net work of triangles over its whole surface, and determining with mathematical precision the true site of every important point. The Revenue Surveyor is laying down the boundaries of every village, and determining the size and productiveness of every field. The Marine Surveyor is ascertaining the capacity of its rivers for navigation, and the means by which their beds may be enlarged and deepened.[1]

He expanded on his vision for the Punjab and beyond:

> The country is intersected by numerous large rivers which flow from north to south. The main lines of communication run east and west. Along these lines Military stores must pass and Troops must March from Hindoostan to Peshawar. Along these lines the qafilahs [caravans] must find their way from Cabul and Central Asia to Hindoostan and take back the manufactures of Great Britain, in return for the products of their own country.[2]

In order to carry all this out, and to administer the vast new territory, he went on:

> Cantonments have to be formed, stations to be laid out, Civil and Military Buildings of all descriptions have to be built. For these purposes expert designers, skilful architects, and clever artificers are urgently required ... a large and a steady demand for all classes of Civil Engineers may be confidently anticipated.

This was a plea to enlarge Roorkee College, which had been established in 1847 'for the instruction of Civil Engineers'. (Coincidentally, the same year saw the establishment of the first independent school in England to teach architecture.)[3] The college was an important boost for the profession and the first such institution in the subcontinent. It had begun 2 years earlier, with a class to train a few local young Indian men in basic engineering techniques so they could assist with work on the adjoining Ganges Canal. This was an ambitious engineering project aimed at irrigating the Doab—the area between two rivers, the Ganges and the Jumna—and exploiting its agricultural resources. The governor general Lord Hardinge had been 'determined' to push this through, although it is clear that preparations and manpower had not been factored in. The word 'emergency' was used to describe how the project progressed, together with 'great engineering difficulties', and it was clear there was an immediate need for well-trained experienced civil engineers.

A number of incentives were offered to tempt students to the college. There were three categories, the first being for British candidates, who had to be under 22 years old, literate in English and with a knowledge of geometry, algebra, mensuration (measurements), spherical trigonometry and mechanics. These entry requirements for young men from government colleges seem high, but if they qualified for Roorkee they got travelling expenses, free accommodation and a monthly allowance of Rs40, so the rewards were high too. These were the men who would become civil engineers. The second category was for non-commissioned British officers and private soldiers who were to be trained as overseers in the Public Works Department. They had to provide a 'certificate of character' and would be accommodated in barracks. The third category was for 'native youths desirous of instruction in surveying, levelling and plan drawing'. They had to have a fair acquaintance with 'arithmetic in the native form' and be able to read and write Urdu using the Persian characters.

'A few native lads' were already being instructed in levelling by Major W.E. Baker, the newly appointed director of the Ganges Canal. Classes began formally on 1 January 1848, only to be interrupted by the Second Punjab War, when staff (and students) marched to the Front to fight, which meant an absence of 2 months before they could resume their studies. Although Roorkee was a civil engineering college, it was anticipated that many of its students would be drawn from the three Presidency armies of Bengal, Bombay and Madras, as well as the British army. The army was perceived as 'one of the sources whence scientific agency is most easily supplied. There are in the Indian Army many well informed and highly educated men who have much taste and capacity for Civil Engineering'.[4] If Roorkee did indeed attract young army men, this meant that, even after the Public Works Department was freed from the Military Department, the military ethos was continued in civil building for many years.

Thomason was neither an engineer nor a military man; he had been trained as a civil officer specialising in administration at the East India College at Haileybury, rather than the Military Seminary at Addiscombe. In fact, Thomason's drawn plans for the enlarged Roorkee College carry a strong likeness to Haileybury itself, with the front elevation mimicking the Hertfordshire college. Thomason was also a supporter of elementary schooling in the vernacular languages for village children and had established nearly 900 small schools for this purpose in the north-western provinces. He now ordered 'improvement and superintendence' in the village schools within a radius of 50 or 60 miles of Roorkee, whose pupils could potentially graduate to the college in the third category. Thomason's plans were eagerly accepted and acted upon, so that by 1854 the enlarged college was ready. The main building stands today virtually unchanged as the oldest of the Indian Institutes of Technology, with departments including engineering, architecture and planning.

That same year, 1854, also saw a significant move towards general higher education in the three Presidency cities. The president of the

London-based Board of Control, Sir Charles Wood, wrote to the governor general, Lord Dalhousie 'that the time is now arrived for the establishment of universities in India, which may encourage a regular and liberal course of education by conferring academical degrees as evidence of attainments in the different branches of art and science'.[5] As we have seen, Muslim and Hindu colleges had been established in the late eighteenth century at Calcutta and Benares, but Wood's proposal advocated something different. The Presidency Universities, as they became known, were to be secular and based 'on the model of the London University'. This was an important distinction. London University in 1854 was not an actual college, but an administrative headquarters and degree-awarding body. What is today University College London was the first secular college to be established in England and controlled by London University. It was distinguished from the universities of Oxford and Cambridge, which then restricted admittance only to professed members of the Church of England.

Wood's despatch was remarkably far-reaching and liberal, suggesting among other proposals that the Company should support female education (which was already being done in missionary schools). While teaching was to be in local languages at primary level, including reading and writing, education would be switched to English at higher levels. Wood believed that an English education would enhance the 'moral character' of Indians, who would then be able to enter the Company as civil servants. At the same time, government schools were to be opened in every district, private schools given grants, and Indians 'given training in their mother tongue', which meant they would be taught to read and write. It took another two decades before Calcutta's Senate House was built in College Street, and the first students to sit the entrance examination in 1861 had to use the Town Hall. Both Bombay and Madras followed with their own universities, incorporating earlier institutions like Elphinstone College and each following the guidelines laid down by London University.

Apart from the three Presidency cities with their new universities, the recognisable pattern of an anglicised town was beginning to emerge on the plains of India and in its hill stations. The town might be near an existing Indian settlement and share the same name, but it would be separate. A cantonment would be attached which might predate the town. Typically, there would be administrative buildings where Company officials worked, computing the land revenue and dealing with taxes, crime and civic affairs. The chief official might be a commissioner who lived in his own grand bungalow. The treasury, one of the most important buildings, would be guarded by *sepoys* who were also stationed around the *kacheri*, the local court, where petty cases and disputes were heard. The prison would be nearby for those sentenced or awaiting trial.

In these towns, a church had been built and consecrated, and there might be a smaller church in the cantonment known as the garrison chapel. Inevitably, there would be a cemetery which had been consecrated by a visiting bishop but was separate from the church and away from residential areas. The style of tombs had changed considerably over the previous half century. The spectacular tombs in South Park Street Cemetery, Calcutta, which had been closed in the 1820s, did not bear crosses, something which still has never been satisfactorily explained, since all but one of those interred were nominally Christian.[6] Far grander than anything in Britain, this cemetery was an elite city of the dead, every pathway flanked by substantial domed kiosks, fluted pillars, soaring obelisks and enormous pyramids. Appropriately, Sir William Jones' tomb was the largest, with its inscription commemorating a man 'who feared God, but not death'. These grandiose tombs were erected for the same reasons as the equally splendid houses along Chowringhee: labour was cheap, materials (brick and *chunam*) were cheap, and those buried here were wealthy Britons (unlike the paupers buried in the Bhowanipore cemetery), as ostentatious in death as they had been in life.

It may seem strange that there are fashions in death, but the monumental structures of the late eighteenth century gave way to something much simpler and less ostentatious. The Evangelical movement had led to a more overtly religious tone which is reflected in plainer tombs with stone crosses and, increasingly, biblical quotations at the end of the inscriptions. Stone angels started to appear on some graves, which led local people to call them *pari*, or fairies, because they had wings.

Apart from churches and cemeteries, the new towns had Banks, post offices, 'Europe' shops, lending libraries, hotels, clubs, theatres, Freemasons' lodges, assembly rooms, stables and the Company *bagh* (garden). These were all foreign interventions that distinguished a European, primarily British, settlement from a traditional Indian town, and they were almost exclusively for the use of European inhabitants. In appearance, the 'White Town', as it was called (to distinguish it from the 'Black Town'), was considerably more spacious, with its wide, tree-lined streets—one of them inevitably called The Mall—and metalled roads.

Bungalows had their own large compounds, with servants' quarters tucked away at the rear. A visitor to the White Town would be struck immediately by the sense of space; the cleanliness of the streets, which were swept and watered daily; the absence of noise and the absence of smells, not only from spices and incense, but from animals and unprocessed sewage. The temperature was different too. Mud-brick houses in narrow streets reflect the heat outwards, as anyone who has cycled along a country path through a village at night will have noticed. This meant that the *pukka* brick-built European houses were both colder in winter and warmer in summer, particularly when the sunlight was not deflected by the intricate pattern of walls and shaded courtyards as it was in the old city.

Statues of British dignitaries were erected in public places in the White Towns and the Presidency cities. The majority of them were installed after the Uprising—to British heroes like Sir James Outram—but Lord Cornwallis, who had twice been governor general, was the first figure to be memorialised in the early nineteenth century. His statues were erected in Calcutta, Bombay and Madras, each of them funded by public subscription in India and sculpted in Britain before being shipped out and prominently displayed on tall pedestals.[7] While British statues have been meticulously catalogued, enabling us to know where each one stood and where it stands today, little attention has been paid to their impact on the local population. Hindus have a long tradition of making statues of their gods and goddesses, which continues today especially in Bengal at the time of Durga Puja. Hindu statues at the time were made from clay and painted in vivid colours. The idea of an unpainted metal statue was thus completely foreign, although such statues may have been occasionally acknowledged with a marigold necklace. For orthodox Muslims, any kind of representation of the human form was forbidden, so they would have averted their eyes and hurried past.

Many of the different institutions of a typical mid-nineteenth century White Town and their concomitant buildings had originated early in the life of the Company's three Presidency cities, which set the pattern for later urban developments elsewhere. For example, the idea of a Bank as an organisation, rather than a person lending money, had begun in 1683 when the Madras Bank was established by a Company agent, William Gyfford. With a large balance of sterling capital, the Bank lent money at 6 per cent, and much later, after a number of mergers, it became the Imperial Bank of India in the early twentieth century. In Calcutta, the agency house of Alexander & Co. had set up the Bank of Hindustan in 1770 and started issuing its own banknotes. The Bank existed for a little over 60 years before collapsing shortly after the financial failure of the agency house of Palmer & Co. in Hyderabad. Agency houses were private organisations that dealt with the movement of money and goods between Britain, the subcontinent and settlements further east. They accepted deposits from Europeans (but not Indians) and lent money at the Company's standard rate of 12 per cent. Europeans with money to invest bought East India Company bonds, which were redeemable in England. Since these were not available to Indians, except by proxy, the old system of money-lending and borrowing persisted, as it does today, particularly in rural communities.

From the mid-eighteenth century, there are records in all three Presidency cities of post offices acting as a depot for both receiving post and despatching it, using the well-established system of cross-country dak runners, men carrying letters and small parcels who were accompanied by a drummer to scare off wild animals. The Company made attempts to regulate the transmission of mail in its own territories, but these were not formalised until the Indian Post Office Act of 1837, which allowed the government to grant licences to suitable people to convey letters by post from place to place.[8] Income was generated by levying inland postage duties, and postage could be paid either on receipt of the letter or on its posting. Curiously, it was found necessary to add a clause which hints that no new convenience comes without its drawbacks:

> The person to whom [a letter] is delivered shall not be bound to pay the postage if he returns the letter or packet unopened, but if he opens the same, he shall be bound to pay the postage due thereon; provided always, that if the letter or packet shall appear to have been maliciously sent for the purpose of annoying the person to whom it is directed, the Post Master General ... shall remit the said postage.[9]

Letters arriving by ship (steam postage, as it was called) meant an extra levy for the recipients, but at the same time there was a long list of people, including bishops and judges, who were exempt from paying postage on their correspondence, which led to criticism from the general public. If a letter remained uncollected at a post office for more than 3 months, it was sent to a designated 'dead-letter' general post office in one of the three Presidencies, and a list of unclaimed post was published in the local Official Gazette. If it still remained unclaimed after 18 months, the postmaster could open it and the contents, if valuable, would be paid into the government treasury. Once the idea of postage stamps was introduced in 1852, indicating that a letter had been paid for at source, this led to competition among different areas as each issued their own stamps; the Red Scinde Dawk, as it is known, is equivalent to the British Penny Black in its rarity.

Early European travellers in the subcontinent were limited in their choice of overnight accommodation, which is why the majority travelled by boat, anchoring at night. Caravanserais on the outskirts of cities provided shelter for travellers on horseback or cart, as we have seen, but the idea of a more sophisticated urban establishment open to the public was slow to develop. The earliest hotel was probably Spence's in central Calcutta, established in 1830. Government dak-bungalows in rural areas were set up a decade later, and, as the name suggests, they were connected with the dak runners or postal carriers, although the bungalows were used as staging posts where mail was handed over rather than providing overnight accommodation for the runners. In fact, it was almost exclusively Europeans who occupied the dak-bungalows, apart from Indian servants accompanying travellers.

Clubs became an almost essential element of social life in British India and catered for all classes of European society, from tea planters to diplomats. Women, however, were initially excluded, and when they were admitted they were often confined to certain rooms. The Bengal Club in Calcutta was the prototype, established in 1827, because there was at the time nowhere 'for those who constitute the society of Calcutta ... where they can spend an idle half hour agreeably'. Its first members were senior military and administrative men, and its constitution was modelled on that of the Oriental Club which had opened 3 years earlier in London. The Bengal Club also provided sleeping rooms for 'mofussil [upcountry] members visiting Calcutta'.[10]

In its exclusion of women, these early clubs resembled secular gatherings of Indian men, who would meet at each other's houses for cultural functions like *mushairas* (poetry sessions) or at specific areas to watch cock fights, animal fights or *pehlwani* (wrestling). Women were also excluded from Freemasons' lodges, of course, but they were welcomed at theatres, with a few even allowed on stage as performers. There was a vibrant tradition of play-acting in the Hindu community, with annual performances of *Ramlila* based on the Ramayana story but these were held in open, public spaces, not in a dedicated building. The assembly rooms were where Europeans of both sexes could meet and socialise, enjoying dancing and charity-raising events, as well as serving as a town hall for civic functions. Europe shops were self-explanatory, selling imported alcohol and a wide selection of expensive tinned goods, as well as patent medicines and laudanum, which was widely used as an analgesic. The Company *bagh* was another meeting place for both sexes, where walks were taken in the evenings, often to the music of a regimental band playing popular tunes from the bandstand.[11]

A typical White Town in India thus formalised a number of important functions like banking, postal communication, entertainment and the reception of travellers. Some of these were taken up by the Black Town, particularly post offices, where the expense of sending letters and packets was outweighed by the convenience of being able to communicate across long distances with friends, relatives and trading partners. For illiterate people, there were scribes who sat outside the post offices, ready to write letters for those who could not. By the mid-twentieth century, the scribes had been replaced by typists with small, portable typewriters.

In residential areas, the fashion for over-large town houses like those along Chowringhee in Calcutta had lessened, due in part to changing habits among the Europeans. It was now far less easy to make a fortune in India than it had once been. Reforms and restrictions in Company practices meant that the days when a 'nabob' like Francis Sykes could go home with a fortune were gone. There was also more of an expectation that one would indeed go home as transport links improved and journey times diminished with the arrival of steamships. Robert Pott's great house at Afzalbagh, the payment of bribes to his predecessor John d'Oyly and his comparatively early death at thirty-eight in India were seen as outdated relics of the previous century. The development of the hill stations meant that more time could now be spent in a healthier climate and led to less emotional and financial investment in the Indian plains by ordinary Britons. Coupled with the revival in Christian beliefs of humility and modesty emphasised by the Evangelical movement together with the arrival of missionaries, an overly extravagant house became somewhat anachronistic.

The *Calcutta Review* noted in 1845 that there had been 'a very striking reduction of the average mortality' as jungles were cleared, marshes drained 'and thick walled, well-raised houses erected, whilst simultaneously with these important changes, sobriety and moderation have steadily advanced'.[12] The raucous eighteenth century had given way to the sober nineteenth. Company officials now were moved to different stations on average every 3 years, so it was no longer sensible to build one's own house but to hire a bungalow instead. Accommodation was provided for some posts, although this could vary in quality. The engineer John Sprot found on his transfer to Nasirabad that he had been allocated 'a small bungalow with one large room, two very small ones, and a "zenana khana" behind, into which the bedroom opened, the walls being about ten feet high ... three sides of the house were surrounded by a wide-raised verandah', which was enclosed so his staff and draughtsmen could work there.[13] This was bachelors' accommodation; had Sprot been married, he would have had to hire somewhere larger and more suitable and pay for it out of his own pocket.

There are few written or painted descriptions of these rented houses, because their inhabitants did not feel the same kind of attachment to them. The days when Lady Impey's bedroom would be charmingly depicted by an Indian artist, down to the very details of her dressing table ornaments, were gone, and there is a noticeable gap of interior views until early photographs appear. Only George Atkinson's illustrated book *'Curry and Rice' on Forty Plates; or, the Ingredients of Social Life At 'Our Station' in India* (1859) gives some idea of the type of furnishings which may have been customary, including large *punkahs* and the familiar and comfortable *muda* chair of woven cane in a bedroom.

One noticeable and important change in houses was the introduction of window glass. Small pieces of coloured glass were sometimes used for decorative effect in local houses, but the idea of large panes of plain glass was something new and foreign. By the early nineteenth century, the majority of European-style town houses were glazed, as were many of the humbler bungalows. This in turn affected the design of buildings and had implications for security, ventilation, light, privacy and health. Exterior walls could now be fenestrated and internal doors glazed. It also, subtly, altered European attitudes to India, which could now be experienced at one remove, without the inconvenience of smells, noise, insects, dust, wind and rain, but which then required an internal cooling system of ceiling-mounted *punkahs* and thermantidotes. Glass windows in imported carriages allowed passengers to view the passing scenery in close-up and comparative safety, thus disengaging them from the street bustle, beggars and eager shopkeepers.

There were problems with importing glass, of course, not just of breakages in transit but of getting the glass cut to fit the frames and the tendency of even well-seasoned wood to warp and crack the glass. But these difficulties were balanced out by the cheapness of the glass and its ready availability. Glass sold at Fatehgarh and Lucknow, though imported through Calcutta a thousand miles distant, was little more expensive than the wholesale price in London: 8x11-inch panes could be bought for a rupee each, and the largest size, 20x30 inches, for Rs3 each.[14] These were of course transparent glass panes, but there were other kinds of glass too, including opaline, or opaque glass, which is produced by adding different substances, such as chalk. Opaline objects had been produced since the seventeenth century in Europe, mainly for decorative ornaments like vases, but it was also used for clock faces on towers, where the face was lit up by a light source behind it.

Once this use for opaque glass was realised, clock towers became fashionable, both as a focal point of multi-storeyed buildings or as stand-alone constructions. Gas lamps were used to illuminate the faces, until they were replaced by electric lights. Clock towers were often prominent in White Towns, sometimes as part of a church tower, as was the case with Christ Church, Shimla, or sometimes freestanding in a public place. By the end of the nineteenth century, clock towers had sprouted all over India, not just in British India but in the capitals of princely states too, like Udaipur in Rajputana. They were known locally as *ghantaghar*, literally 'bell house', where periods of time had been marked by striking a metal bell. As this method of time-keeping fell out of use, the word came to mean a clock tower.

Time is a surprisingly emotive issue. Even in a small country like England, clocks were not synchronised until railway trains started to run across county boundaries, when it was found that Bristol time, for example, was eleven minutes behind London time. There were protests against the synchronisation of time, with towns continuing to use local time until the late 1840s, when Greenwich Mean Time was introduced as the standard time. Variations in the Indian subcontinent were obviously much more pronounced, with local times tied to the rising and setting sun. It was not until 1870 that 'Madras time' was agreed to be the standard time for the whole subcontinent, with a meridian line passing through the Madras observatory.[15] Bombay, however, was the last to hold out, and for decades 'Bombay time' remained about thirty minutes behind the rest of India.

This was simple stuff compared to the introduction of the twelve-hour clock used by Europeans in India, where the ancient unit of time had been the *pahar*. One *pahar* was about three hours long, and there were eight *pahars* in a day and a night. At the spring and autumn equinox, the *pahars* were of equal length, but during the summer the daytime *pahars* increased while night-time *pahars* decreased. The term *do pahar* is still a synonym for the afternoon, though other named *pahars* are no longer used. Change did come, although not without resistance and there are unreferenced reports of rebel *sepoys* shooting at clock towers during the Uprising of 1857.[16] This would not be surprising. Clock towers were one of the most visible signs of foreign occupation in British India, a barrier to a more leisurely way of life and also, if one wishes to stretch the analogy, a white (clock) face lording it over the humble Indian townscape.

If time itself differed throughout the subcontinent, then so did the calendar. Hindu calendars, of which there were many attached to various regions and sects, were based on both lunar and solar cycles. Some are retained today for religious ceremonies and astrological forecasts, while the subcontinent has otherwise adopted the Western (Gregorian) calendar. Although the Hindu population greatly outnumbers that of the Muslim and did so throughout the Company period, Mughal rule meant that the Islamic (*hijri*) calendar was used in official correspondence and other written documents. The extensive use of Persian by Company officials before the nineteenth century meant they became familiar with the *hijri* calendar, and it was reasonably easy to transpose dates, although there were variables according to when the new moon was sighted, which affected the length of the last month of the calendar and thus the start of the new Islamic year.[17] This is why the beginning of Ramadan is not fixed to a specific date, like Christmas, but moves around over the years. Tipu Sultan, the ruler of Mysore, attempted to reconcile the lunar and solar years to produce the *mauludi* calendar, but this did not exist long enough to establish itself and died with him in 1799.

Britain was late in adopting the Gregorian calendar which had been in use in Europe since the sixteenth century, replacing the previous Julian calendar. An Act of Parliament in 1750 introduced the new style calendar which was to come into force 2 years later, giving people time to plan ahead. But it has previously been unclear whether and when this was adopted in British India. However, an examination of the burial register in St John's Church, Calcutta confirms that the Company was aware of the change and had informed its officials. There were two burials on 1 September 1752. The following day, 2 September, John Richmond, the Sixth Mate of the ship *Godolphin*, was buried. Then there is nothing until burials begin again on 14 September, when the letters 'N.S.' are added in the margin, standing for 'New Style': Wednesday, 2 September 1752 was immediately followed by Thursday, 14 September.

One could argue that no deaths occurred in Calcutta during the missing 11 days, but this would be most unlikely given the high annual death toll at the end of the monsoon season and the number of daily deaths in August, the preceding month.[18] Whether information about the new style calendar reached all Company officials in the subcontinent, and whether all of them understood the implications and acted on them, will probably never be known. There was also an added tweak to the reforms that moved the end of the British fiscal year from 25 March, Lady's Day, to 5 April by adding on the 11 days, which is why the British tax year begins on 6 April. However, this was not replicated in British India, where the fiscal year had traditionally run from the beginning of May to the end of April. The tax year in India today begins on 1 April.

There were many other anomalies that the Company sought to bring into line, to manage and to control. Everything in this vast country was different: not only its customs and languages, about which nothing could be done, but its calendars, currencies, weights, measures and distances. All of these were gradually being standardised, eliminating the former rational units that were based on what was to hand.[19] The *kos*, which, as we have seen, varied in length throughout India, was overtaken by the standard English mile, which in turn was superseded by kilometres. In 1840, the East India Company's one-rupee silver coin was issued from the three Presidency Mints bearing the head of Queen Victoria. This was an attempt to standardise an impressive array of local coins, including the Bengal sicca rupee—which diminished in value as it grew older—the Bombay rupee and the Arcot (Madras) rupee, all of which differed slightly in value. Then there was the gold mohur, the Madras (star) pagoda, the French Porto Novo pagoda and the Tranquebar dollar, as well as other trading currencies from Mocha, Batavia and China.[20] It was a rich, if confusing, mix, particularly when goods were traded across the country and different weights and values had to be calculated. These anomalies, as the Company saw them, were either reconciled or in some cases simply abolished, though some Indians perversely continued to use them. The term 'imperial measures' should not be taken lightly.

The passage of time led not only to observable changes like the standardisation of coinage and the new buildings with new functions erected by Company engineers in an altered landscape, but also to less visible shifts in attitude among the British in India, some good and some less good. Two examples conclude our study of empire-building. The first, and most important, was the changing view on slavery.

In 1833, Parliament passed the Slavery Abolition Act which excluded 'Territories in the Possession of the East India Company'. The reasons why India, as the largest Company possession, was omitted are complex and had much to do with the loose definitions of slavery and bonded labour. We have seen that Sir William Jones, founder of the Asiatick Society, had a slave boy, which he justified by stating that 'nearly everyone' in Calcutta at the time (1785) had slaves too.[21] These were often children who had been sent down the Hooghly by boat in the hope of saving them from famine further upriver. It was a pragmatic solution, of sorts, and the Company was reluctant to interfere. The *Calcutta Gazette* carried notices offering rewards for absconded slaves rather as one might advertise for a lost dog.

But as the Evangelical movement grew in Britain, the Board of Control was put under pressure to act. The Atlantic slave trade was condemned, but not the trade that saw Africans shipped to India by Arab traders. Distinctions were drawn between the African slave trade and the domestic slavery tolerated by the Company, and in fact Henry Prinsep, secretary to the government of India, complained that 'if Negro slavery had never existed as a topic to be preached upon in England and Europe' then slavery in India would never have become subject to Parliamentary law.[22] So it was not until the Indian Penal Code of 1860 was passed by the British government that it became an offence to own a slave in India.

The Company was alert to the fact that African children were still being shipped into India by Arab slave traders, who have escaped the criticism given to their counterparts in the West, and in the early 1850s it set up an African Asylum in the heart of Bombay at Sonapur. The Asylum had connections with the Church Missionary Society and was funded in part by the British government. Visiting inspectors submitted detailed reports in order to obtain a further grant.[23] Before the Asylum was established, freed child slaves had been placed in the charge of the Bombay Police department, where the commissioner of police said it had been 'a source of much anxiety ... to find the means of suitably disposing of such Children'. He welcomed the African Asylum as being 'most useful to the Government in relieving it of the charge of children of tender age liberated from time to time' from slavery. Now they could be placed safely in an institution 'where they will receive a suitable education to enable them to earn their livelihood, and also receive such moral and religious instruction as will tend to make them good members of the Community'. In 1856, he added, seven children who had been 'imported into Kurrachee in a state of slavery' were sent to the Bombay Asylum, and the Arab slave trader who had imported them was fined Rs1,500, which was paid to the Asylum for their upkeep.[24]

The school inspector found twenty-nine boy pupils enrolled in the Asylum on 2 March 1859. Of these, seven were absent because they had been sent to be vaccinated. It was reported that some of the boys spoke a dialect called Mozambic, while the rest spoke Somali. The twenty-three girl pupils, who were taught separately, were mainly Abyssinian and Somali, which showed that the children had been trafficked from different parts of Africa. They were all being taught Hindustani or Marathi, as well as English, because India would be their home now. The girls were taught needlework, cooking and other domestic skills, while the boys were encouraged to play athletic games, including cricket, and were found apprenticeships so they could support themselves.[25]

While some British attitudes had softened (and there was often a gap between Company policy and public opinion), others had hardened. The initial sense of curiosity about India and respect for its people, so evident in *Asiatick Researches*, had long since disappeared. Familiarity had indeed bred contempt. The wearing of 'native dress' by Europeans may seem a trivial example but it emphasises the shift in perceptions. Eighteenth-century British women stuck firmly to

Western dress, apart from wearing 'turbans' or colourful headgear. (This was in spite of a warning by 'Hindoo Stuart' that the iron busks in their corsets ran the risk of being struck by lightning, and that they would look better in saris.) At the same time, European men were happy to be painted wearing Indian clothes, and there is a particularly fine portrait by Sir Joshua Reynolds of Captain John Foote, captain of a Company ship, in full Mughal dress, wearing a *patka* (waist scarf) and turban. This was a favourite portrait of Reynolds, and a comparison of the dress (which still survives), shows how accurately he captured the gold-thread embroidery of the semi-transparent muslin.[26] The wearer died in 1768; 50 years later he would have been thought eccentric, and by the 1850s he would have been shunned by British society.

There is also the poignant story of a retired soldier and later Company man, Captain Savary, who was invalided out of the Bengal Native Infantry but decided to remain in India. He married an Indian woman and converted to Islam, adopting the comfortable local dress of a respectable Muslim. Because he spoke Urdu and had integrated into Muslim society in Lucknow, where he lived with his wife, he was sometimes called upon by the British Resident to find out what was going on in the old city. But Savary offended successive Residents by turning up to the smart British compound in 'native dress'. His usefulness in relating the Indian point of view to out-of-touch Company officials did not make up for what he wore and what he believed in. (Unfortunately, neither his dress nor his faith could save him during the Uprising and he was murdered by rebel *sepoys*.)

By contrast, many Anglo-Indian men had adopted a particular kind of dress that unconsciously reflected their mixed heritage. It was largely Western, but with an Indian coat, a 'smoking cap' rather like a fez and lace-up shoes to distinguish them from their fellow countrymen who wore *chappals* (sandals).[27] Their women, however, chose to wear Western dress, including the fashionable crinoline. Dress was a distinctive way of declaring one's identity, and while this had not seemed particularly important at the beginning of our study in 1690 when there were only a small number of Britons in the subcontinent, it certainly was by the end as they drew themselves apart from the local people. The term 'gone native' to describe a

Briton who had adopted Indian dress or Indian ways remained an insult well into the 1960s, when the hippie invasion saw a complete reversal of this notion.

In the difficult task of summarising changing British attitudes towards the subcontinent, it would be fair to say that the sense of wonder and enquiry exemplified by the Asiatick Society in its early days had been lost by 1800. As the new century dawned, Indians were increasingly seen as characters in an antique land, unchanging and unwilling to change. It was one of the Company's most serious errors to underestimate the desire for progress among the people it ruled. Nor did it do much to exploit indigenous talent. It was also slow to recognise and adopt technological innovations from the West that were promoted by enterprising individuals in the face of indifference and penny-pinching. Yet somehow modern India was being constructed, bit by bit, in jerky and uneven steps, and often in greedy and self-serving ways. Nevertheless, the foundations had been laid. The East India Company often got things wrong; but it got some things right too.

GLOSSARY

arrack	alcoholic drink made from fermented sugar cane, rice, etc.
aumeen	supervisor, usually of building/construction
ayah	Indian nanny employed by Europeans
bakhshi	paymaster
bund	steep embankment
cha'oni	cantonment
charbagh	garden laid out in four quarters bisected with paths
chunam	stucco, made from mixing lime, brick dust, sand and a binding agent, often molasses
coolies	labourers, porters
dak/dawk	post
darshan	granting the view of a ruler or holy person
desi	local, or country
diwani	grant from the emperor that allowed the Company to administer the collection of land revenue
durbar	the emperor's court, or a provincial court, it later came to mean the act of paying homage to a ruler
factory	trading place where the factors, or clerks worked at listing exports, imports and shipping, also the warehouse for storing goods
filature	factory for processing silkworm cocoons
farman	written decree, issuing orders or granting permissions
feringhees	foreigners, non-Indians, probably from the word 'frankish', meaning European
ganj	area with shops
Gentoos	Hindus

GLOSSARY

ghantaghar	clock tower
ghat	landing area next to a river, often with steps leading down to the water
godown	warehouse, storage building
gomastas	middleman, someone who negotiates between the producer of goods and the buyer
harkaras	messengers, sometimes assistants, often travelling over long distances
jadu-ghar	literally 'house of magic', the name given to Freemasons' Lodges
jagirdar	someone who holds a jagir, a piece of land, in trust from the emperor or his deputy
jangal	uncultivated land
kaccha	raw, or unbaked, when applied to bricks
kacheri	courthouse
kos	unit of distance, varying across different parts of the subcontinent
lakh	hundred thousand
madrasa	school, now associated with Muslim theological scholars
mansabdar	man who could provide 5,000 soldiers for the emperor
mistri	carpenter, skilled workman
Moors	eighteenth-century word for Muslims
mushaira	poetry session
nawab	deputy for the emperor, later a title for a provincial ruler
nawab nazim	title of the Bengal rulers
nawab wazir	title of the Awadh rulers
pahar	unit of time, about three hours
pahari	of the hills
peons	messengers, foot servants
pir	Muslim saint or holy man
pukka	ripe, proper, when applied to kiln-baked bricks
qila	fort
ryot	peasant, someone who tills the land

GLOSSARY

sati	the act of burning a dead man's widow on a funeral pyre
sepoy	Indian soldier
serai	lodging place for travelling people and animals
shikari	hunter
subahdar	man who administers a subah, or province of the Mughal Empire
tarras	floor made with pottery and clay
thagi	the act of robbing and murdering travellers, carried out by thags (thugs)
thana	police station
zamindar	landholder or land-owner

NOTES

INTRODUCTION

1. See Chapter 3 for analysis of the Bhowanipore Burial Registers.
2. The celebrated model of Tipu's Tyger in the V&A Museum is supposed to represent the death of the commander-in-chief's son.
3. Tipu had developed effective artillery rockets which were later copied in England by William Congreve.
4. See Holden Furber *John Company at Work: A Study Of European Expansion In India In The Late Eighteenth Century*, Harvard University Press, 1948, pp. 23–5.
5. Edmund Burke's speech on Mr Fox's India Bill, Parliamentary Papers, 1 December 1783.
6. See Rosie Llewellyn-Jones, *A Fatal Friendship: The Nawabs, the British and the City of Lucknow*, OUP Delhi, 1985, p vi.
7. The embassy was withdrawn following the Soviet invasion and the compound and building handed to Pakistan. It was destroyed in September 1995 during anti-Pakistan riots.
8. Little Calcutta, see Chapter 2.
9. The most serious looting that took place was when the British regained control of the wealthy city of Lucknow in March 1858 and sacked the king's palace in a 2-day orgy.
10. The fourth *nawab* of Awadh, Asaf-ud-daula, was notorious for demolishing his citizens' houses in Lucknow. See *A Fatal Friendship*, pp. 197–8.
11. See Michael Fisher, *The Travels of Dean Mahomet*, University of California Press, 1997.
12. Tanks, also known as cisterns, are filled by rainwater and surface water, wells are excavated to reach water underground.
13. Kambalposh's book went through several editions in Urdu and was published in English in 2014 under the title *Between Worlds: The Travels of Yusuf Khan Kambalposh*, OUP Delhi, translated by Mushirul Hasan and Nishat Zaidi. There are a number of unfortunate mis-transliterations of English names and superfluous footnotes.

1. MERCHANTS OR SOLDIERS?

1. *Diary and Consultation Book for Affairs of the Rt. Hon'ble English East India Company*, 24 August 1690. These books were kept at each of the Presidency towns, Madras, Bombay and Calcutta. Quoted in Cotton, H.E.A., *Calcutta Old and New; A Historical and Descriptive Handbook to the City*, revised edition, 1980, p. 7.

2. *Armenian Holy Church of Nazareth*, twenty-five-page booklet, no author/publisher given, from the Church at 2, Armenian Street, Kolkata, 700 001.

3. Cotton, op. cit., p. 9.

4. When Job Charnock's successor at Cossimbazar, William Hedges, went to pay his respects to the new *nawab* at Murshidabad, he was forced to hand over 30,000 rupees to get the ships of the season released.

5. See Frederick Danvers, *The Portuguese in India*, Vol. II, 1966, p. 247. Danvers does not make the connection between 'the town of Golin' and Hughli.

6. Milo Beach and Ebba Koch (eds), *King of the World: The Padshahnama*, 1997, p. 59.

7. Joseph Tieffenthaler, *Description historique et géographique de l'Inde, 1786–88*, Vol. I, p. 455.

8. *The Trading Post of the Dutch East India Company, Bengal*, painted by Hendrik van Schuylenburgh, 1665. Rijksmuseum, Amsterdam.

9. See E.W.C. Sandes, *The Military Engineer in India*, Vol. I, revised edition, 1997, p. 32.

10. *Map of Fort Gustavus at Chinsura*, from the VOC Archives (OBP Bengalen, 1743) at the National Archives, The Hague, Netherlands.

11. The dimensions of the first Fort William were: North Wall, 113 yards; South Wall, 161 yards; East and West Walls, 236 yards each.

12. Charles Wilson (ed.), *Old Fort William in Bengal, a Selection of official Documents Dealing With Its History*, 1906, p. 13.

13. Sandes, op. cit., p. 36.

14. Titles of officials changed throughout the early years of the East India Company. When Fort William was declared a Presidency in 1699, the chief official became the President. Before that, he was referred to as Agent, or Right Worshipful Agent. The first British Governor of Bengal was Sir Robert Clive, appointed in 1758.

15. Wilson, op. cit., p. 23.

16. Dihi Calcutta, or Dee Calcutta, refers to the central area of the town around Fort William mainly inhabited by the British. The term was in use as late as the 1780s. Its original meaning is 'a village', harking back to the three villages of Sutanuti, Calcutta and Govindpore rented by Charnock.

17. Wilson, op. cit., p. 39.

18. Sandes, op. Cit, p. 33. The term 'Moor' was a generic description for Muslims. Hindus were referred to as 'Gentoos', a corruption of the Portuguese for 'a gentile' or heathen.

19. Wilson, op. cit., p. 15.

20. W.W. Hunter, *A History of British India*, 1912, p. 245, footnote 1.

21. Hunter, op. cit., p. 242.

22. Ghulam Husain Salim, *Riyazu-s-Salatin*, trans. Maulavi Abdus Salam, 1902, p. 260.

23. See the so-called 'Child's War', an attempt by Sir Josiah Child, Governor of the Court of Directors in London, to interfere with negotiations between the Company in Bengal and the emperor. English possessions were seized by Aurangzeb, and the Company suffered a humiliating climb down and had to make grovelling concessions before trading rights were re-established.

24. Wilson, op. cit., p. 46.

25. Ibid., p. 45.

26. This was not an uncommon device used to make a structure seem stronger than it actually was. The idea was to imitate the granite from which the Red Fort at Delhi was constructed.

27. Wilson, op. cit., p. 57.

28. Ibid., p. 82.

29. Ibid., p. 62.

30. Ibid., p. 90.

31. Subhas Chandra Mukhopadhyay, *British Residents at the Darbar of Bengal Nawabs at Mushidabad, 1757–1772*, Delhi, n.d., p. 31.

32. Sarkar, Jadunath (ed.), *The History of Bengal*, Vol. II, 1948, pp. 411–19.

33. John Zephaniah Holwell, *India Tracts by Mr Holwell, and Friends*, 1764, pp. 139–41. The administration of Calcutta at this period was divided between two *zamindars*—the White Zamindar, John Holwell, and his *bête noir*, the Black Zamindar, Govindaram Mitra.

34. Holwell listed the following districts when estimating the population: Dihi Calcutta, Sutanuti, Govindpore, Bazar Calcutta, Jan Nagar, Baag Bazar, Lal Bazar, Santose Bazar. In addition, there were four districts not directly under the Company but within the town: Simlea, Molunga, Mirzapore and Hogulcourea.

35. Wilson, op. cit., p. 136.

36. Ibid., p. 135.

37. The temple, parts of which still exist, is commonly known as the Black Pagoda, not because of its colour but because it was built by the Black Zamindar, Govindaram Mitra.

38. Jorasanko is today best known for the large family house of Rabindranath Tagore, which is now a museum.

39. Ives, Edward *A Voyage From England to India in the Year 1754* ..., 1773, p. 91.
40. The best account of the events leading to the capture of Calcutta by Siraj-ud-daula and the fate of those in Fort William is by Noel Barber, *The Black Hole of Calcutta: A Reconstruction*, 1965. See also Partha Chatterjee, *The Black Hole of Empire*, 2012, which takes as its starting point the memorial erected by John Holwell to his dead companions.
41. Ives, op. cit., p. 110.

2. ENGINEERS, ARCHITECTS AND BUILDERS

1. There is a twentieth-century parallel in St Martin's Garrison Church, New Delhi, designed by Arthur Shoosmith. Completed in 1931, it is a fortress-like defensible building in the military cantonments.
2. Charles Wilson (ed.), *Old Fort William in Bengal: A Selection of Official Documents Dealing With Its History*, London, 1906, p. 171.
3. Ibid., p. 172.
4. Ibid., p. 178.
5. *A Plan of Calcutta and the Adjacent Country, by Foresti and Ollifres Drawn in 1742*, British Library K. Top. 115.40.
6. E. W.C. Sandes, *The Military Engineer in India*, Vol. I, revised edition, 1997, p. 54.
7. Wilson, op. cit., p. 244.
8. Ibid., p. 205.
9. Sandes, op. cit., p. 90.
10. Wilson, op. cit., p. 115.
11. Ibid., Captain Barker to the Board at Fort William, 13 June 1757, p. 123.
12. Ibid., p. 124.
13. Ibid., William Frankland's Minute, 20 June 1757, p. 125.
14. Court of Directors Minutes, 9 March 1763, quoted in Michael Mark Chrimes, 'Architectural dilettantes: Construction professionals in British India 1600–1910. Part 1. 1600–1860: The age of the dilettante,' *Construction History*, vol. 30, no. 2, 2015, pp. 15–44.
15. Home Department, Public Branch, 1 December 1783. No. 23, National Archives, New Delhi.
16. 'Translation of Newton's *Principia* into Arabic Under the Aegis of the East India Company: A Rumour Turning into a Myth,' K. Razi Naqvi. https://www.researchgate.net/publication/351120100.
17. As a young engineer, John Sprot (later Lieutenant General) was ordered to start a 'famine road, for the purpose only of "keeping the wolf from the door" of the starving population' near Delhi in 1856. He was given a

grant 'to expend on these poor people', the work taking 4 or 5 months until the monsoon, when the labourers returned to their villages. John Sprot, *Incidents and Anecdotes in the Life of Lieut-General Sprot, etc.* [Told by himself], Vol. I, 1906, pp. 49–50.

18. Sandes, op. cit., p. 80.

19. Thomas Williamson, *The East India Vade-Mecum*, Vol. II, 1810, p. 213.

20. Bengal Judicial Proceedings, August 1825–October 1826. No. 62. E. de la Combe to W.B. Bayley, 18 August 1825. India Office Library and Records.

21. Ibid., No. 65. C. Mouat to J. Craigie, 8 September 1825. India Office Library and Records.

22. Owain Edwards. 'Captain Thomas Williamson of India,' *Modern Asian Studies*, vol. 14, no. 4, 1980, pp. 673–82.

23. Williamson, op. cit., Vol. II, p. 6.

24. Ibid., Vol. I, p. 515.

25. William Dalrymple, *White Mughals: Love and Betrayal in Eighteenth-century India*, p. 351.

26. Alfred Spencer (ed.), *Memoirs of William Hickey (1790–1809)*, Vol. IV, 1948, p. 133.

27. Wilson, op. cit., p. 226.

28. Purna Ch. Majumdar, *The Musnud of Murshidabad (1704–1904)*, 1905, p. 179.

29. K.M. Mohsin, 'Murshidabad in the eighteenth century,' in *The City in South Asia*, Kenneth Ballhatchet and John Harrison (eds), Routledge, 1980, p. 82.

30. Rosie Llewellyn-Jones, *A Very Ingenious Man: Claude Martin in Early Colonial India*, Oxford University Press, 1992, p. 55.

31. Bisheshwar Prasad (ed.), *Fort William India House Correspondence, 1770–1772*, Vol. VI, p. 64.

32. Jan Lucassen, 'Working at the Ichapur Gunpowder Factory in the 1790s,' *Indian Historical Review*, Sage Publications. Part 1 published in Vol. 39 (Issue 1), Part II published in Vol. 39 (Issue 2), 2012.

33. Moumita Chowdhury, 'Production of gunpowder in early modern India, 1757–1849,' *Journal of History*, Vidyasagar University, West Bengal, Vol 5, 2016–17, p. 80.

34. Ibid., p. 76.

35. Stephen Wilson, 'Reports and documents of the East India Company in regard to the culture and manufacture of cotton-wool, raw silk and indigo in India,' *Journal of the House of Lords*, Vol. 62, 13 May 1830, pp. 1065–8.

36. Karolina Hutková, *The British Silk Connection: The English East India Company's Silk Enterprise in Bengal, 1757–1812*. PhD thesis, Department of History, University of Warwick, 2015, p. 109, et seq.

37. Bengal Public Consultations, 3 January–26 May 1774. Report dated 9 May 1774. India Office Library and Records.

38. Prasad, op. cit., pp. 14–15, 66.

39. Bengal Public Consultations, 3 January–26 May 1774. 9 May 1774 quoting letter dated 30 October 1771, India Office Library and Records.

40. Ibid., letter from Claude Martin to James Wiss, dated 14 July 1773.

41. *Reports and Documents Connected With the Proceedings of the East-India Company in Regard to the Culture and Manufacture of Cotton-Wool, Raw Silk and Indigo in India*, 1836, p. xi.

42. James Rennell to Revd Gilbert Burrington, 31 August 1765. Home Misc. Series. Letters of Major James Rennell, 1758–1785. India Office Library and Records.

43. Wilson, op. cit., pp. 1067–8.

44. H.N. Sinha (ed.), *Fort William India House Correspondence, 1757–1759*, Vol. II, 1957, p. lvii.

45. John Sharples, 'Calcutta Mint, Medal & Coin Makers, Kolkata, India, 1757–1952,' in Museums Victoria Collections, 2005. https://collections.museumsvictoria.com.au/articles/1879.

46. Sue Tungate, *Matthew Boulton and the Soho Mint: Copper to Customer*. PhD thesis, Department of Modern History, University of Birmingham, 2010, p. 210; see also Chapter 3, 'The Technology of Coining,' pp. 99–184.

47. Sharples, op. cit.

48. *Grace's Guide to British Industrial History*. Institution of Civil Engineers: Obituaries for 1861. William Nairn Forbes. www.gracesguide.co.uk.

3.   THE SPIRIT OF ENLIGHTENMENT

1.   John Ford, 'Travelling With Claude Martin,' in *The Estate of Major General Claude Martin at Lucknow: An Indian Inventory*, Llewellyn-Jones, Rosie (ed.), Cambridge Scholars Publishing, 2021, pp. 29–30.

2.   Lord Teignmouth, *Memoirs of the Life, Writings, and Correspondence of Sir William Jones*, 1807, pp. 400–1.

3.   O.P. Kejariwal, *The Asiatic Society of Bengal and the Discovery of India's Past, 1784–1838*, Oxford University Press India, 1999 p. 35.

4.   Ibid., p. 54.

5.   Teignmouth, op. cit., p. 417.

6.   Ibid., p. 418.

7.   Thomas Hardwicke, 'Narrative of a Journey to Sirinagur,' in *Asiatick Researches: or, Transactions of the Society Instituted in Bengal for Inquiring Into the History and Antiquities … of Asia*, vol. vi, no. ix, 1801, pp. 309–81.

8. Ibid., p. 371.

9. See William Dalrymple (ed.), *Forgotten Masters: Indian Painting for the East India Company*, Bloomsbury Publishing, 2019.

10. Richard Axelby, 'Calcutta Botanic Garden and the colonial re-ordering of the Indian environment,' *Archives of Natural History*, pub. Society for the History of Natural History, Edinburgh University Press, vol. 35, no. 1, 2008, pp. 150–63.

11. George King, *Annals of the Royal Botanic Garden Calcutta*, vol. iv, 1893, p. vii.

12. Bisheshwar Prasad (ed.), *Fort William India House Correspondence, 1770–1772*, vol. vi, National Archives, New Delhi, 1960, p. 476.

13. King, op. cit., vol. iv, pp. ix–x.

14. R.K. Kochhar, 'Madras Observatory: buildings and instruments,' *Bulletin of Astronomical Society India*, vol. 13, pp. 287–302.

15. D.B. Diskalker, 'Foundation of an observatory at Lucknow,' *Journal of the United Provinces Historical Society*, vol. x, pt. 1, 9–10 July 1937, pp. 10–11.

16. For the fuller story, see Rosie Llewellyn-Jones, *A Fatal Friendship: The Nawabs, the British and the City of Lucknow*, 1985, pp. 65–74.

17. India Political Consultations. H. Torrens, Political Secretary to Government of India to J. Caulfield, Acting Resident at Lucknow, 22 June 1840, India Office Library and Records.

18. Matthew Edney, *Mapping an Empire: The Geographical Construction of British India, 1765–1843*, University of Chicago Press, 1997, p. 24.

19. William Lambton, 'An account of the trigonometrical operations in crossing the peninsular of India and connecting Fort St. George with Mangalore,' *Asiatick Researches*, vol. x, 1811, pp. 290–384.

20. R.K. Kochhar, 'Science in British India. II. The Indian response,' *Current Science*, vol. 64, no. 1, 10 January 1993, pp. 53–62.

21. Gilchrist's stated dislike of Indians did not stop him from fathering a number of children by Indian women. Three of his daughters accompanied him home to Edinburgh where they all married well.

22. *The Indian Vocabulary to Which Is Prefixed the Forms of Impeachment*. The British Library online catalogue gives Weeden Butler as the author, but there is nothing to indicate this in the obituary of the Revd Butler published in *The Gentleman's Magazine*, vol. 93, pt 2, 1823.

23. John Borthwick Gilchrist, *A Dictionary, English and Hindoostanee, in Which the Words Are Marked With Their Distinguishing Initials; as Hinduwee, Arabic, and Persian etc.*, 1786, p. ii.

24. See Bernard S. Cohn, *Colonialism and Its Forms of Knowledge*, University of Princeton Press, 1996.

25. Alfred Spencer (ed.), *Memoirs of William Hickey (1775–1809)*, Vol. II, 1948, pp. 173–5.

26. For a detailed history of the newspaper, see Andrew Otis, *Hicky's Bengal Gazette: The Untold Story of India's First Newspaper*, Tranquebar Press, 2018.

27. Kathleen Blechynden, *Calcutta Past and Present*, 1905, p. 158.

28. Kochhar, op. cit.

29. Parimala Rao, 'Modern education and the Revolt of 1857 in India,' *Paedagogica Historica International Journal of the History of Education*, vol. 25, nos 1–2, 2016, p. 25.

30. Rosie Llewellyn-Jones, 'The lost graves at Bhowanipore Cemetery,' *Chowkidar: Journal of the British Society for Cemeteries in South Asia (BACSA)*, vol. 13, no. 1, 2012, pp. 1–3.

31. Charles Lushington, *The History, Design and Present State of the Religious, Benevolent and Charitable Institutions*, 1824, p. xlviv.

32. Bishop Reginald Heber, *Narrative of a Journey Through the Upper Provinces of India*, Vol. 1, 1827, p. 42.

33. Christopher Hawes, *Poor Relations; the Making of a Eurasian Community in British India, 1778–1833*, Routledge, 1996, p. 22.

34. Theresa Hubel, 'In search of the British Indian in British India: White orphans, Kipling's *Kim* and class in colonial India,' *Modern Asian Studies*, vol. 39, no. 1, February 2004, p. 242.

35. Lushington, op. cit., footnote p. 292–3.

36. Anonymous, 'Old Hospital Records,' *Indian Medical Gazette*, vol. 38, no. 1, January 1903, p. 7.

37. Lushington, op. cit., p. 299.

38. Lushington, op. cit., p. 295.

39. Waltraud Ernst, *Mad Tales From the Raj: The European Insane in British India, 1800–1858*, Routledge, 1991, p. 18.

40. For example, the Surrey County Lunatic Asylum, now Springfield University Hospital, south-west London, was built in open countryside following a legal ruling that counties should provide their own asylums funded by a local levy. It also had its own dairy and water supply.

41. Lushington, op. cit., p. 303.

42. British Library blog, November 2018, by Margaret Makepeace, Lead Curator, East India Company Records.

43. H.E.A. Cotton, *Calcutta Old and New: A Historical and Descriptive Handbook to the City*, revised edition, 1980, pp. 133–7. Lottery winners were selected by a roulette-type wheel being spun.

44. Guy Robinson and O.L.J Milliagan, *Lodge 'Star in the East' No. 67 E.C.: Two Hundred and Forty Years of Freemasonry, 1740–1980*, 1980, p. 7.

45. Jessica Harland-Jacobs, *Builders of Empire: Freemasons and British Imperialism, 1717–1927*, University of North Carolina Press, 2007, p. 85.

46. Lushington, op. cit., p. xxviii.

4.   JOINING THE PARTS TOGETHER

1.   Undated (early August 1786) letter from Claude Martin. Original correspondence, Ozias Humphry, vol. iii, 1784–7, HU/3/f 101, Royal Academy of Arts, London.

2.   Susan Gole (ed.), *Maps of Mughal India Drawn by Colonel Jean-Baptiste-Joseph Gentil, Agent for the French Government to the Court of Shuja-ud-daula at Faizabad, in 1770*, Kegan Paul International, 1989.

3.   *Carte générale du Cours du Gange et du Gagra, dressée sur les Cartes particulieres du P Tiefentaller, J. Missionnaire Apostolique dans l'Inde.* M. Anquetil du Perron, Paris, 1784.

4.   Joseph Tieffenthaler, *Description historique et géographique de l'Inde* .... M. Jean Bernouilli, Berlin, 1786–91, vol. iii.

5.   Jean Deloche, *Transport and Communications in India Prior to Steam Locomotion*, Vol. I, Oxford University Press, 1993 p. 122.

6.   Ibid., pp. 153–8.

7.   For a more nuanced view, see Kim Wagner, *Thuggee: Banditry and the British in Nineteenth-Century India*, Primus, 2015.

8.   Deloche, op. cit., Vol. I, p. 198.

9.   James Rennell, *A Description of the Roads in Bengal and Bahar*, 1778, p. i.

10. R.H. Phillimore, *Historical Records of the Survey of India*, Vol. I, 1945, p. 295.

11. Ibid., p. 196.

12. James Rennell, *Memoir of a Map of Hindoostan or the Mogul Empire*, 1788, p. vi.

13. Ibid., p. ix.

14. George Chesney, quoted in E.W.C. Sandes, *The Military Engineer in India*, Vol. II, 1935, p. 60.

15. Amitabha Gupta, 'Mysterious towers: Relics of the visual telegraph,' 23 March 2019, www.livehistoryindia.com. Only one British semaphore tower remains, in Surrey on the route between London and Portsmouth.

16. George Chesney, *Indian Polity: A View of the System of Administration in India*, 1894, pp. 274–5.

17. From the manuscript diary of Emily Shakespear, entry dated 28 June 1814. Royal Society of Asian Affairs, Haileybury.

18. Parliamentary Papers, Part 2, Vol. 10, 6 December 1831–16 August 1832. Appendix 25, pp. 675–9.

19. Ibid., pp. 680–90.

20. Ibid., p. 715–21.

21. Ibid., p. 710.

22. Rowland Macdonald Stephenson, *Report Upon the Practicability and Advantages of the Introduction of Railways into British India* ..., 1844, p. 63.

23. In 1795, two steam engines made by Boulton & Watt were sent to Claude Martin at Lucknow, Ozias Humphry's host, followed by a third in 1797. See Rosie Llewellyn-Jones, *A Very Ingenious Man: Claude Martin in Early Colonial India*, Oxford University Press Delhi, 1992, pp. 128–9.

24. Clive Dewey, *Steamboats on the Indus: The Limits of Western Technological Superiority in South Asia*, 2014, p. 63.

25. 'Papers regarding the coal mines of Cutch,' Report of Captain John Hawkins, August 1827–May 1829 and 10 November 1827, Major Pottinger to Mr Secretary Norris. IOR/F/4/1131/30216 India Office Library and Records.

26. Dewey, op. cit., p. 60.

27. Parliamentary Papers, op. cit., p. 67.

28. Ibid., p. 675.

29. Bengal Proceedings, 4 February 1852–29 December 1853. Report dated 25 November 1851, p. 37, India Office Library and Records.

30. Ibid., 4 March 1852, No. 7, and see the report by C.H. Lushington, dated 18 September 1851 and bound into this volume of the Proceedings.

31. Asok Mukhopadhyay, 'Howrah Railway Junction Station, Howrah, 1854,' 18 November 2015, puronokolkata.com.

32. Henry Hyde Clarke, *Colonization, Defence and Railways in Our Indian Empire*, 1857, p. 138.

33. *The Spectator*, 6 September 1856.

34. Hyde Clarke, op. cit., p. 237.

35. HMSO, *Statistical Abstract Relating to British India From 1840 to 1865*, 1867, pp. 57–9.

36. Ritika Prasad, *Tracks of Change: Railways and Everyday Life in Colonial India*, 2016, pp. 32–3.

37. Edwin Arnold, *The Marquis of Dalhousie's Administration in British India*, 1865, pp. 241–2.

38. Jeffrey Kieve, *The Electric Telegraph: A Social and Economic History*, 1973, p. 22, et seq.

39. 'Experiments on the communication of telegraphic signals by induced electricity,' *The Journal of the Asiatic Society of Bengal*, Vol VIII, January–December 1839, New Series. Calcutta 1840. Article VI, September 1839, pp. 714–31.

40. W.B. O'Shaughnessy, *The Electric Telegraph in British India*, 1858, p. iv.

41. Ibid., O'Shaughnessy p. vi.

42. Rosie Llewellyn-Jones. *Engaging Scoundrels: True Tales of Old Lucknow*, Oxford University Press, 2000, p. 141.

5. CANTONMENTS, COUNTRY HOUSES AND HILL STATIONS

1. Robert Clive to the Select Committee Fort William on 10 July 1765. Select Committee Proceedings 10 August 1764. National Archives, New Delhi. Quoted in Christopher Cowell, 'The *kacchā-pakkā* divide: Material, space and architecture in the military cantonments of British India (1765–1889),' *ABE Journal Architecture Beyond Europe*, vol. 9–10, 2016, p. 16.

2. Arthur Broom, *History of the Rise and Progress of the Bengal Army*, vol. i, 1850, pp. 533–6.

3. See Rosie Llewellyn-Jones, *A Very Ingenious Man: Claude Martin in Early Colonial India*, Oxford University Press Delhi, 1992, pp. 37–41 for a detailed account of the White Mutiny.

4. Public Records Department, Archibald Campbell to Warren Hastings, 17 December 1772, No. 9. National Archives, New Delhi.

5. Ibid.

6. Bisheshwar Prasad (ed.), *Fort William India House Correspondence 1770–1772*. National Archives, New Delhi, 1960, Public Letter from the Court of Directors, 23 March 1770, vol. vi, pp. 23–7.

7. Ibid., p. 26.

8. Ibid., p. 145.

9. George Thomas, the eclectic Irish mercenary and one-time ruler of a small north Indian kingdom, died at Berhampore in 1802 on his way down to Calcutta. See the author's entry for Thomas in the *Oxford Dictionary of National Biography*. Lyon Prager, the Jewish diamond merchant who died in 1793, is buried in the nearby Cossimbazar cemetery.

10. See Sharon Murphy's *The British Soldier and His Libraries, c. 1822–1901*, Palgrave Macmillan, 2016 for a comprehensive account.

11. Letter from William Tolley, Barrack Master at Monghyr, to George Vansittart, Chief, and Council of Revenue at Patna, dated 26 April 1773. No. 3. Public Proceedings 15 April–29 June 1773. National Archives, New Delhi.

12. Zoë Yalland, *Traders and Nabobs: The British in Cawnpore, 1765–1857*, Michael Russell Publishing, 1987, pp. 30–1.

13. Rosie Llewellyn-Jones, *A Fatal Friendship: The Nawabs, the British and the City of Lucknow*, Oxford University Press, 1985, pp. 8–9.

14. Yalland, op. cit., p. 40.

15. Giles Stibbert, commander-in-chief to Warren Hastings, governor general, 2 August 1784, Public Consultations, Home Dept, No. 21, National Archives, New Delhi.

16. Llewellyn-Jones, *A Fatal Friendship*, op. cit., p. 116.

17. Thomas Lumsden, *A Journey From Meerut in India to London During the Years 1819 and 1820*, 1822, pp. 14–15.

18. Yalland, op. cit., p. 40.

19. Alfred Spencer (ed.), *Memoirs of William Hickey (1775–1809)*, Vol. III, 1948, p. 236.

20. Ibid., p. 237.

21. Rosie Llewellyn-Jones, *The Louisa Parlby Album: Watercolours From Murshidabad 1795–1803*, Francesca Galloway, 2017.

22. A. Qamaruddin and M. Roy, *Murshidabad Affairs (1821–1850): Records From the Berhampore Collectorate*, 1995, p. 183.

23. *Gazetteer of the Simla District 1904*, new edition, Indus Publishing Company, 1998, p. 11.

24. Edward Buck, *Simla, Past and Present*, 1904, p. 6.

25. Victor Jacquemont, *Letters From India; Describing a Journey in the British Dominions of India* ..., Vol. I, Edward Churston, 1834, p. 226.

26. Godfrey Mundy, *Pen and Pencil Sketches, Being the Journal of a Tour in India*, Vol. I, 1832, pp. 226–7.

27. Buck, op. cit., p. 12.

28. Mundy, op. cit., Vol. 1, pp. 240–1.

29. Raja Bhasin, *Simla: The Summer Capital of British India*, Penguin, 1994, pp. 171–2.

30. Mundy, op. cit., Vol. 1, pp. 188–9.

31. Dane Kennedy, *The Magic Mountains, Hill Stations and the British Raj*, Oxford University Press Delhi, 1996, p. 10.

32. Queeny Pradhan, 'Empire in the hills: The making of hill stations in colonial India,' *Studies in History*, vol. 23, Sage Publications, 2007, p. 36.

33. Virgil Miedema, *Murree: A Glimpse Through the Forest*, Amur Maple Books, 2002, p. 17.

34. Kennedy, op. cit.,, p. 136.

35. *The Imperial Gazetteer of India*, Vol. 22, new edition, 1908–31, p. 379.

36. Emily Eden, *Up the Country: Letters Written to Her Sister From the Upper Provinces of India*, Vol. I, 1866, p. 163.

37. Richard English, 'Himalayan state formation and the impact of British rule in the nineteenth century,' *Mountain Research and Development*, vol. v, no. 1, 1985, pp. 61–78.

38. Mundy, op. cit., Vol. I, p. 229.

39. Ibid., p. 181.

40. D.C. Kala, *Frederick Wilson ('Hulson Sahib') of Garhwal, 1816–83*, Ravi Dayal, 2006, p. 43.

41. Fanny Parkes, *Wanderings of a Pilgrim in Search of the Picturesque During Four-and-Twenty Years in the East*, Vol. II, 1850, p. 274.

42. Kala, op. cit., p. 101.

6.   THE PASSAGE OF TIME

1. Sir James Thomason, *Account of Roorkee College Established for the Instruction of Civil Engineers With a Scheme for Its Enlargement*, 1851, p. 15.
2. Ibid., p. 15.
3. This was the Architectural Association School of Architecture in London, established as an alternative to the apprentice system then in place.
4. Thomason, op. cit., p. 16.
5. Sir Charles Wood's Educational Despatch from the Court of Directors, London, 19 July 1854. National Archives, New Delhi.
6. Major General Charles Stuart, of Irish birth, became known as 'Hindoo Stuart' for his advocation of Hindu beliefs, values and costumes. He did, however, concede to burial in a Christian cemetery under a tomb resembling a small Hindu temple.
7. See Mary Ann Steggles, *Statues of the Raj*, BACSA, 2000.
8. Post Office Act, 1837, Act No. XVIL, passed by the Governor General of India in Council, Calcutta 24 July 1837.
9. Ibid., paragraph XXI.
10. H.E.A. Cotton, *Calcutta Old and New: A Historical and Descriptive Handbook to the City*, revised edition, 1980, p. 755.
11. A tune often taught to bandsmen was 'The girl I left behind me,' an eighteenth-century folk tune of Irish origin, popular with naval and military bands.
12. 'The sick room in India,' *Calcutta Review*, January–June 1845, p. 78.
13. John Sprot, *Incidents and Anecdotes in the Life of Lieut-General Sprot, etc.* [Told by himself] Vol. I, p. 52.
14. Thomas Williamson, *The East India Vade-Mecum*, Vol. II, 1810, pp. 45–6.
15. Ritika Prasad, *Tracks of Change: Railways and Everyday Life in Colonial India*, Cambridge University Press, 2016, pp. 135–6.
16. The Latkan Darwaza in Lucknow had a clock face suspended between two substantial towers, hence its name. The clock and gateway were in a prominent position outside the British Residency and were severely damaged during the Uprising.
17. See my discussion on Islamic dates in *A Man of the Enlightenment in Eighteenth-century India: The Letters of Claude Martin, 1766–1800*, Permanent Black, 2002, pp. 53–6.
18. Photograph of the 1752 Burial Register (author's collection).
19. Diamonds, for example, were measured in *ratti*, the nominal weight of the toxic seed of the Rosary Pea plant.
20. Holden Furber, *John Company at Work*, 1948, p. 349.
21. Cotton, op. cit., p. 192.

22. Nancy Gardner Cassels, 'Social legislation under the Company's Raj: the Abolition of Slavery Act 1843,' *South Asia: Journal of South Asian Studies Australia*, vol. xi, no. 1, 1988, p. 61.

23. See Joseph Earl Harris, *The African Presence in Asia: Consequences of the East African Slave Trade*, Northwestern University Press, 1971.

24. Home Department Proceedings, Education Branch. From Mr A. Young, Chief Secretary to Government, Bombay to Cecil Beadon, Secretary to Government. Nos 1–3, 29 April 1858, National Archives, New Delhi.

25. Home Department Proceedings, Education Branch. Report by W.H. Newham, Assistant at the Bombay office of the Director of Public Instruction, to Mr A. Young, Chief Secretary to Government, Bombay, 3 March 1859, National Archives, New Delhi.

26. The portrait is in York City Art Gallery, England.

27. John Walker Sherer, *Daily Life During the Indian Mutiny: Personal Experiences of 1857*, 1898, p. 30.

BIBLIOGRAPHY

Anonymous. *The Indian Vocabulary to Which Is Prefixed the Forms of Impeachment*. Printed for John Stockdale, Piccadilly [London], 1788.

Arnold, Edwin. *The Marquis of Dalhousie's Administration in British India*. London: Saunders, Otley, and Company, 1862, 1865.

Barber, Noel. *The Black Hole of Calcutta: A Reconstruction*. London: Collins, 1965.

Beach, Milo and Koch, Ebba (eds). *King of the World: The Padshahnama*. London: Azimuth Editions, Ltd., 1997.

Bhasin, Raja. *Simla: The Summer Capital of British India*. Haryana, India: Penguin India, 1994.

Blechynden, Kathleen. *Calcutta Past and Present*. London: W. Thacker & Co., 1905.

Broom, Arthur. *History of the Rise and Progress of the Bengal Army*. Calcutta: W. Thacker & Co., 1850.

Buck, Edward. *Simla Past and Present*. Calcutta: Thacker, Spink & Co., 1904.

Chatterjee, Partha. *The Black Hole of Empire*. Princeton, NJ: Princeton University Press, 2012.

Chesney, George. *Indian Polity: A View of the System of Administration in India*, 3rd ed. London: Longmans, Green & Co., 1894.

Cohn, Bernard S. *Colonialism and Its Forms of Knowledge*. Princeton, NJ; Chichester, UK: Princeton University Press, 1996.

Cotton, H.E.A. *Calcutta Old and New: A Historical and Descriptive Handbook to the City*, revised edition N.R. Ray (ed.). Calcutta: General Publishers, 1980 [1909].

Cox, J.L. *Reports and Documents Connected With the Proceedings of the East-India Company in Regard to the Culture and Manufacture of Cotton-Wool, Raw Silk and Indigo in India*. Printed by order of the East India Company, London, 1836.

Dalrymple, William. *White Mughals: Love and Betrayal in Eighteenth-Century India*. New York: HarperCollins, 2002.

Dalrymple, William (ed.). *Forgotten Masters: Indian Painting for the East India Company*. London: Bloomsbury Publishing, 2019.

Danvers, Frederick. *The Portuguese in India*. London: Frank Cass & Co., Ltd, 1966 [1894].

Deloche, Jean. *Transport and Communications in India Prior to Steam Locomotion*. Vol. 1 Land Transport. Delhi: Oxford University Press, 1993.

Dewey, Clive. *Steamboats on the Indus: The Limits of Western Technological Superiority in South Asia*. Delhi: Oxford University Press, 2014.

Eden, Emily. *'Up the Country': Letters Written to Her Sister From the Upper Provinces of India*. London: Richard Bentley, 1866.

Edney, Matthew. *Mapping an Empire: The Geographical Construction of British India, 1765–1843*. Chicago, IL: University of Chicago Press, 1997.

Ernst, Waltraud. *Mad Tales From the Raj: The European Insane in British India, 1800–1858*. London: Routledge, 1991.

Furber, Holden. *John Company at Work*. Cambridge, MA: Harvard University Press, 1948.

Harris, Joseph Earl. *The African Presence in Asia, Consequences of the East African Slave Trade*. Evanston, IL: Northwestern University Press, 1971.

Gazetteer of the Simla District 1904, new edition. New Delhi: Indus Publishing Company, 1998.

Gilchrist, John Borthwick. *A Dictionary, English and Hindoostanee, in Which the Words Are Marked With Their Distinguishing Initials; as Hinduwee, Arabic, and Persian etc*. Calcutta: Stuart and Cooper, 1786.

Gole, Susan. *Maps of Mughal India Drawn by Colonel Jean-Baptiste-Joseph Gentil, Agent for the French Government to the Court of Shuja-ud-daula at Faizabad, in 1770*. London, New York: Kegan Paul International, 1989.

Harland-Jacobs, Jessica. *Builders of Empire: Freemasons and British Imperialism, 1717–1927*. Chapel Hill, NC: University of North Carolina Press, 2007.

Hawes, Christopher. *Poor Relations: The Making of a Eurasian Community in British India, 1778–1833*. London: Curzon Press, 1996.

Heber, Reginald. *Narrative of a Journey Through the Upper Provinces of India*. London: John Murray, 1827.

Holwell, John Zephaniah. *India Tracts by Mr Holwell, and Friends*. London: T. Becket, 1764.

Hunter, W. W. *A History of British India*. London: Longmans, Green & Co., 1912.

BIBLIOGRAPHY

Hyde Clarke, Henry. *Colonization, Defence and Railways in Our Indian Empire*. London: John Weale, 1857.

The Imperial Gazetteer of India, new edition. Oxford: Clarendon Press, 1908–31.

Ives, Edward. *A Voyage From England to India in the Year 1754* .... London: Edward and Charles Dilly, 1773.

Jacquemont, Victor. *Letters From India; Describing a Journey in the British Dominions of India* .... London: Edward Churston, 1834.

Kala, D.C. *Frederick Wilson ('Hulson Sahib') of Garhwal, 1816–83*. Delhi: Ravi Dayal, 2006.

Kejariwal, O.P. *The Asiatic Society of Bengal and the Discovery of India's Past, 1784–1838*. Delhi: Oxford University Press, 1999.

Kennedy, Dane. *The Magic Mountains: Hill Stations and the British Raj*. Delhi: Oxford University Press, 1996.

King, George. *Annals of the Royal Botanic Garden Calcutta*. Calcutta: Bengal Secretariat Press, 1893.

Llewellyn-Jones, Rosie. *A Fatal Friendship: The Nawabs, the British and the City of Lucknow*. Delhi: Oxford University Press, 1985.

Llewellyn-Jones, Rosie. *A Very Ingenious Man: Claude Martin in Early Colonial India*. Delhi: Oxford University Press, 1992.

Llewellyn-Jones, Rosie. *Engaging Scoundrels: True Tales of Old Lucknow*. Delhi: Oxford University Press, 2000.

Llewellyn-Jones, Rosie. *The Louisa Parlby Album: Watercolours From Murshidabad 1795–1803*. London: Francesca Galloway, 2017.

Llewellyn-Jones, Rosie (ed.). *The Estate of Major General Claude Martin at Lucknow* Newcastle-upon-Tyne, UK: Cambridge Scholars Publishing, 2021.

Lumsden, Thomas. *A Journey From Meerut in India to London During the Years 1819 and 1820*. London: Black, Kingsbury, Parbury & Allen, 1822.

Lushington, Charles. *The History, Design and Present State of the Religious, Benevolent and Charitable Institutions*. Calcutta: Hindostanee Press, 1824.

Macdonald Stephenson, Rowland. *Report Upon the Practicability and Advantages of the Introduction of Railways into British India* .... London: Kelly & Co., 1844.

Majumdar, Purna Ch. *The Musnud of Murshidabad (1704–1904)*. Murshidabad, India: Saroda Ray, 1905.

Miedema, Virgil. *Murree: A Glimpse Through the Forest*. Washington, DC: Amur Maple Books, 2002.

Mukhopadhyay, Subhas Chandra. *British Residents at the Darbar of Bengal Nawabs at Mushidabad, 1757–1772*. Delhi: Gian Publishing House, n.d.

Mundy, Godfrey. *Pen and Pencil Sketches, Being the Journal of a Tour in India*. London, 1832.

Murphy, Sharon. *The British Soldier and His Libraries, c. 1822–1901*. London: Palgrave Macmillan, 2016.

Otis, Andrew. *Hicky's Bengal Gazette: the Untold Story of India's First Newspaper*. Chennai, India: Tranquebar Publishers, 2018.

O'Shaughnessy, W.B. *The Electric Telegraph in British India*. Printed by the Order of the Court of Directors, London, 1858.

Parkes, Fanny. *Wanderings of a Pilgrim in Search of the Picturesque During Four-and-Twenty Years in the East*. London: Pelham Richardson, 1850.

Phillimore, R.H. *Historical Records of the Survey of India*, Vol. 1. Dehra Dun, India: Office of the Northern Circle, 1945.

Prasad, Bisheshwar (ed.). *Fort William India House Correspondence, 1770–1772*, Vol. 6. New Delhi: National Archives, 1960.

Prasad, Ritika. *Tracks of Change: Railways and Everyday Life in Colonial India*. Delhi: Cambridge University Press, 2016.

Qamaruddin, A. and Roy, M. *Murshidabad Affairs (1821–1850) Records of the Berhampur Collectorate, West Bengal*. Calcutta: K.P. Bagchi & Co., 1995.

Rennell, James. *A Description of the Roads in Bengal and Bahar*. London: Court of Directors of the Honorable East India Company, 1778.

Rennell, James. *Memoir of a Map of Hindoostan or the Mogul Empire*, 1st edition. 1788. Printed for the author.

Robinson, Guy and Milligan O.L.J. *Lodge 'Star in the East' No. 67 E.C.: Two Hundred and Forty Years of Freemasonry. 1740–1980*. Calcutta: The Statesman, Bengal, 1980.

Salim, Ghulam Husain. *Riyazu-s-Salatin*, trans. Maulavi Abdus Salam. Calcutta: The Asiatic Society, 1902.

Sandes, E.W.C. *The Military Engineer in India*, Vol. 1. Chatham, UK: Institution of Royal Engineers, 1933; republished Uckfield, UK: Naval & Military Press, 1997.

Sarkar, Jadunath (ed.). *The History of Bengal*, Vol. 1. Dacca: University of Dacca, 1943.

Sherer, John Walker. *Daily Life During the Indian Mutiny: Personal Experiences of 1857*. London: Swan Sonnenshein & Co., 1898.

Sinha H.N. (ed.). *Fort William India House Correspondence, 1757–1759*, Vol. 2. New Delhi: National Archives, 1957.

Spencer, Alfred (ed.). *Memoirs of William Hickey (1775–1809)*, 2nd edition. London: Hurst and Blackett Ltd, 1948.

Sprot, John. *Incidents and Anecdotes in the Life of Lieut-General Sprot, etc.* [Told by himself]. Printed for private circulation, Edinburgh, 1906.

Steggles, Mary Ann. *Statues of the Raj*. London: BACSA, 2000.

Teignmouth, Lord. *Memoirs of the Life, Writings, and Correspondence of Sir William Jones*. London: Brettell, 1806.

Tieffenthaler, Joseph. *Description historique et géographique de l'Inde*. Berlin: M. Jean Bernouilli, 1786–91.

Thomason, Sir James. *Account of Roorkee College Established for the Instruction of Civil Engineers With a Scheme for Its Enlargement*. Printed by order of the Honourable Lieutenant Governor of the North Western Provinces. Agra, India: Sikandra Orphan Press, 1851.

Williamson, Thomas. *The East India Vade-Mecum*. London: Black, Parry & Kingsbury 1810.

Wilson, Charles. *Old Fort William in Bengal*, a Selection of Official Documents Dealing With Its History. London: John Murray, 1906.

Yalland, Zoë. *Traders and Nabobs: The British in Cawnpore, 1765–1857*. Norfolk, UK: Michael Russell Publishing, 1987.

INDEX

Tir

&

Tide

Wait for no
Man on the
Severn

B. A. Lane

Time and Tide Wait for no Man on the Severn

B. A. Lane

Designed produced and Published by
Douglas McLean
at
The Forest Bookshop
8 St John Street, Coleford, Glos. GL16 8AR

Printed in Great Britain by
AMCL Cinderford

ISBN 0 946252 29 7

Working the Severn Estuary

An artist's impression of the first Severn Barrage proposed in 1933, but on learning the damage it would do to the environment the project was dropped. It was proposed where the second Severn crossing is to be built; which the author believes is also a mistake.

1

Working the Severn Estuary
- Avonmouth to Sharpness

To learn the secrets of River Severn navigation, it is important to begin as I did, at an early age. One of the earliest things I learned was an old proverb - 'Treat Sabrina with respect and she will treat you the same, but abuse her, then she will most certainly abuse you.' Anyone who ever ventures out onto the Severn estuary would do well to remember this.

The best teachers of the Severn's mysteries were the old sailing pilots. These men were experts. Navigating with only the wind for power, they sailed the Bristol Channel looking out for ships to pilot to Sharpness and Gloucester. They would love to describe their work in detail to anyone interested. It is sad that after the coming of engine power much of the knowledge died out with them.

My own father was a pilot. I remember when, during my school holidays, I spent many a time with him on board the 'Berkeley Castle'. This was the pilot's base at Portishead. One day I asked one of the other pilots where all the mud and silt came from along the Swash. The Swash was the bank between Avonmouth and Portishead, long since excavated to build the new Portbury dock. His answer was 'The only way you will learn, is to come out in the boat with me and I will teach you'. He kept his word. I spent two days with him drifting in an open boat on the ebb and flow of the tides. I learned the hard way and I have never forgotten. It is no wonder that the pilots of today know their jobs so well. They had very good teachers in men like this. Sadly there are none of the old sailing pilots alive today. With their advice, much of the latter day construction work in the Severn Estuary would have been more satisfactory and not cost the taxpayer so much money in repairs. In my experience, the 'powers that be' never seem to listen anyway.

It was important that the masters of all the craft working Severn learned the channels of the river. Good navigation skills were essential to survival. Like myself, all the men on board the river craft had to master the channels and also study and put into practice traversing the

'Berkeley Castle' 1939
Pilot's house-boat in Portishead hole between the swash and the shore at Portishead.

river from Avonmouth to Sharpness and back. This, in all winds and weathers without going aground. We memorised the marked channel of lights, perches and buoys. Also the tides and the currents and how they behaved in certain parts of the river. We would know how the tide came into the river first up the deep water channels. We had a saying then, 'The Bedwins, Bull, and Lyde would be covered by the tide at three hours to high water Sharpness time'. I have watched these points in the channel often and find this true, even allowing for the different heights of tides. Once these points submerge, the tides spread over the sand banks and rocks. Here, early on tide the speed of the water would increase, making very difficult and dangerous currents in the river.

One of these danger areas is around the Charston rocks. Here the tide would increase from Gruggy rock and whip across the Charlston channel. This caused a current that could put us into a very difficult situation if we did not expect it. It would turn us towards the channel to the tiny Chapel Island, the spot where the River Wye flows into the Severn.

Chapel Island was so called because there was once an ancient Celtic chapel built upon it, dedicated to a little known early saint, St. Tegla, said to be the martyred daughter of a king of Gwynedd. The ruins of an old chapel, St Twrog's Chapel, can still be seen on the island.

Once past this island, we would have to turn in towards the Lyde rock and proceed into Slimeroad to turn up toward the next point; Inward Rocks. If we were not careful, the force of tide here pushed our vessel towards the cliff. When we reached the Inward Rocks, we would then have to turn across the river to follow the leading lights. There was treacherous current here and high and strong tides could drag us down towards the Shepperdine Sands. This current had once capsized a craft the 'BP Explorer' with the consequent loss of all hands.

As the tide was dragging at our vessel, we would watch the marker lights through the starboard windows of the wheelhouse and the marker perch on our port bow. Once we reached this perch, the river current would completely change and we could then head toward the leading lights at Shepperdine. This was because the tide would be running from Narlwood rocks, which altered the whole flow of the

Dumb barges being towed empty to Avonmouth tied together, no-one steering them. 1950

Vessels moored alongside; making their way to Avonmouth down the South shore. 1948

tide in this vicinity. Here, we had to turn into the main channel up towards the fishing house channel. Then we would have to pass the Hills Flats buoy and then Hayward buoy, turning in until we could turn up through the Berkeley Pill channel, where there is another perch built upon the Bull Rock. This is marked to tell how much water is on the sill at Sharpness at that time of tide. From this point we would proceed towards the landmark we called the Swinging light on the shore south of Sharpness. This light lets all vessels know it is prudent to swing head to tide here, before entering the tidal basin at Sharpness docks.

We learned other ways of navigating to Sharpness to enable us to use the river when the tide was getting too low for docking.

Before the war, the tide time at Avonmouth was limited to three hours before and three hours after high-water. This curtailed docking time at Avonmouth and Sharpness, so our local knowledge was quite an advantage.

In those days, all motorised or steam engined craft had to tow the unmotorised dumb barges. Because the men were paid by cargo, our short cuts were essential to get our money at the end of the week, as well as vital to successful docking.

For instance, if we were late on tide we would count the girders on the Lyde Light to calculate whether there was enough water to navigate from inward rocks to the Guskar rocks on the Lydney side, then across the sand to Berkeley Pill. This saved time by taking the short cut to Berkeley Pill and Sharpness and docking within the tide time. We could also carry on up the river channel from the Inward rocks, past the Guskar rocks, on up the Severn shore to Lydney, then across the river to Sharpness dock. Otherwise, without the short cut, we probably would not have enough time left to dock.

By making this crossing it enabled us to do more work in the channel. We also had to know that when the tide had reached its height at Sharpness and was on the turn to ebb. This same tide was still flowing up river for another ten minutes at Lydney.

Navigating South from Sharpness to Avon was a different technique than traversing the river. During the 1940's, a tug might leave Sharpness with as many as six general cargo barges in tow. With this load it could take him all his time to tow to Avonmouth. Later, this was reduced to four barges up and down river. So on arriving, he would have the barges double up and alongside one another. He would either moor them on the pier until the next tide, or go to anchor in a safe spot. Consequently, the anchor gear had to be in good working order.

The craft towing dumb barges would have the dumb craft alongside, but on leaving Sharpness they had to tow against the tide. As this was before the construction of the Berkeley and Oldbury Power Stations, there was a clear run down inside the perches, the Haywards and Hills Flats buoys, then across the river following the shipping channel down. If we knew our river and tides, we could go straight down on the English side of the channel using marks according to our draught and the time and heights of tide. We would always keep watch on the passenger ferries working the river from Aust to Beachley.

If we were using the South shore channel, a good navigation aid was the coal fired power station at Portishead. We lined one chimney stack behind the other, there were four chimneys, so we had to know which two we could use to indicate we were on the right course for the channel from New Passage Hotel to Avonmouth. This could save us a lot of time.

Later in 1947, came improvements to the docks and the docking time at Avonmouth was increased by two hours. Four hours before and four hours after high water. This increased our cargo rates, because if we went in on one tide and out on the next, this gained us an extra tide.

It was during this time that the increase in river traffic began. Sometimes there were as many as thirty craft sailing in and out of Avonmouth and Sharpness Docks.

Sometimes, once we were out of Sharpness dock, empty and bound for Avonmouth Light Ship, the tanker and cargo craft towing dumb barges would tie alongside one another. Weather permitting, three dumb barges and three motor towing craft would moor to one another on the end of their tow ropes. To hold the rudders in position a stool would be jammed under the steering wheel. The centre towing craft was the only one that steered. The crews then had hours of welcome relief not having to steer from Sharpness to Avonmouth.

After the nuclear power stations were built many of our favourite short cuts down the south shore channel were ended. We could still use some; over Hills Flats to Shepperdine, and from the Lyde to

Avonmouth. This was possible as long as the grain ships or timber ships were not moored to Northwich mooring buoy, to be lightened by the 'SS Leitrim' into grain barges bound for Sharpness. Timber ships were also lightened using the ships' derricks. Tugs were also in attendance. This channel from the Lyde took us down past the New Passage, then Pilning shore to Avonmouth.

I have not yet written anything about the war years. I have already put a paragraph into my first book 'Severn Tanking' when I recalled an incident when we were bombed, but here I want to relate an incident when we were mined. It concerns a general cargo vessel, the 'MV Severn Transport'. She was on passage to Cardiff from Gloucester and was making her way across the channel to the E & W lightship. However, unbeknown to the master and crew, the Germans had sown mines the night before, some of them magnetic. The master was at the wheel, and the engineer was in the engine room. The deck hand was standing on the companion way ladder and the boy lay on his bunk, which in fact saved them both when the mine struck. Because the deck hand was resting his arms on the top of the hatchway to the deck and his feet were resting on a step, when the mine burst he just fell to the cabin floor. The boy in his bunk was also unharmed and they both rushed on deck to find the captain. Captain Rowles was injured and on the floor of the wheelhouse and the engineer, his son, Mr Wilfred Rowles was calling for help in the engine room. The fuel tank had fallen across his legs trapping him and injuring his feet. They freed him and struggled to get him on deck. When they got his father out on deck with him they saw that the lifeboat had been blown in two; length ways. They got the two injured men into the good half, the buoyancy tanks were under the thwarts and still functioning pushed it over the side, jumped in, and sat and watched the 'Severn Transport' sink.

A few hours later, a Navy mine sweeper picked them up and transferred them to Barry hospital for urgent medical attention. The Navy in the meantime put an embargo on shipping in the channel until it had been swept and cleared of mines. This procedure happened many times during the war.

Another occurrence in the river was the appearance of mines that had broken free from their moorings. One such happening I recall was when a skipper towing three craft bound for Avonmouth, saw something strange in the water. Upon investigation he found it to be a mine, so he quickly got away from there. Also, there was a firing range situated at New Passage and one day whilst vessels were on passage for Avonmouth, a vessel was making its way down the south shore past this firing range when they were practising. They must have had their sights wrong on the machine guns and the bullets rattled against the ships port side, and when they arrived at Avonmouth the skipper was soon ashore to report it to the Harbour Master; as his crew and he were very frightened. There was also a target buoy moored on Shepperdine Sands for bombing practice for aircraft. We all gave that a wide berth, especially when practice was taking place.

2

Safe Anchorage

During windy or foggy weather we had to be sure of our ability to anchor and sometimes would sail up onto the mud shore to be in a safe place. There were three well-known places where we could lay in safety, Shepperdine, Slimeroad and Mathern Ouze. Shepperdine was in front of the navigation lights. In this area, if we wanted to be underway in time to dock at Sharpness or Avonmouth, we could not go ashore until about three hours ebb water. Consequently, as the tide started to flow, our vessel would float in reasonable time to be off the mud flat and to make our way up channel to Sharpness.

This rule also applied to craft bound for Avonmouth. However, in their cases if light, they could float and be away a little earlier than the loaded vessels.

Many is the master that has been grateful to the Shepperdine light keeper, who lived in the cottage nearby. In fog he could strike a bell set in his garden and guide us into a safe haven. This bell was once the bell of the ship 'Atlas' then later the dock bell at Gloucester. Knowing the river, he could shout to tell us where and what time to drive ashore so that we could be safe until the next tide.

Slimeroad was right under the leading light. Here the mud sloped steeply down to the waters edge. If we had beached, as the tide receded, our vessel would slide into the water. While sliding down the bank we had to be careful when tide started to flow as we would be floating far too early to get underway.

Mathern Ouze was between Charston Rock and the mouth of the River Wye. Here we had to be careful as to the time we put our craft ashore. The area is a large expanse of flat mud, so if we went ashore too early we would have to wait a long time before we were afloat to resume our passage. It was because of this that we would learn why the currents occurred in certain parts of the river and what caused them. This knowledge, when navigating the river, was invaluable to the masters that took the trouble to learn. I hear men today claim they can get all the information from their computers. But we, the old rivermen, know that the incalculable ways of the River Severn are beyond any computer. It takes a lifetime to learn Sabrina's secrets, but even then she will often come up with something to surprise you.

A safe anchorage for ships to be lightened to navigate over sill into the Sharpness docks. 1935

3

Fog in the river

The masters of every craft working on the river agreed that the Severn fogs are the most alarming occurrence. In my early days on the Severn, when my vessel, like most working craft, would be towing another, I had to be very careful in fog conditions. I had to be sure that my towing craft did not turn too quickly, because the towing rope could snap up, snatch in half and cast the tow adrift. Whenever this happened, we had urgently to find the dumb barge and its crew to pick them up into tow again before they became helplessly lost in the fog. In a flowing tide this could be difficult and would often become desperate, as men's lives would depend upon us finding them.

On foggy mornings, the masters and crew of most of the power craft moored in the Sharpness basin, would meet on the entrance wall to discuss such things as the current visibility and weather condition. Some of the masters would be contemplating whether to try sailing by the 'Times and Courses', studied and recorded by the masters on calm, clear days. With clock and compass, they had carefully plotted the times and courses taken under similar tow and tidal conditions. Below is an example from my own, taken going up-river with my engine at 600rpm:

Cockburn Buoy to Charston	NE x N½N	5½ miles	26 min
Charston to Chapel.	E x N½N	2 miles	12 min
Chapel to Lyde	NE x N	½ mile	3 min
Lyde to Slimeroad	NNE	1 mile	8 min
Slimeroad to Inward Rocks	NE	¾ miles	8 min
Inward Rocks to Shepperdine	E	3 miles	9 min
Shepperdine to past Hills Flats buoy	NE x E½E	1 mile	11 min
Hayward Buoy to Conigre lights	E x S	½ mile	8 min
Fishing House to Berkely Pill	NE½E	1 mile	12 min
Berkely Pill to Sharpness	NNE	1¼ miles	10 min

Four vessels on mud, as a safe haven in fog at Slimeroads. 1960

Even Pilots had trouble in fog. Ship aground at Shepperdine. 1960

Tug, 'Resolute' high and dry after tide left her on the Oldbury Power Station cooling lake wall. App 1970

Two Tankers on the mud at Slimeroad, a safe haven in fog. 1959

19

Many bad incidents have occurred in the Severn fogs. Sabrina has taken and has not always returned. She has kept her secrets.

I remember once the 'SS John' loaded with coal, sailing out of Lydney. She ran into fog at Aust. With the ebb tide running very hard at Charston Rock she dragged into the strong current, then onto Gruggy rock. Here subsequent tides fragmented her until she was no more.

Another time, the tug 'Severn Iris', bound for Sharpness, had four general cargo vessels in tow. She ran into fog at Berkeley Pill. While trying to reach the haven of Sharpness dock, the ropes between the tug and the first and second craft parted. The first craft was an extra large grain carrier, the 'Fox Elms'. The tug picked up the second, third and fourth craft, but could not find 'Fox Elms' in the fog. The 'Fox Elms' crew, aware of their danger, decided to take to the lifeboat. They landed safely on the Purton side of the river above the Severn Railway Bridge. The 'Fox Elms' was never seen again.

Towing in fog by motor vessels was eventually abandoned. This was not only because of the 'Fox Elms' disaster but also because of another incident that happened in the Severn above Gloucester Dock. I will relate to this later in this book.

4

Mishaps in the Channel

Off Sharpness in both fog and clear weather, there were many unexpected incidents and losses of life where several large vessels went down. The 'MV Ramses II' loaded with maize and bound into Sharpness, was aided to dock by two large tugs from Avonmouth, one on aft and one on the bow. When they reached Sharpness, she was swung head to tide, off Sharpness piers. Whilst swinging, the tow rope on the bow tug parted and the pilot had to have full speed to turn her head to tide, or to drive her round. Without the aid of the tug she ran onto the Lydney Sands where she broke her back. Eventually she was broken up on the spot.

Another vessel loaded with grain broke down off the piers at Sharpness, and the two tugs trying to dock her could not hold her against the tide. The tug crews, scared they may be dragged into trouble, cut the tow ropes. The ship then drifted up past the old dock entrance and grounded on the Prinn sands, south of the old Severn Railway Bridge. It later took five tugs to pull her off at high water. When she was finally free it was ebb tide. As they approached Sharpness entrance, instead of swinging head to tide, they tried to tow her into the dock on the down stream run. They went through the South Pier on the ebb tide and she was gradually towed out and into the tidal basin over the outer sill and moored in the basin. This vessel was the 'MV Tynemouth'. I witnessed this event. It was a spectacle I will never forget.

A few years later, a vessel called the 'SS Stancliff' loaded with match wood logs for Price Walker & Co. of Gloucester and for Morelands, went aground just north of the piers at Sharpness and broke her back. She was unloaded into lighters out in the river and then cut into two. Then they towed the bow section and later her after-end to the yard at Newport. The two halves were reunited in dry dock, but with an extra section inserted to make her twenty feet longer. She was renamed 'Gripfast' and then returned to sea.

The first losses of life on the Severn that involved tankers, were when two motor tankers were towing one dumb barge, loaded and

21

running to Sharpness. The vessels were the 'MV Severn Traveller', the 'MV Severn Carrier I', and the 'Severn Venturer'. The 'MV Carrier I' broke down and the 'MV. Severn Traveller' could not hold both vessels against the tide. All three drifted up toward Purton where they hit the sand banks and the tide rolled them over. Five out of eight crew members were lost. The 'Severn Carrier I' and the 'Severn Venturer' were subsequently towed into Sharpness tidal basin. The 'Severn Venturer' and 'MV Carrier I' still upside down, were righted by the wrecking barge used for this sort of work.

The 'MV Severn Traveller' ended right side up, on the Frampton sand bank, and you could walk round her if you knew where to step to avoid the quick-sands. The authorities at the time asked for volunteers to search for bodies. Men that knew the river were put in charge of two young boys to search. I was twelve years of age at the time and was one of those boys. This incident happened in 1936.

The next tragedy involved a Shell tanker, deeply laden with oil, on passage from Swansea to Gloucester. It was night time. She evidently turned late at Inward Rocks and was traversing across the channel crab fashion to tide, which pushed her down toward the Shepperdine Sand. Afterwards, another master said he had seen her navigation lights, then there was nothing. He had no idea what had happened, but whilst lying off Sharpness pier before docking he saw something black drift up by on the tide, which he thought must have been the underside of the 'MV BP Explorer'. Again five men had lost their lives. She finally drifted ashore at Awre where she was later relaunched, taken to Sharpness, rebuilt and renamed the 'MV BP Driver'. About eighteen months later she was lost again on the Welsh coast at the Nash Point. Thankfully, this time there was no loss of life. After this she was finished for good and scrapped.

A few years later, there were about thirty craft on passage from Avonmouth and Swansea to Sharpness and when they got to the Berkeley Pill they all ran into sudden dense fog. Most vessels swung head to tide to try to find Sharpness dock in safety. The bell for fog warning was switched on at the North Pier, but the two vessels 'MV Wastdale' and 'MV Arkendale' had gone on by, having been sucked together by each others' turbulence. When two of these flat bottomed and sheer sided craft came together like this they could not part easily.

The Severn Bridge Disaster, 'Arkendale' and 'Wastdale', 1963

The Severn Bridge after the collision by the tankers 'Wastdale' and 'Arkendale'. 1963

24

One was carrying petrol and the other black oil. With a lighted heating boiler on board, this was a volatile combination. They drifted upriver, hopelessly unable to discover their position, until they collided with the Sharpness Railway Bridge. Running across the bridge was a gas line. This fractured upon the impact. The escaping gas from the bridge and leaking petrol and oil from the tankers were ignited by the boiler fire. There was a gigantic explosion. Two of the bridge arches collapsed onto the tankers and seven men lost their lives. The remains of the two unfortunate craft can still be seen today at low water on the Frampton to Purton Sand. The Severn Railway bridge was later condemned and demolished. A vital rail link was lost.

'Severn Carrier I', one of the first incidents involving tankers, with loss of life. App. 1936

'Ramses II' with broken back, between Lydney and Sharpness.

26

Bow and stern halves of 'SS Stancliff' prior to towing to Newport, an extra 20ft inserted and sent back to sea as the 'SS Gripfast'.

Bow section of 'SS Stancliff'.

Avonmouth Lock packed ready for sailing.

Sailing out of Avonmouth.

Bad weather off Avonmouth. Vessels bound for Sharpness.

Bad weather off Avonmouth.

29

Bad weather off Avonmouth.

Schnieder propelled craft, sailing for Swansea out of Sharpness. 1968

Prior to sailing for Swansea. Schneider propelled craft. 1968

Craft in Sharpness Basin, prior to sailing. 1950

Ship being towed out Stern first, before sailing.

5

Docking at Sharpness

Sailing out of Sharpness was quite an easy procedure. All one had to do was to keep up to the end of the South Pier and the tide would do the rest. However, docking into Sharpness with a loaded ship was a different proposition. We had to be able to judge the height of tide and the speed of the tidal current in order to get into the slack or slow running water behind or between the North and South piers. If we were towing when we reached Berkeley Pill on passage up river, and the tide was anything over 24ft 6ins on Sharpness outer sill, all we had to do was shorten the tow rope to about 60ft. In the case of tugs with a tow of four craft, they all had to be shortened to about 30ft each.

If our motor craft was towing one dumb barge, we could swing towards the Swinging Light. Provided the signal mast on the dock head was flying the correct signal for docking, we could, using the power of the engine, slowly drop back with the tide to dock. The dumb barge would then keep out in the tide, also to drop back to dock. Then the motor craft would drop back close to the south pier. When the bow was about two feet off the end of the pier, all speed would be put on the engine. The vessel would then be turned in, clearing the end of the pier by just two feet and the stern end would gradually pull the dumb barge in and up to the pier. This also had to be done by the tugs.

The vessels would then proceed into the tidal water basin and slip the tow rope. The crew man on the dumb barge would pull the rope in and the dumb barge would proceed alongside the motor craft where the master of the motor craft could handle both together. He was also solely in charge of both craft at all times.

A tug docking with four barges had to hang off the Swinging Light, waiting until the tide flow and pressure eased. They could then drop back and drop in, making sure the last craft cleared the North pier. Many a craft was dropping back when the duty man has put the signal up on the signal arm. They have been as far back as the South pier. In this case the power craft could not hold these craft up to tide. They would drop back to clear and then drop into the slack water behind the North Pier until the tide eased. They were then able to tow into slack water. There was no room for error as lives could have easily been lost as a result of any mistake.

It was also difficult to dock two dumb barges with one power barge. We had to shorten our tow ropes the same as the tugs did. All the craft were of similar size and took power from the engine. The master would drop in close to the pier, until the first dumb craft was in the slack water. Then he turned on in for the entrance. This enabled him to pull his second barge in with him. This was a very difficult manoeuvre indeed. He would then have one dumb barge each side of the motor craft for easier handling.

6

The Graveyards

As the old wooden lighters began to get beyond repair, they were taken to those parts of the Severn river bank which, due to erosion, required reinforcement. A few were stored in the old timber pond at Sharpness, but it was soon realised that the old hulks could be put to good use. One area that needed strengthening was between Purton waste weir and the Severn Railway Bridge. The old lighters were towed out on a big tide up the river from Sharpness dock and positioned in the weak part of the river bank. A few planks were then knocked out. As the tides washed over the hulks they soon filled with Severn mud and became part of the bank thus strengthening it. In later years the river bank south of Lydney pier also became very weak. Consequently, the dead craft that became available were taken there and put alongside one another. This built the bank up and also strengthened Lydney south pier removing the threat of Lydney dock and canal disintegrating and closing down.

During the war there were some concrete built barges introduced onto the waterway at Sharpness and Gloucester, but during their lifetime their structures became cracked from impacting against walls and other craft. After the war, because of the high cost of repairs, they suffered the same fate. They were towed up onto the bank near Purton and sunk to strengthen the bank between the river and the canal.

7

Knowlege of the Channels

Yes, men who were masters of tugs, general cargo craft, tankers and even the pilots, had to study every aspect of the river. They had to know every current and tide and how their vessels reacted in the river. They were good, extremely good, at their jobs. It was nothing for them to be navigating up or down channel with only two foot of water under their keels. Even pilots piloting ships of at least eight to nine thousand tons had to know exactly where they were and always to know what water was under their vessel. That is why the perch at Berkeley pill has two foot markers, which gives them the opportunity of knowing how much water was on the sill at Sharpness outer gates, for safe docking with large ships.

Skippers of the general cargo craft and the tankers had to know the deep water channel all the way on up river from Gloucester docks to Stourport-on-Severn, or, if they had larger craft of over two hundred tons carrying capacity, then up as far as Worcester.

Ship 'Etna', loaded with timber cargo, having moved in a gale at sea.

When the ill-fated Severn Railway Bridge was under construction, there was a large black wooden building erected on the canal bank, the Purton side, to accommodate the workers, known locally as the Black Hut. When the bridge was completed it was turned into two bungalows, back to back. The first engineer on the bridge and his family lived in one half until it was demolished in 1934. He worked for the Great Western Railway Company. The other half was inhabited by an employee of the Canal Company and his family, as it was quite a large building. Because the Black Hut was tarred all round it never rotted outside, but inside sadly it was a different story. So it finally had to be demolished. The only thing that remains now is a pile of wall bricks that are the remnants of the wash house, or the salmon house.

Opposite the Black Hut was the timber pond. This was for seasoning bulk timber and was known as Marshfield. There was also a lay-by here used to lay ships up. Going on from here we came to the two Purton canal bridges, then on again to the Patch bridge at Slimbridge. The land around here was known as the New Grounds and was used in the war years to grow potatoes for the war effort. There was a warehouse here used to store the crop. Later it became a camping and equipment sales site. The New Grounds became the Slimbridge Wild Fowl Trust.

Continuing up river we sailed through the Cambridge Arms Bridge. Just up above here was the entrance to the river Frome, which when in flood, carried silt down to settle in the canal. Next was the Frampton Splatt and on to Frampton bridge. Then we came to Cadbury's factory, where the longboats were loaded with chocolate crumb or raw chocolate for transporting to Bournville. The longboats were owned by Fellows Moreton and Clayton, the Severn Canal Carrying Co. and the Birmingham Canal Navigation Company. There was also one coal carrying barge named the 'Severn Collier' that transported the coal from the coal tips at Sharpness, to this factory at Frampton. Above here, adjacent to the Splatt Bridge, a grain silo was built for transhipping English wheat brought in from farms.

From here, we came to the boat yards at Saul and then the junction of the Stroud Water canal. This was a very busy place in those days. It still is, but pleasure craft are the main customers now.

The Stroud Water Canal has now been cut in two by the M5 motorway. The last craft to go up here was the Severn and Canal long boat the 'MV Swan' loaded with Asphalt blocks. It was two days before Christmas 1940, a very icy day and the canal had frozen over. The crew of the longboat was a Mr and Mrs Sammy Patoe.

Life on a longboat was very hard. I can recall Mrs Patoe standing on the bow with a hook shaft, pushing the ice away while her husband was alternating ahead and astern to break the ice as they came out of the lock at Whitminster. I witnessed this scene when, riding my bicycle home to Sharpnesss, I stopped on the bridge over the canal for a rest.

It seems that the history of the canal from the junction on to the Castle Bridge has been forgotten, but many years ago when the canal was first built it became a haven for smugglers. When the Brigantines and the Barques used to dock at Sharpness bound for Gloucester, they had to be towed up the canal by teams of horses. At Sharpness they were boarded by a customs officer who accompanied them to Gloucester. At the Castle the vessel was usually moored up in the lay by and the customs officer traditionally was invited to partake in a drink at the Castle Inn. Whilst he was drinking the smugglers were of course, busy getting and conveying cases of tea, bales of silk, casks of wine and other dutiable goods into the privacy of their warehouse, whence it was subsequently transported to London. However, this business had a tragic end, in consequence of a drunken quarrel of two wagonners. One of them informed against his companion. The wagon and its incriminating freight were seized and the poor fellow in charge, his name still borne in the locality, was hanged under the vindictive penal code of the day.

The smugglers' warehouse was built with stones which bore the same masons' guild marks are to be found on the Norman work of Gloucester Cathedral. The stones undoubtedly came from the old Norman Castle at Moreton Vallance three quarters of a mile away.

After leaving the Stroudwater Junction the next interesting place is the Pilot at Quedgeley. Here was a very large petrol and oil depot, with the wharf on the right hand side. As larger vessels started carrying here, the canal bank had to be opened up on the opposite side

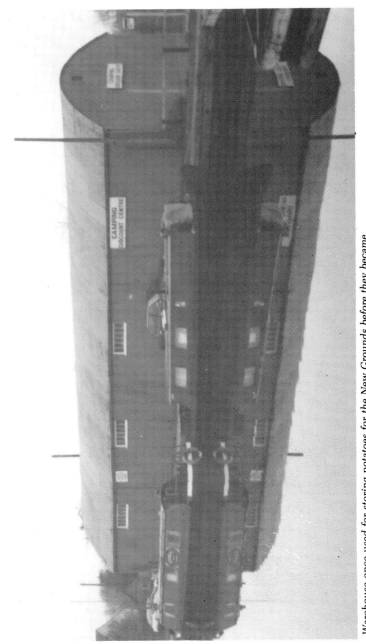

Warehouse once used for storing potatoes for the New Grounds before they became the Wild Fowl Trust. 1942.

Entering the canal for Shell Depot at Quedgeley. 1971

'Vindicatrix' sea training ship, prior to sailing for Newport and the breakers yard.

Another ship being turned around prior to locking out for sailing.

'Vindicatrix' going to the breakers.

Vessels entering Sharpness Dock, prior to sailing. 1968

Gas-water barges moored in the dock at Sharpness. 1950's

50

Two tankers 'Regent Jill' and 'Regent Lady' prior to sailing from Sharpness. 1938

'Mayflower' leaving Sharpness Docks for Gloucester in June 1991.

View from High Bridge at Sharpness showing old black bungalow on the canal bank. 1926

Two ships at Marshfield lay by, between Sharpness and Purton. 1920

'Severn Side' loaded with wheat bound for Reynolds Flour Mill at Gloucester proceeding up the canal at Purton. 1980

The 'M.V. Berkeley' rounding Purton Upper Turn, bound for the Depot at Quedgeley, Gloucester. 1971

Ship being towed up the canal. Photo taken at Purton. 1925

Purton Upper Bridge.

Two large tankers passing at Splatt Bridge in the canal. 1970

Tug built at Stroud.

The Junction. The crossing of the Stroudwater canal and the Gloucester and Berkeley canal.

The entrance to the Stroudwater canal and the lock gates of the canal to Framilode built in 1826 and closed in the early 1900's.

to allow these large tankers to swing round to make their way back down to Sharpness light ship.

From the Pilot we proceed up to the two mile turn outside Gloucester dock and Hempstead. On the right hand side here was a water dock for bulk timber to season. Then came the saw mills owned by the Morelands Match factory adjacent to the A38. They were always very busy here unloading match logs from the lighters. Lighters were brought up the canal from Avonmouth and Sharpness after being loaded out of deep sea freighters into these craft. Morelands once owned two of their own motor craft named the 'River King' and the 'Sunrisen', but these were later sold to a firm in Worcester and used for carrying wheat. Above here was a wharf for discharging ashore a spirit for use in the manufacture of gas, and for loading waste water for discharge into the Channel. Above this wharf was a little dry dock, used for the repair of small craft and worked in conjunction with the dry dock at Saul junction. It is still being used to this day. Above this came Hempstead bridge. The working quays from here went all round the docks to Monk Meadow timber ponds. The warehouse at the Hempstead Bridge was used exclusively for the storing of Calcium Carbide. This was very dangerous. It gave out a very highly explosive gas even under the slightest damp condition. Therefore it had to be kept completely dry and it was watched day and night.

As we proceeded, just above this area there were timber lighters moored bow to stern up as far as Fosters Mill. This was the Gloucester timber yards and mills. As all the building timber for every conceivable building job went through here it was always a very busy site.

The Foster Mills were also invariably busy with oil seed and animal feed milling. The raw material was brought up from ships at Sharpness and Avonmouth, mostly by their own barges. They owned the largest dumb barges on the waterway.

From here we went through the Llanthony Bridge and into Gloucester dock. Here was the home of the Severn Canal Company and their dock constantly contained their long boats and barges. It was possible to walk from one side of the dock to the other across them. Another dock was reached through the main dock, through a cutting

Cadbury's factory at Frampton, where the chocolate crumb was loaded for Bourneville into long boats.

The lock gates to Framilode canal with the date plaque in place.

The junction of the two canals; Stroudwater and Gloucester to Sharpness canal. Photograph taken in 1978.

with a bridge. The inner arm incorporated a mill and building firm with a concrete warehouse on the quay.

One of the vessels to come here belonged to Smiths of Bristol the 'SS Calcaria'. She was so big she got stuck on the bottom in the Llantony bridge-hole. She was hauled out by two tugs and then towed through and into the Old Arm (as it was termed) for discharging. This was in the year 1935. The mill in this dock was run by Priday Metford & Co., who had their own fleet of craft bringing wheat to the mill. This fleet has also now finished along with the mill in the dock owned by Reynolds and their fleet of craft. Around the dock were warehouses for many other products, including sack repairers to the mills and other establishments.

Across there is another lock that leads back into the river, there is a railway line and turntable, since removed, to enable firms with railway wagons to use that side of the dock. These warehouses were used to store salt brought down from Droitwich. Over the years, the walls became saturated with the salt and the birds flocked on to the walls to peck the salt out of the mortar. Eventually the birds weakened the joints much the buildings had to be demolished.

At the end of this quay were two dry docks and repair yards always in constant use. The quays here were often two or three lighters deep. The work load was colossal in this dock. Many firms used the buildings including, stevedore firms, offices and other amenities related to the docks.

There was also a man that owned two motor long boats, which traded out of Gloucester to Birmingham and other areas in the Midlands. This was Charles Ballinger who always carried goods for Morelands Match Factory. As he had the sole carrying rights he always had plenty of work.

Back out through Llanthony Bridge were the moorings for the tug fleet. Their towing office was on the roadside close to the bridge. All the way down this wall, which was owned by the Railway Company, were rail sidings and moorings for lighters. These were moored two and three abreast as far down as the green bank, as it was called. This was a piece of ground outside the jurisdiction of the Railway Company and was approximately 100 yards long. There was another quay wall running along and into Monk Meadow oil dock. This wall

One of the 1,000 ton tankers making its way to Gloucester oil dock. 1970

*One of the Bristol Colliers belonging to A. G. Smiths, a regular trader to
Gloucester. 1930*

Pair of tankers proceeding to the Rea Bridge. 1941

Approaching the Rea Bridge in the canal, from the bank. 1941

65

Even pilots made mistakes on the canal. 1950

Jammed in ice, waiting for tugs to free them in the canal. 1963

Tugs acting as ice breakers in the canal and towing a string of barges up through to Gloucester. 1963

Gloucester Docks, 1930's.

Docks at Gloucester in the 1950's.

'Empire Laird' proceeding out of the lock to go astern onto jetty.

"Empire Laird" moored at jetty outside Gloucester lock with the power station in the background.

70

The Coaster "Empire Laird" proceeding through Gloucester lock into River Severn.

'Regent Jill' on the stocks in Gloucester dry dock. 1950

'Regent Swift' in Monk Meadow Dock.

constantly had tankers moored two abreast. They were large tankers capable of carrying somewhere in the region of two to three hundred tons from Swansea to Worcester. These craft were owned mostly by J. Harkers Ltd. of Knottingley.

In the late 60's the Shell B.P. Company brought out a fleet of six tankers with a new type of rudderless propelling equipment called Schnieder Propelling Gear. This was found to be useless in these shallow waters. They were forever breaking down because if a blade fouled an underwater object and was damaged, the vessel had to be taken to the repair yards and the whole propelling unit replaced. Trips were lost to the men and the Company lost money.

We now entered the Monk Meadow Dock. This was an area used by the oil companies. There were oil tanks and also compounds all around, for storage of oil. Then there was a silo for the storage of the grain brought in from the farms, for loading onto ships for export. Just inside Monk Meadow was another small mill where linseed oil was extracted. They had a small barge approximately twenty feet long and eight feet beam, named the 'King'. This was loaded here and taken across to Fosters Mill and discharged for resale.

At Monk Meadow there was always something moving or being moved. They also had twenty four hour security in operation in case of fire.

On below Monk Meadow dock was another large timber pond. This was yet another area for seasoning bulk timber. This pond was used continuously with very large timber bulks made into rafts.

9

The Canal

The Gloucester and Berkeley Canal was a very busy waterway. There were craft moving up and down ceaselessly. To traverse the canal in the early years you had to book a time and a Passman. Because the bridges were in two halves, one side had to be opened by the resident bridge man and the other by the Passman. The Passman was a man that began from Purton by opening his half of the bridge and then riding his bicycle on from bridge to bridge to pass you through the canal to Gloucester, Hempstead or vice versa. Sometimes, if you were going from Gloucester to Sharpness for tide and there were a number of craft or coming off tide the other way, there would be two passmen, one to open the bridges and the other to shut them. It was a long hard ride, worse if there was a head wind. There were twelve bridges. Later they were made single span. Passmen then became redundant.

Sometimes the wind was so strong it was impossible for the Passmen to work. In this case vessels used to push these bridges open with their bows or to pull them open with a rope. It was a very precise operation to avoid damage. However, if it wasn't done nothing could move on the canal and it would soon get fouled up with craft. Tides would be lost and trips would be lost.

10

The Graveyards

The 'Spry' was rescued from the old basin at Worcester and taken to the Ironbridge Museum for restoration, but most of all the other craft were inspected and condemned as beyond repair in the boat yard at Saul and sent out to become breakwaters. Two of the vessels regularly inspected at Saul and repaired, were the two pilot cutters 'Berkeley Castle' and 'Alaska'. Run and maintained by the Sharpness Channel pilots, these two craft were built from oak trees donated to the pilots by the Earl of Berkeley. The 'Berkeley Castle' was keeled and built with a single oak tree but the 'Alaska' was built by the residue of the tree and as there was not enough of the trunk left, it had to be built with a split keel. However, because of the iron bolts that were used, she soon rotted away. When she was first condemned she was at Sharpness, moored in the old dock small lock entrance. She was then moved into the old dock basin, but later had to pay the price and was put behind the old dock pier where she finally rotted away.

The 'Berkeley Castle' was bought by a man named George Partridge of the milling family of Pershore. When he was using it as a house boat at Tewkesbury in the mouth of the river Avon it caught fire and it was gutted opposite Healings Mill, on what is known as Tewkesbury Ham. That was the last of the pilot cutter 'Berkeley Castle'.

11

Bad Weather in the Canal

In high winds the canal could be treacherous. In such conditions, particularily in strong cross winds, we struggled hard to keep our craft up to the wind. Our vessels had to be screwed through the bridges at speed to avoid the gale forcing our stern aground or damaging the propeller on rocks in the canal bank. If the motor craft was towing a dumb barge, it was twice as difficult to hold it up to wind.

Very often, the canal swinging bridges were pushed off their plinth when the winds blew hard. The Canal Company kept special jacks and other equipment, which enabled them to put them back on in a couple of hours if this happened.

When gales were forecast, the masters of all vessels were given information on the weather conditions at all ports in the Severn Estuary by the harbour masters. If there was heavy wind blowing, the strength of the wind would be given, such as 'gale force six' or 'gale force eight'.

Our tankers, sat very low in the water. When loaded they had a freeboard of about 2 foot. Because of this they were nicknamed 'Severn Submarines'.

If a gale was forecast in the region of force eight, everything was lashed down and covers put over the hatches. The ventilators would be turned away from the wind and stoppers inserted to prevent water entering the cabins and engine rooms.

I remember one particular night well. We were sailing out of Sharpness bound for Avonmouth, but the Harbour master omitted to tell us that the wind was going to increase to storm force eleven. The tide was at its peak when we left Sharpness. By the time we got to the Aust or Beachley points, the wind was very severe. There were three of us bound for Avonmouth and the elements began to pound us mercilessly. We finally got to Charston and turned for Avonmouth. I had to struggle with the wheel to keep her head to sea and wind. By this time we had been on passage for about three hours and had yet to reach the safety of Avonmouth. We eventually made it after four hours.

The harbour master had been watching all of us and had kept his men on duty, so as I approached the entrance he had his men open the gates of the lock. I entered and he made his men close the gates to enable them to take our mooring ropes. He did exactly the same for the other two vessels. When he had all three in the lock he lifted us up in the dock and then came to all three of us and told us off. He asked why we had been out there in such atrocious weather. We all said the same thing, that we had not been warned about wind conditions. As he thought the last vessel to dock had appeared to be in difficulties, he demanded a written report from the master. The other master and I were excused.

Afterwards, when we went below to the cabins, it took hours to put them tidy before we could have a rest. I then found I had lost my spare anchor. Its lashings had parted. Also, the lifeboat had come loose and gone back against the wheelhouse and also moved that. We all considered ourselves lucky to be safe.

This was one incident, but there were many others. I remember a friend of mine belonging to the Severn Motor Yachting Club who wished to go with his yacht to Barry. He duly engaged a pilot and they sailed out of Sharpness with a wind force four. When he reached Avonmouth the vessel started to dance a little. The Pilot who was used to this just carried on, but on looking at the owner and wife, he saw that they were very uncomfortable. He then said to him 'Are you frightened Sir?' 'No' he said, 'I am not frightened - I am bloody petrified!' Needless to say, they did get to Barry. The owner then engaged the coxswain of Barry Lifeboat to take her back to Sharpness for him. The owner and his wife caught the train back. He told me afterwards 'I am not going out there again for all the money in the world!' I know he never did.

When the tankers were loaded, however much water came on board it always ran back off, but with the cargo craft it was different. If ever their canvas hatch covers were ripped in heavy weather they would almost certainly sink. So they just did not sail out into bad weather and as the tug masters were aware of this, they had to be careful as well.

There were many days and nights when we had to brave heavy weather. The one at the beginning of this chapter was one of the worst I can recall and I believe the other two skippers, like myself, will never forget it.

Another hazard on the canal was fog. In these conditions, we had to keep a look-out at all times as there were many smaller craft moored to the bank. One touch from one of our large craft could sink them.

When in fog, we approached a bridge, the bridgeman used a whistle to tell us the bridge was open. Sometimes he walked down the bank to help to guide us through. Some said the bridgemen only come off their bridge to avoid getting 'a wet shirt' if the bridge was hit into the canal! This actually had happened on several occasions so it was not such a joke. Being without propellers, the dumb barges were very hard to handle. If they were not in a dead straight line for the bridge hole, they would invariably collide with it.

In fog in the canal, the length of the craft had to be taken into consideration before moving. The tugs were at an advantage for their wheelhouse was more or less on the bow and their visibility was unimpeded. Whereas, the barges and tankers had their wheelhouses aft, so the helmsman had to look the whole length of the craft before he could see anything. This is why the skippers wanted a certain amount of visibility before moving in the canal, as much damage could be caused by running into other craft, bridges and jetties.

In severe icy weather, the canal used to freeze over and tugs were employed as ice breakers to keep the canal open. But in the very severest weather, these same tugs had to tow a fleet of motor powered vessels through. One tug would break the ice whilst the other towed. All craft were moored together and with their combined engine power, helped get through to Gloucester or Sharpness. Very often ships would jam in the ice and a tug was sent to pull them free. If a loaded craft was proceeding up the canal and a light craft down, and they attempted to pass, invariably the ice would collect and build up between them. Then they would become stuck fast, unable to move ahead or astern. Again the tugs would come to the rescue.

The outer gates at Sharpness dock would often freeze up. If this happened the harbour master and his men had to break the ice with hook shafts where the gates came together and the heel of the gate had

'Wave', a passenger boat on the canal at Frampton, one of two. The other one was the 'Lapwing', 1928

The Harbour Master and his men breaking the ice on the entrance gates to try and open them. 1962

Crew of the 'John Harker' walking on the ice in the canal.

to be cleared before they could be opened for tide. We all dreaded navigating in ice, as our job was made twice as hard. In extreme cold our ropes would freeze solid and could snap in two.

In the early years there were two passenger steamers, the 'Lapwing' and 'Wave', plying the canal. Every bridge had a nearby landing stage for embarking and disembarking passengers. The two craft used to run twice a day from Llantony Bridge to Sharpness High Bridge. They would also carry parcels, if the customer was prepared to put them aboard and arrange for someone to collect them at their destination. It was a two hour service.

12

Passing up the Severn from Gloucester

Passing up the river Severn to the Midlands was a very hard task in bad weather. In flood water or when the water was at summer level, the river was very busy from early morning until late at night. If our vessel was bound out of Gloucester to the Midlands, we would leave Gloucester docks at five in the morning. Vessels would pass through the lock into the river in turn. By the time all had left the lock that were waiting to leave, the craft that were on passage from Sharpness were commencing their locking out into the river. Additionally, craft coming down river from Worcester had also began to arrive and required locking in. This lock was often congested. Gloucester lock was, until the 60's, hand operated. Improvements came when the lock was mechanised and fewer hands were needed to work it. However, the time spent in filling and emptying was no quicker, so our speed was not improved by all this mechanisation.

Here in the late 1940's a wharf was built opposite the lock on the Castle Meads for three new coastal craft to unload coal from South Wales. This never worked. The river men all knew just why this could not have worked and had said so beforehand. However, those in control thought they knew better. The three coastal ships were built, but just as predicted by the rivermen, could not be used because there was always a silt bar outside the lock. This was formed by the lock water being let out into the river.

When the vessels were lowered into the river, they had to navigate up the quay wall until their sterns were clear of the lock, go out into the centre then reverse back to get onto this new wharf. But they used to foul onto the silt bar and could not get back to their berth. Consequently, the coal fired power station had to be bunkered by coal from rail wagons brought onto the Castle Meads sidings. The three coasters the 'Empire Reaper', 'Empire Rancher' and 'Empire Laird' were sold. The 'Empire Laird' met its fate in the Newport river in South Wales, breaking its back across a bridge after breaking away from her moorings.

On the quay at Gloucester lock was a berth for four tugs, which were always busy towing timber lighters and various barged goods from Gloucester up to Worcester or Stourport-on-Severn. Sometimes this was done two at a time. In the early days they used to tow up to six longboats where they joined the canals, to be towed by horse or mules on into the Midlands. In latter years, craft with aluminium ingots, dried fruit, butter and other food stuffs were being transported to the depots on the river side, at Worcester and Stourport-on-Severn.

Before the large wharves were built the quay wall above Worcester bridge on the port, or left hand side of the river, was used as a discharging wharf for a lot of these perishable goods. The jibs of the vessels' mast and structure lifted their load ashore straight onto lorries as there were no warehouses there.

There was continuous movement of craft from Gloucester lock. There were four tugs based on the quay wall at Gloucester. Barges or lighters were locked down to the same level of the river and the tug that was ordered for them would go back down the quay wall to the lock entrance and tow out up the river to Worcester or Stourport-on-Severn.

The river from the lock up as far as the tar works is not very wide and very winding. This made it very risky to navigate. To pass one another either way you had to run alongside. It was difficult to negotiate bridges, such as the Westgate road bridge and the Gloucester Railway bridge. In the early years, the road bridge was a stone archway and was very precarious, but it was taken down in the early 1950's and replaced with an iron bridge. The railway bridge was a swing bridge, but wasn't used as such. The centre table was held up by six pillars about five foot across, so the width of the navigational part was not very wide. In later years, the outer pillar in the navigable part was taken out making the arch wider. Even so, when we were making up towards the bridge we had to blow the ships' siren to see if anything was coming the other way. A look-out had to be on the bow at all times, watching and listening for any craft going up or down through the river.

It was very dangerous for any craft to navigate the length of the parting from Gloucester lock to the Butler's tar works at Sandhurst.

Once the vessels had cleared the tar works, the river widens to twice its width and we could navigate without a look-out, from here to Worcester, or up to Stourport-on-Severn, as long as we knew the deep water channel as taught to us by the old river men. There were no better teachers than the old long boat and lighter men, most of whom had been brought up on the river and knew all the tricks. They were invaluable as teachers.

The Haw Bridge after demolition.

'MV Darleydale' after hitting Haw Bridge.

Entering Tewkesbury Lock.

Haw Bridge being dismantled.

Haw Bridge being dismantled.

13

The First Length

The fast tidal length of the river was from Gloucester to Tewkesbury, If tides were 24ft 5ins at Sharpness they lipped the weir at Gloucester, Hempstead or Maisemore and lifted the river height up from here onward. A large bore tide could lift the water up as far as Diglis or Worcester Lock.

After clearing Ashleworth Quay we were on the way to Wainlode Hill. Here was a difficult shallow right opposite the cliff. After clearing this, on our starboard side was an island of sunken Severn long boats. Clearing the island, we came to the entrance of the Coombe canal. The lock here had been dismantled and replaced by stop gates to prevent flood water going into the canal and filling all the low ground. From here we came to Haw bridge, now only of single span; the original bridge having had three arches. Because of a collision by a tanker named the 'MV Darleydale', it had to be demolished and the new one built. The original bridge was built of cast iron, and the skipper was maybe over cautious careful in navigating the bridge. He dropped down into the arch, went in under the side and hit the ironwork. It collapsed onto the wheelhouse and killed the master.

When the 'MV Darleydale' demolished Haw Bridge I consider my crew and myself thankful to the Police Force. That night I was running back to Gloucester Quay with the 'Regent Jill' for the morning tide at Sharpness. The river was in full flood and I approached Tewkesbury lock with the full intention of going over the weir. The lock keeper was waving a red light on the island and I sent my mate forward to see what was wrong. He came back to tell me that the message was that the 'Darleydale' had hit an arch down. As there were two others I decided to carry on and take one of them. As I approached the White Lion pub up above the bridge I saw a car flashing its headlights and a flashing blue light on its roof. I then decided to stop. I turned my bow into the port bank where the force of the water turned me round and I

Upper Lode Lock gates being replaced after repair.

Tankers pumping over Upper Lode Lock for cargos to be carried on up the river.

92

Upper Lode being cleaned out.

Upper Lode Lock being cleaned out.

'Severn Traveller' and 'Regent Swift' proceeding out of Upper Lode Lock. 1953

dropped across to the starboard bank alongside the farm house and the car. My mate threw a rope ashore, this was put round a tree and the end thrown back aboard and made fast. I walked forward to see what was wrong. The police sergeant told me all three arches were down and in no way could I carry on. I was thankful he had stopped me! I then had to stop the 'Regent Swallow' from attempting the same thing and he moored alongside me. Both of our craft and crews' lives had been saved.

Passing on up river we had to cross and recross the river up to the White Lion, keeping within the deep water channel and up to the basket makers. Then to the salmon draft, where they long net for salmon. Next to the Yew Tree, and then on to the Lower Lode to pass the lower entrance to the River Avon. We then made our way on up to the Upper Lode bottom cutting, which took us into the lock. Here we would lock up to get into the next river length. The bore tides from here to Worcester Diglis lock have made as much as ten inches at this point, much to the surprise of many river men. This reminded everyone of the power of the bore tides, which could level the lock at Tewkesbury. Many is the lucky vessel that has navigated the Upper Lode lock at Tewkesbury with all four gates open without having to lock up. This saved them much time.

Most river men liked to clear the parting before the tides came up behind them. Then they could certainly move up river at speed. The tide would be rising and taking them with increased velocity along all the shallow places, such as Wainlode, Haw bridge, the White Lion and the fishing draft, where sand banks were formed. All these places could be navigated at full speed. With the aid of a good tide, the time between Gloucester lock to the Upper Lode lock at Tewkesbury could be cut by at least an hour. No river man worth his salt would miss the opportunity of running with a good tide.

When leaving Gloucester lock, with the river at summer level, we had to contend with a bed of mud right up as far as Ashleworth Quay. We had to stop several times to go into astern with our propeller, this cleared the mud, silt and leaves from it. If we did not do this we would lose all power and would not make any headway on our passage up the river.

Coming down from Worcester, empty. Mythe Bridge, Tewkesbury.

Shell Tanker going towards Mythe Bridge, Tewkesbury.

'Regent Jill' proceeding to lock at Worcester.

Illegal towing of a Tar Barge.

98

If we were towing and had to 'clear the prop', we had to be careful to set the tow rope once we went ahead again. If we were towing two dumb barges, we had to be twice as careful. If we parted our tow ropes, we had to go back to pick up the barges and join our tow up again. We also had to ease our speed over shallows so that the dumb craft did not run across the shallow channel and go aground. It has been up to two or three hours before we have been able to pull them off into deep water once again. This has happened with motor craft on their own. A tug has had to be sent to pull them off the shallow into deep water. Then of course, the cargo has been that much later being delivered. The cargo was late in being delivered which was very annoying if it was expected by waiting lorries.

Tewkesbury Upper Lode Lock is what is termed as a tidal lock. It used to have a tidal basin and lock but now is just one complete unit. It can hold four ordinary size craft or lighters. This is an advantage to the transport on the river as it saved time for them. If they blew their sirens for the lock and there was room enough, the lock keepers would get them in. It also saved water when the river was at summer level.

When leaving Tewkesbury lock we passed the entrance to the River Avon. We looked to the Healings Mill then approached Mythe Bridge. Here, the old long boatmen used to fill their water butts because, it was said, the river bed just above the bridge is full of springs and the water very pure, clear and clean. From here the river is quite deep right up as far as Sandy point where it winds in a figure 'S'.

From above Mythe Bridge to the Sexton Lode Rail bridge, since demolished, was the underground Air Ministry petroleum Ripple Depot served by the river tankers. Up river on the starboard side was the water extraction point for the City of Coventry. Onwards we passed through Upton-on-Severn. Here the river has some very shallow areas. Just above the bridge at Upton is a bad sand bank bottom which had to be negotiated with great care.

Travelling on, we came to Stoke Hill where there is a rock bottom. All vessels treat this hazard with great caution. On rounding this corner into Severn Stoke, there is a nice length of water up to the Rhyde. Here was a very shallow run. The cliff was on our port side. The channel was very close to our starboard side shore and we had to adhere to it. When clear of this we were into a stretch of comparatively deep water to Clevelode. It was here in the 1950's that rocks had to be blown out of the channel with explosives because the deeper craft were hitting the bottom too frequently.

Rounding this we entered what was commonly known as the five mile hole. Here we had a shallow channel right up the river to the beginning of Kempsey Bay, as it was known. Entering Kempsey Bay we pass the first yacht club moorings then on up the bay to the Upper Kempsey Yacht Club moorings. Through here we approached the River Teme. Once we had passed here we came to an extremely shallow part of the river. On the starboard side there is a long line of sunken long boats put there in an effort to hold the bank in position. This is the reason for the shallow channel here.

Then on we went up to Diglis Locks. Here there are two river locks, one large and one small. In the late 50's the small one was widened in the lower part of the lock This was because our vessels could not lock down as the tankers were all 19ft 6ins wide and the lock about 18ft 6ins. Prior to this, the large lock had to be used for all vessels, which took a long time when vessels started to congregate above and below the lock.

Tug 'Enterprise' and tow entering Worcester Dock.

101

Diglis lock being cleaned out.

Diglis large dock under overhaul and cleaning out. New gates being put into place.

Men cleaning out Diglis large dock.

Lifting out Stopping Baulks from the bottom of Diglis Lock.

Lifting Stopping Baulks out and letting water back in to fill lock.

103

Pumping lock out at Diglis prior to cleaning and repairing, with tankers pumping cargo over lock as a Tewkesbury Upper Lode Lock.

'Shell Steelmaker' reversing out of oil basin into top cutting, prior to turning and proceeding to lock.

104

Worcester General Cargo Berth for unloading all imports from Bristol Channel ports. 1950's

'Deerhurst' from Tewkesbury entering Worcester Diglis lock going to load English
wheat at the General Cargo Berth. 1950's

'Deerhurst' proceeding out of Diglis lock into top cutting.

14

Diglis Lock and Worcester Length

All the equipment for repairing the locks was at Worcester and the vessels moored here were to do with this type of repair work. The workshops were on the island because it was important to keep all the operation in one place. Also in this top cutting, was a mooring basin for discharging tankers up to 400 tons and on the opposite shore was a berth for timber vessels. All spaces were taken up almost every day of the week.

After we passed from the upper cutting back into the river and were about 200 yards clear of the cutting, we came to a new quay. This was the Diglis quay. This quay was for discharging of all sorts of goods, including perishable items. A few of the vessels, owned by Bristol firms, carried up to 300 tons. Some of their crews were Bristol men and some were river men employed by the Severn and Canal Carrying Company including ex-longboat men.

Just above this berth is another boat lock for the canal. A grain barge carrying approximately 140 tons named the 'River King' and another, the 'Sunrise', used to trade to the flour mill. In general it was quite busy in this area.

From here on up through Worcester town was a beautiful stretch of water. On our starboard side we passed the Diglis Hotel and then came to an avenue of trees. Here was the Cathedral with its well-kept grounds sloping down to the wall of the river walk.

Next we came to the Worcester Road Bridge consisting of five stone arches, badly marked as a result of vessels colliding with it when the river was in flood. All vessels needing to negotiate this bridge in summer level had to use the second arch from the port side, because none of the others were deep enough. The quay just above the bridge on the port side was for discharging cargo before the other wharf at Diglis was built. Not far from here, on the other side, was another jetty, built after the war for discharging coal. It was never satisfactory though, because the water was not really deep enough at this point.

Then on through the Railway Bridge, to approach Worcester Racecourse where, in the years before and just after the war, there were two swimming pools in the river. Chained to the shore, they rose and fell with the water against concrete pillars. They were not used too often as, I believe, mostly the water was too cold for comfort. They were simply river water running through wire mesh fencing. Past the swimming pools, we came to a boathouse owned and run by the Worcester College for Boys, and then on up to the racecourse length.

The short length of river from the boathouse to the Dog and Duck ferry was said by the longboat men, to be one of the deepest parts of the river. Indeed, I have seen a river man dip a twenty foot long shaft here and not touch bottom. But from the ferry to the top end of the racecourse it is very shallow, which struck me as most peculiar. Then we came to the intake for the Worcester Water Works, built after the war. On past here and bound for Bevere, the river winds round some very shallow areas up to the Camp Hotel, then it straightens out into Bevere Lock or nicknamed, Camp Lock, for obvious reasons. Then we would go into Camp Lock. Most of the tankers were designed to fit this lock, especially the dumb craft, for they had to be pulled in tight against the upper gates. Once one gate was shut, the rudder was put up behind it. Then the other gate was shut before they could be lifted up in the lock, to proceed into the next pound or length.

Above this lock was an entrance to a weir cutting, and when tugs or motor barges were towing up river they had to make sure the bow of their craft was up against the bank while the craft they were towing was locked up. If this was not done they could be swept into the weir cutting by the pressure of the water.

'Regent Linnet' rising up on Bevere Lock. 1958

'Regent Linnet' going into Bevere Lock prior to entering next length of river. 1950's

Tug 'Severn Active' entering Holt Lock with 'Sabrina' and 'Severn Falcon' in tow, bound for Stourport. 1950's

15

Bevere to Holt Lock

Once clear of Bevere lock we progressed out of the cutting. There was a further weir cutting on our starboard side creating an island known by the rivermen as Camp Island. Once out into the river and going on, we came to the Droitwich Canal lock. This is now disused but the lock-house is privately owned and very well looked after. Just upstream is another river entry known as the Droitwich river. This river is used by yachts traversing into the boat-yard just the other side of the A38, which is approximately one mile from here. Carrying on up the river from here we came to Hawford Rovings and Grimly Sands.

In summertime this was a favourite spot for bathers. The sand here stretched right out three quarters of the width of the river. The channel winds its way to Holt Castle boathouse, then very close to the overhanging trees by the Holt Wharf Hotel. The river bottom from the boathouse to the hotel is very hard rock, so it had to be navigated with great care. Once clear of the Wharf we were opposite the Holt Fleet Hotel. Then we were under Holt Bridge and into Holt Lock.

Once locked up at Holt we had to navigate at slow speed until we cleared the cutting. Then we would have to clear the propeller of twigs and leaves before we continued on to approach the Lenchford Inn and boat moorings. We would pass here at reduced speed then head up river to another bad shallow called Shrawley Wood. Again we would drop our speed until up over the shallow and on to Chitters Ditch. Here was a stream coming into the Severn from the hills on our port side. Then on again to Hampstall, were there is a submerged bar of rock stretching from one side of the river to the other. This could be very dangerous to all vessels. Once over this we could navigate on to Lincombe Lock passing some moorings on our starboard side. Tankers discharged here into the Air Ministry Depot on top of the cliff, known as Lincomb Hall.

Next we would come to Lincombe Lock. On the starboard side is the old river entrance where water only used to flow into the Severn after

Discharging berth at Stourport just outside Lincombe top cutting. 1950's

General cargo vessel 'Severn Merchant' just clearing top cutting at Lincombe with mast and jib ready for discharging. 1950's

Upper jetty for handling general cargo with loaded craft waiting their turn. Also long boat waiting to proceed up into Midlands after loading aluminium ingots. 1950's

Top jetty and craft unloading aluminium ingots. Stourport 1950's

The Regent Oil Depot at Stourport-on-Severn. 1950's

The Northern Section of The Regent Depot in Stourport. 1950's

115

The 'Regent Linnet' approaching the Depot. 1958

Loaded tanker about to discharge at Regent Depot, Stourport-on-Severn. 1950

116

'Regent Lark' empty, ready for return journey to Gloucester. 1958

'Regent Linnet' on Regent Depot about to discharge with John Harker craft 'Nancy' passing by after discharging at Power Petrol Depot. 1958

117

heavy rainfall. There is a small pedestrian bridge here where people can see down river towards Hampstall. In the lock, we could see the bottom of the top gates resting on the upper sill. The lift from the bottom level to the top is approximately eight feet, making the top water level about six feet on the sill. This is the approximate amount of water craft can draw to enable them to get to Stourport-on-Severn. So before they load, owners are informed as to the draught they can load to, to reach their destination.

Having cleared the lock we could approach our place of discharge. Two hundred yards outside the cutting was a large general cargo wharf. Up another hundred yards there was a further wharf for timber and next to that was another wharf used for aluminium ingots. Now it is a yacht repair yard and the old timber yard has been excavated to make a mooring dock for the yachts. Above this was the first of the oil jetties; one for Fina Oil. The second and third jetties were for Regent Oil and then the next two for Russian Oil Products, but later taken over by the Regent Oil. About half a mile further on were the Power Petrol depot and jetties, then the Power Station and a little higher up, was the entrance of the Staffordshire canal. It was a very busy little place. Alas, it is all finished as far as commercial craft is concerned.

The river from Gloucester to Stourport-on-Severn is one of the prettiest rivers in the country. The change of seasons and colours was a beauty to behold and enjoyed by all men working the river.

16

The Change of River during Winter

I have described the river in summertime but it is very different in the winter, when there is fog and fresh water floods. In flood, when the river water rises, instead of looking for shallows to find the deep water channel you have to look for tops of trees and bushes growing in the river bank. If, going up river, we did not get behind the corners of the river, the full force of the flood water would stop our headway and it would put many hours on our journey.

Turning round light ship to go down stream in flood water, much inreased the speed of passage home. Leaving Stourport-on-Severn with the river full of water and being able, if the water was high enough, to navigate over the weirs, saved us hours in locking time. The trip from Stourport-on-Severn to Gloucester could take four and a half hours instead of the usual six or seven hours.

All this river work came to an end in the late 70's. The last vessels to use this river were two vessels carrying wheat up river from Avonmouth to Avon and Healings Mill in Tewkesbury. The first of the mill's vessels to finish were the 'MV Deerhurst' the dumb barges 'Bushley' and 'Apperly'. They had purchased two more 'MV Tirley' and 'MV Chaseley' but even these finished. This was the final death knell of navigation of cargo craft on the river Severn.

Running Worcester Bridge in flood water and pushing up through with bare clearance. A regular occurance during floods. Approx. 1955

17

Flood Water; Bridges and Weirs

In flood conditions, whatever his craft, the master had to be sure he could negotiate all the bridges. This was not so much a problem for tankers for we could load with water as ballast. Even so, the masters had to be extremely careful. At Worcester road bridge for instance, we could use any arch going up loaded, but coming down the only one we could use was the middle one.

Our favourite method of passing through in flood was to run at speed at it. Very precise judgement was essential. Many is the craft that has hit the arch and lost wheel house or ventilators when in the process.

We had ways of telling if there was sufficient space to go through bridges. These were in the form of certain landmarks on the shore. One was the hand rail on the bottom lock gates at Bevere Lock. Another, the fence below the boat house at Worcester Racecourse where, when the water was up to the top rail, we knew we could just go through with the wheel house up. Additionally, the lock-keepers telephoned the water heights were up river from lock to lock.

If we needed to take water ballast in, we could do so with the cargo pump. Vessels without a pump could do so with the help of the depot they were discharging at, who filled them with water.

I remember when once leaving the depot at Stourport having filled my tanker with water ballast. The river was 21ft 6ins at Worcester and rising fast. When I arrived at Bevere lock the lock keepers informed me it was then 22ft 6ins at Worcester lock. I said 'Well I've had it until the water drops at Worcester Bridge'. They told me that the 'Regent Swift' and the 'Severn Traveller' were tied on the quay above the bridge but said, to my astonishment, 'If you have the guts your craft will go through', I told them that my vessel stood six inches above the hand rail, and no way would it go through. Those two lock keepers said 'Believe us, you will go through if you do what we say'.

They described how I should ease my craft to just ticking over at the Dog and Duck ferry, half way up the racecourse, until I cleared the

Gloucester lock with flood water above the level of the dock.

Stourport lock at summer level height of water.

Stourport Lincombe, top cutting at summertime.

Barge 'Rosa' jammed under Westgate Street road bridge in flood water.

Two of three tankers leaving Gloucester Lock in flood water. History was made that day. It was the first time they went through the lock when floods made the dock and river the same height.

Two tankers negotiating the old Haw bridge, following after one another.

Upper Lode Lock. Photo taken from deck of tanker about to go over weir.

Tewkesbury Abbey, taken from deck of tanker, across the Tewkesbury Ham in flood.

Lincombe lock in flood with water up to bars on lock gates.

pillar of the railway bridge. Then I must pile on all the speed I had aiming for the pillar between the second and middle arch of the bridge. Then, when I was three quarters of the way to the road bridge, I was to head for the centre of the middle arch. I decided to have a go.

I had the fright of my life. As she entered the bridge her bow dipped down and the stern rose up. At this point I was high enough to actually look through the balustrade of the bridge. As her bow went out the other side it rose and the stern dipped down and with great relief, we cleared the arch.

If I had not had faith in those two lock keepers, who were two ex-longboat men and knew a good deal more about the river above Gloucester than I, I wouldn't have dared try it. But thanks to them I was on my way to Gloucester Docks and another trip under my belt.

Once the water started to rise, the general cargo craft were unable to traverse the river at all. If the water rose when they were above Gloucester, they became trapped and had to be laid up. They were then a liability to their owners. Consequently, they tried not to let them go above Gloucester when flood water was imminent. They would then be used instead to carry from ports in the Bristol Channel to Gloucester. I have seen a dozen general cargo craft moored in a line, above the railway bridge at Gloucester, because they were unable to get under the bridge. Also, many empty general cargo craft were moored at Stourport-on-Severn waiting for the water to recede so that tugs could take them down river. Large tankers had a problem at Haw Bridge, the Mythe Bridge and the Black Bridge at Gloucester in the same way we had at Worcester.

Although problems were caused by running with the flow of the water down river through these bridges, there was another method. This was dropping down through, stern-wise, by putting a rope out through the bow leads and on to the shore. We had to do this to make sure we could get under bridges without hitting them. At Worcester, a man would be put ashore to attach a rope onto a bollard on the quay wall. The vessel was then dropped through stern first. When the vessel had cleared the bridge the man on the shore dropped the rope into the water for the men on board to pull it in. The man on shore would then sprint across the bridge, get back on board and the vessel would be turned round to get under way again.

At Gloucester, under the railway bridge it was unfortunate for the larger craft. First, in order to get under the bridge, they would unbolt and drop their wheelhouse. Then they would have to go all the way back to Gloucester quay and proceed into Gloucester lock stern first, to turn round again in the dock. In the meantime, they would have put the wheelhouse back up and everything back to ship shape again. As these vessels came past the marker board at the entrance to Sandhurst Ditch, they knew what they had to do at the bridge. About half a mile from the railway bridge up river there was a large piece cut out of the starboard bank. When they approached this area they could put their bow here, which gave them room to swing. Their sterns would then be clear to drop stern first to Gloucester lock. The unfortunate thing was that there was one girder that hung just three inches below the others and that was the most arduous part of getting through. Other obstacles in our way were the empty cargo lighters moored above the bridge that were unable to get through until the floods dropped.

18

Leisure

Once a year, the first Saturday in September, at Stourport-on- Severn, there was a large carnival, with a procession on the roads and through the town. But there was also a river carnival and I have seen tugs, motor cargo vessels all decorated up and entered in the carnival river procession by the various firms. In earlier years longboats too were decked up and entered, but whether the owners had given permission or not, I'll never know.

All my time of working on the Severn we got on well with the yachtsmen. Whether they were from privately owned or hired craft we made friends with them. There was hardly a cross word between us. We used to moor at the public houses along the river and enjoy a good summer evening with them whenever we could spare an hour ashore. I made friends with quite a few and one yacht owner based at Tewkesbury aboard a large cabin cruiser named the 'Maid of the Mist' became a good friend. He once confided in me that the yacht owners, hired craft-owners and club members up and down the river were told if you get in trouble such as going aground, and you see a tug or tanker coming, hold a rope up and the skipper will come to your aid. If he has to pull you off the bottom he will be very careful and your vessel will be good hands.

After a days work, especially on a hot summers day, we used to moor near a public house, get into our bathing costumes and tie a ladder to the ships side. Then over into the river for a swim. If yachts were also moored, their crews would often imitate us.

One place we used to swim regularly was by the Wharf Hotel at Holt, where we moored to the pub jetties. After turning out time it was 'over the side lads'.

One evening, when we were returning light ship we came down river to moor at the Wharf Hotel. I could see a large Bathurst hire cruiser from Tewkesbury moored at the jetty. On the deck were two young men, a young lady and a man and woman. We had made our minds to go for a drink followed by a swim in the river. It would have been difficult for us to moor unless they moved up about two feet, so my engineer asked them. They did this while I went down river about a hundred yards and proceeded to swing round. Trees overhung the river on both sides and I was limited for room. I managed to get round and proceeded back up river to the jetty. We moored within two feet of the cruisers stern end. I inspected my tanker to ensure all was safe and then we proceeded into the Hotel to meet the landlord Mr. Flynn and have a few beers. The people from the cruiser also came into the hotel. The gentleman came up to me and said 'Good evening Captain, Would you and your crew like to have a meal with my family and me?' Needless to say, we accepted and it was the beginning of a good night.

During the meal the gentleman and I got talking. He said 'I was absolutely amazed when I watched you swing that large vessel in so confined a space and moor her up so efficiently and neatly. None of my men could do that and their vessels are only a sixth of the size.' I was very intrigued at the authoritative way he spoke. I asked him what his line of work was. He casually remarked 'I am the master of the "HMS Illustrious"', astonishing my crew and myself. He told us that for his annual leave he liked to hire a cruiser somewhere or other. As the talk progressed, the landlords eldest daughter came and asked if we were going swimming at closing time as we always do, this I agreed to. I then had to explain to the gentleman and his family. I asked if they would like to join us. He said 'but its nearly dark' My cabin boy laughed and said 'It won't be, you'll see'. When we got back aboard after our customary help with the washing up and sprucing the pub up we went aboard, rigged the ladder over the side and fixed all the clear lights we had. Then in to the river we all went for a swim before turning in.

We were away early next morning and Mr. Flynn was about and saw us move away. He was in the Birmingham police force and had to be, like us, away early each morning.

This is the sort of thing that happened up and down the river with river men on all craft and at quite a number of the hotels and pubs that had deep enough water outside for us to moor up; Tugs and general cargo craft included. It also made the time more enjoyable spent with each other and in each others' company. I know when we met that cruiser again during the next two weeks the family were all on deck to greet us. I know they had a holiday to remember, as did many others who spent time with river men.

19

The Life

It could be said that the river men had to keep two homes. This was expensive especially when we had to buy our food for aboard and for home. Our pay was a pittance, which made men do certain things they should not have done, to help make ends meet.

We could all cook and if the vessels were fitted with a cooker it was well used. However, some of the lighters did not even have a proper cabin or sanitary equipment. Life could be very hard for the crews of these vessels. If they had to spend a night on board it was usually with an overcoat huddled in a corner somewhere to keep warm. While working the river, they often saw cabbage, sprouts or any vegetable growing on the river side. It was not long before someone jumped ashore to help themselves. Of course, some of these goods sometimes found their way home with the men.

Most if not all craft carried a shot gun, so the poor Severn ducks lived a perilous life. Most of the men were good shots and they did not miss much. Even pheasants were fair game. The favourite place for shooting them and also hares and rabbits was Wainlode Hill. Many a man was put ashore here to pick up game that had been shot.

There were plenty rabbits to catch and even a bit of salmon poaching helped with life and to eke out the wages.

There were many things done by the men to help out on board tankers. For instance, even though the cargo had seals on all the outlets to try and stop one getting cargo out, the men had more ways of 'milking' the cargo than even the most cunning of the designers could have dreamt about. This was done by nearly all the skippers to help make ends meet. They could even keep enough in when discharged and were able to milk it out when the depot representative had inspected and declared them to be empty.

This was a way of life instilled into them more or less by the employers because they kept them so short of wages that the men were forced to fiddle to try and make more money on the side. Any extras were shared with all the crew members to boost their wages a little. In some cases they rigged up a small pump to pump petrol or diesel into forty gallon drums to sell to people who were willing to buy it. Even farmers up the river were glad of it to keep their costs down. It was nothing to see a tractor with trailer with forty gallon drums being loaded from a tanker out in the country. It was easy to do this because they were out of sight of any roads or buildings.

When general cargo vessels were carrying edible goods like sultanas, butter, nuts and suchlike, this could turn the river into the biggest barter area in the west and midlands. It was not unusual to see a vessel carrying one of these cargoes, go alongside a tanker and the transfer of goods take place. I have seen a fifty six pound box of butter opened on a cabin table, the butter cut into cubes and wrapped into grease proof paper then taken home by the crew. Lunch on board that day was a quarter inch thick slice of butter on a thick toasted slice of sandwich loaf and eaten with relish.

It was not unusual to see a bargeman walking home after mooring up, with two carrier bags full of goods for home. Many of the men also kept chickens to keep the family in eggs, so another perk was to sweep the holds of empty grain craft, bag it up and carry that home to feed their hens or rabbits. I don't think anyone begrudged them for doing this because of what how little they were paid for the hours they had to work.

The tanker men were the worst paid as far as hours were concerned. They would leave Sharpness on one tide to Avonmouth and return that evening. This consisted of fourteen hours work. The next morning they would leave Sharpness for Stourport-on-Severn at 5.30 a.m, arrive at Stourport at 4.30 p.m, discharge their cargo, which could take two hours, then back to Worcester Lock by 8.30 p.m., making another fifteen or sixteen hour day. Then from Worcester the next morning at 5 a.m. arriving at Sharpness about twelve noon making a seven hour day; thus enabling them to have a couple of hours home with the family. The total a trip of approximately 37 hours, was done twice a week, for very little money.

The general cargo men were worse off than the tanker men as far as pay for their job was concerned, so it was no wonder the fiddling went on.

I know that these men were moved from vessel to vessel and I have known them to go aboard a timber lighter to take it to Stourport-on-

The Stourport river carnival was entered by the river men with the blessing of their individual companies. Severn Enterprises dressed overhaul, for it was always held on the first Saturday in September every year.

Stourport-on-Severn general cargo jetties as it is now, all work has finished on the River Severn.

Severn, with no cabin or any proper facilities and have to be aboard until they reached their destination. It was a very hard life indeed. In the winter the only heat on board to keep them warm was an old five gallon oil drum with holes in to convert it to a brazier and placed on the deck.

Why did they do this work? It was because it was a way of life they liked. It was out in the open air and they were their own bosses. We enjoyed the life and there was not another job anywhere, with comradeship like the life on the Severn.

Yes, Sabrina had her drawbacks but as I said in the beginning of this book if you treated her with respect she'd treat you the same way. The only ones that did not were the craft owners who kept their men on such low pay. It did not matter where the barges were from, it was like belonging to a big family. You saw no one in trouble if you could help them in anyway. At Stourport-on-Severn I have seen Gloucester men as they were so called, drinking and working alongside Birmingham boatmen. There were Severn and canal men, men and families on board Fellows Morton and Clayton boats, and the Birmingham canal boats all working and living in harmony, unloading the two hundred ton barges and loading the longboats with their cargo for transporting into the Midlands. The comradeship of these river men and canal men was something to behold. I am very proud to say I was one of them and lived in their company.